THE CAROLINA BRATTONS

THE CAROLINA BRATTONS

Courage, Honor, and Country
Since 1766

BY

Patricia West

Tree of Life Memoirs

SEWANEE, TENNESSEE

Library of Congress Control Number: 2016910994

ISBN-10: 0-9973335-2-9
ISBN-13: 978-0-9973335-2-7

Book layout and cover design by Patricia West. Image of American flag from STILLFX/ Shutterstock. Image used as family tree in first three chapters from Morphart Creations/ Shutterstock.

Edited by G. Norman West, PhD

Printed by IngramSpark

Published by Tree of Life Memoirs
700 Haynes Road
Sewanee, TN 37375-4050
www.TreeofLifeMemoirs.com

Contents

Preface

RESEARCHING THE MATERIAL FOR this book about the Bratton family, interviewing descendants who had direct or indirect knowledge of them, and putting it all together has been an amazing adventure for me—an adventure more interesting, inspiring, and fun than I could have imagined.

It began when I was approached by John Gass Bratton, a sixth generation descendant of the Bratton family. I had just completed a talk on the subject of my business as a personal historian at a Rotary Club Meeting in Sewanee, Tennessee. Mr. Bratton asked if I would write his family history, a history that would focus on four of his well-known ancestors from South Carolina. He informed me that the book would entail significant research and a trip to North and South Carolina.

Mr. Bratton, an octogenarian with a quick smile and a kindly manner, was obviously proud of his family and felt that their story would be a significant contribution to the history of South Carolina. His primary reason for wanting the book written was to honor and explore the legacy of his grandfather, Bishop Theodore DuBose Bratton, a man whose position on race relations was very unusual for his times.

One book about one of Mr. Bratton's ancestors had already been written. *General John Bratton, Sumter to Appomattox: in Letters to His Wife*, by Luke Austin, revolves around General Bratton's Civil War activities. Mr. Bratton knew that the general had also been a plantation owner who was active in politics, and he was curious about the rest of General Bratton's life. Another ancestor had immigrated to the American colonies from Ireland, was also a plantation owner, and had fought in the American Revolution. A third ancestor was John's grandfather, a bishop of Mississippi. Finally, there was a cousin who moved to Raleigh, North Carolina, founded a business there, and was a well-known philanthropist. All left admirable and far-reaching legacies, and Mr. Bratton felt that their stories should be preserved and honored in print.

Mr. Bratton's family history sounded fascinating. My response to him, without quite thinking it through, was, "Sure, I'll be glad to do it." I explained that I was not an actual historian but felt that I was good at research and placing individuals within the context of their times. Most of my books had been written by interviewing people, transcribing the stories of their lives, and then shaping them into book form, but this sounded like an interesting change.

Having no real idea of how long or involved the production of this book would be, I accepted Mr. Bratton's offer anyway. I began my quest by doing some preliminary research in the archives at the University of the South, Sewanee, and on the Internet. I traveled to the Carolinas a couple of months later, and to say I enjoyed the trip is an understatement. I was "blown away" by the people I met and their offers of help and hospitality. The Bratton family may not be well-known outside of North and South Carolina, but they seemed to be a fascinating subject to the people I met, all of whom were more than eager to be a part of my journey through the history of this family.

I found out that the book I so quickly said "sure" to took much longer than the six or eight months I had anticipated, but it has been time well spent as far as I am concerned. I learned a lot, developed an even greater appreciation for our nation's history, and made some terrific new friends as a result. I also developed a great admiration for the Bratton family. I hope you will find my journey through the Bratton family history enjoyable and inspiring as well.

Acknowledgments

To all the people who assisted me with this book, I proffer my endless gratitude. This book would have been much less interesting and much more difficult to write without them. They are as follows, with my apologies to anyone I may have left out.

John Gass Bratton has been an ongoing source of encouragement and information. He gave me stacks of information from his personal files on the family and provided several suggestions. Elliot Bratton, his cousin, is an African-American descendant of the Brattons who lives in Maryland. Elliot and I exchanged several phone calls and emails, and he contributed appendix D, "Some Historical Notes on South Carolina's Brattons."

Luke Austin, author of the book about General Bratton, has given me much-needed advice on books to read, subjects to explore, and places to visit for research purposes in South Carolina. He was also kind enough to provide a useful critique of the first draft of General Bratton's chapter.

My trip to South Carolina began with two days at the South Caroliniana Library in Columbia, where archive staff lugged folder after folder of information about the early Brattons to my desk. They also stopped to talk with me about Bratton family history.

After an afternoon at the Thomas Cooper Library in Columbia, I spent the next day at the Fairfield County Museum in Winnsboro. Director Pelham Lyles had arranged for her staff to help me in all ways possible. She even set up an interview with her father, James Lyles, who was ninety-six years old. James had known some of the Brattons and was happy to reminisce. A video of the interview, *The Brattons of Fairfield County*, is now on YouTube. Mr. Lyles and the videographer, Jim Young, took me to visit the cemetery where General Bratton and several other Brattons are buried. We also drove to St. John's Episcopal Church. The church contains memorials to Bishop Theodore DuBose Bratton and to his mentor and uncle, William Porcher DuBose.

Pelham Lyles also provided me with contact information for Penny Renwick, current owner of historic home Wynn Dee, where General Bratton was born. Penny provided me with a photo she had taken of the house.

Eddie Killian, President of the Fairfield Genealogical Association and employee at the museum, stayed at least two hours after closing time to help me locate materials. Suzanne Johnson and James Green also provided assistance.

My next stop was at Historic Brattonsville, a living history and battlefield site near McConnells, South Carolina. I met with Kevin Lynch, the site manager, who provided much information about the property and its history. Kevin also referred me to Michael Scoggins, historian for the Culture & Heritage Museums in York County.

Michael Scoggins deserves a very special thanks. He has done extensive research and writing on the history of Historic Brattonsville and I think he shared just about all of it with me. Without his generosity and encouragement, the chapter on Colonel William Bratton, founder of Brattonsville, would be significantly shorter. We exchanged numerous emails and he allowed me to reprint appendix A, "William Bratton's Military and Civil Service," for the book.

After a trip to the Department of Archives and History in Columbia, I drove to North Carolina. I spent some time doing research at the University of North Carolina in Chapel Hill, and then traveled to Wake Stone Corporation headquarters in Knightdale (just outside of Raleigh). Wake Stone was founded by John Bratton Jr., who died in 2009. I had arranged to interview Johnny and Sam Bratton, two of his three sons who now run the company, and Tom Oxholm, Wake Stone accountant and family friend. They were very generous with their time, spending almost three hours reminiscing about Mr. Bratton and providing me with written materials.

Lucy Bratton Doak of Chapel Hill, sister to Johnny and Sam Bratton, was also very kind and provided me with a telephone interview, email correspondence, and photographs of the John Bratton Jr. family.

Others deserving many thanks are Libby Adamson and Clinton Bagley. Libby is the secretary at the Church of the Advent in Spartanburg, South Carolina, where Theodore DuBose Bratton was rector. She spent much time scanning and sending me information from church histories. Clinton is an archivist at the Mississippi Department of Archives and History. He was also very gracious, communicating with me via phone and email several times, and sending me at least three or four packages of information.

Last, but always most importantly, is my husband, Norman West, Clinical Psychologist and Associate Professor at the University of the South in Sewanee. I wore out his ears more than once discussing this book with him, and he spent countless hours proofreading and copy editing it. He also took over the cooking, housework, and animal care while I stayed on my computer to write, and he even flew down to South Carolina to help me with research.

Introduction

"The songs of our ancestors are also the songs of our children."
—Philip Carr-Gomm

———————☆———————

WE ALL NEED A sense of our roots, and it is especially gratifying when we have reasons to be proud of our ancestors. They can intrigue us, inspire us, and fill us with appreciation.

You will be taken on a journey through one line of the Bratton family and six generations of Brattons. Four prominent members of that line will be portrayed, along with their wives and some of their children. You will travel with the Brattons from Ireland to South Carolina, and then move with them to Tennessee, Mississippi, and North Carolina. You will see how they made the best of their circumstances to become successful, not only by providing for their families but also by contributing to their communities and their states. This is an American success story of Scots-Irish emigrants who hoped for a better life—and found one.

This book will attempt to see the Brattons through the eyes of their times. There will be information about their social, economic, and political environments and personal stories of their triumphs and tragedies. There will be side stories of relatives who were both famous and infamous. Common family themes will begin to emerge throughout the generations, including family strengths and connections, a love of the land and property ownership, and strong moral values. Honor, personal responsibility, patriotism, and faith in God are exemplified in every generation.

The first chapter belongs to Colonel William Bratton, as he was known after the American Revolutionary War. Colonel Bratton was born Ireland in 1742 and settled in the wild backcountry of South

Carolina in the 1760s. In 1766 he purchased land in York County that became a plantation and is now known as Historic Brattonsville, a living history museum and battlefield site. The chapter will take you through the hardships and dangers of the Carolina backcountry and Colonel Bratton's struggles to protect his family and property while fighting Indians and criminals. It details his Revolutionary War activities, his businesses, and his extensive political and civic service. It also pays tribute to his talented wife, Martha, who "doctored" both Patriot and Loyalist soldiers during the Revolutionary War. It describes their children, some of whom became physicians whose children became physicians.

The second chapter skips a generation and follows Colonel Bratton's grandson, John Bratton, who enjoyed a privileged upbringing during antebellum days and married a beautiful, cultured aristocrat. John's life changed drastically during and after the War Between the States, and his family suffered terribly. He became a brigadier general during the war and was wounded twice. Like most people in the South, he lost almost everything. General Bratton managed to restore his family fortune, however, and thus saved his family, including his large "slave family," from destitution. Like his grandfather, he also became very active in local and state politics. His infamous cousin, Rufus Bratton, fled to Canada because of his Klan activities. What was the general's role in the Klan? Read all about it. Also learn of yet another Ruffus, an African American Bratton who was quite possibly one of General Bratton's children.

Theodore DuBose Bratton, one of General Bratton's sons, is the subject of the third chapter. Theodore became a bishop of the Episcopal Church, served as a chaplain in World War I, and spent much of his time before and after the war advocating for African Americans. According to one source, Theodore and his sister were close to Ruffus—the Ruffus who may have been his mulatto half brother—and this may have been a contributing factor to his interest in race relations. His love for all men—of any color—was great and his beliefs were ahead of his time. Additionally, he was also an early advocate of women's rights on many levels. Theodore Bratton felt that a woman's education was just as important—if not more—as that of a man.

Finally, we skip yet another generation and focus on John Bratton Jr., one of Bishop Bratton's grandsons and a member of the Greatest Generation. John grew up during the Great Depression when his father lost his plantation and moved the family from South Carolina to Raleigh, North Carolina. John served with the Marines during World War II, and when he returned home to his war bride and child, he was quickly employed as a civil engineer. A man who believed in the American dream, he took a calculated risk in 1970 and started his own quarry business, a family-owned business that became very successful. This is more than the story of a man who became a self-made millionaire, however. John Bratton Jr. donated a fortune to various charities and became personally involved with many of them, even spending the night on a regular basis at a homeless shelter for men. John was also a conservationist who planned to restore his quarry lands to usefulness after they were developed. He landscaped his quarries when they were built and even consulted with wildlife experts. A lover of the outdoors and the land, he created a farm-like atmosphere whenever possible. John died in 2009, but his children carry on his work and cherish his memory. Interviews with three of them and with the company's CFO can be found in his chapter.

Yes, this is the story of a family led by well-educated, white Christian males whose family, social and business connections, and reputation gave them many advantages. They tended to marry well-educated women who were also from prominent families. This is also the story of a family who learned from its rich heritage to pick itself up when times were bad, and to contribute to their communities in an active, positive way. All were patriots, and all were politically active except for John Bratton Jr., but politics had changed during his lifetime. It moved from a profession that had been considered honorable to a profession considered by many to be divisive and dishonest.

It occurred to me as I finished this book that all four of the prominent families portrayed had characteristics of the Greatest Generation that Tom Brokaw, who wrote a book of that name, described as the greatest generation that ever lived. That's his story and he's sticking to it, but I wonder. Courage, honor, country—and more—seem to have been qualities of the Bratton family throughout the generations.

Chapter One

Colonel William Bratton
From Ireland to Brattonsville

———— ★ ————

WILLIAM BRATTON WAS JUST a boy when he left the Emerald Isle with his father in the mid-1700s.[1] He did not realize he would soon be walking into a wilderness where he would learn to fight like an Indian, become the founder of a plantation in South Carolina, and become active in local and state politics. William, along with many other Brattons who emigrated to the British colonies in North America, just hoped for a fresh start with family and friends.

Life in Ireland had been harsh for most people due to famine, drought, or disease. Between 1717 and 1775, over 200,000 Scots-Irish emigrated from Northern Ireland to America, almost all of them Presbyterians. The social and political climate in Northern Ireland was especially oppressive for Presbyterians from the Ulster province, where William's family lived. The Ulster Presbyterians could own land and businesses but could not vote and had no political power. The British Parliament had the power to make laws binding in Ireland, and "power was held by a small group of Anglo-Irish families who were loyal to the Anglican Church of Ireland and owned the great bulk of farmland."[2] The New World beckoned, promising cheap land, work, and freedom. Immigration to the British colonies was in full gear by the time William and his father began their journey from Northern Ireland.

William's journey began in a sailing ship. Most voyages to the British colonies took six to eight weeks, depending on the weather and the sea-worthiness of the vessel, and all voyages over the Atlantic Ocean were treacherous. Food and water were often limited or foul, and the ships were crowded and disease-ridden. Many immigrants arrived weakened and ill, having lost friends or family during the voyage. According to the journal of Gottlieb Mittelberger, a German who immigrated to the colonies in 1750, few children between the ages of one and seven survived the voyage.[3] Gottlieb described the horrendous conditions:

> During the voyage there is on board these ships terrible misery, stench, fumes, horror, vomiting, many kinds of seasickness, fever, dysentery, headache, heat, constipation, boils, scurvy, cancer, mouth rot, and the like, all of which come from old and sharply-salted food and meat, also from very bad and foul water, so that many die miserably.[4]

William and any relatives who made the trip with him would have probably disembarked in Philadelphia. Before 1720 most Scots-Irish emigrated to Boston, but after some violent episodes arising from intolerance they emigrated to Philadelphia, a more welcoming port and area.

"The Ulster Scots emigrated in groups, generally organized by their Presbyterian ministers, who negotiated with shippers to arrange passage."[5] The Scots-Irish were a tight-knit group, and relatives who had already arrived may have greeted William and his father. They may have entered into a period of indentured servitude to pay for the trip, or they may have arranged ahead of their arrival to settle with other Scots-Irish Presbyterian emigrants.

As we shall see, William Bratton and his descendants were a hardy, brave lot. Before moving on to his arrival in the Carolinas, however, we will review what is known of the Bratton family origins in Europe and William's likely circumstances and relatives in the British colonies.

The Early Brattons

"The origins of the Bratton family can be traced back to ancient Britain and its earliest historical inhabitants, a Celtic people."[6] Many Brattons eventually migrated to the Ulster province of Northern Ireland after 1600 and were numerous there by the eighteenth century.

> We find them most numerous in County Tyrone, but smaller number were also living in County Donegal,

H. M. S. Blonde, by Robert Dampier.

County Antrim, County Armagh, and County Derry—
all areas traditionally identified as the homeland of the
Scotch-Irish Presbyterians who journeyed from Ulster
to the British colonies of North America.[7]

Bratton family members are shown on immigration and passenger
lists in the early eighteenth century, when the first large wave of Scots-
Irish came to the British colonies. Many then migrated further south
or west soon after arriving in Boston or Philadelphia due to the land
prices and other unfavorable living conditions in the northern colonies.

The price of land in Pennsylvania was quite high, according to
Gottlieb Mittelberger's journal, compared with the lower price of land
in the South. Rich Europeans had already bought land "far and near"
from the Indians to resell it, and the price was beyond the reach of most
immigrants. Mittelberger described how much warmer it was in the
South, mentioning South Carolina in particular, and how it produced
"rice in abundance, much cotton, and olive oil."[8]

By the 1740s many of the Brattons were moving from Pennsylvania
to the Virginia frontier. We are not certain if these Brattons included

William or if he stayed behind in Pennsylvania, but ongoing research indicates that William probably had connections with them. Robert Bratton and a man who might have been his brother, James Bratton, both settled in old Augusta County, Virginia, on the Calfpasture River in an area called Brattons Run. The Virginia Brattons served in the Augusta County militia during the French and Indian War (1756–1763).[9] An account titled *Chronicles of the Scotch-Irish Settlement in Virginia* contains extracts from original court records of Augusta County from 1745 through 1800, and numerous references are made to Brattons in the area, including Robert Bratton, his wife, Ann Dunlop Bratton, and their son, Adam Bratton; James Bratton and his son, John; George Bratton; Thomas Bratton; and William Bratton.[10]

≈ ≈ ≈

Who were William's parents, exactly where was he born, and what do we really know about his forebears—or even where he married his wife? Not much is certain, as records are often incorrect or vague, and people's memories can grow dim. We are not even certain about the year of his birth, although his family and obituary indicate it was around 1742 and this book will use that date. No information located to-date hints at the identity of William's mother, but we do have some possibilities, however, regarding the identity of his father.

Several claims have been made about the identity of William's father. Some online family websites have identified him as Andrew Bratton of Pennsylvania, but there is no real proof to back that up. Other sources claim that William's father is the Robert Bratton who lived in Brattons Run in Virginia.

Robert Bratton was a prominent man in Virginia, and his relatives and activities are well documented. With all of this information available, there is nothing that indicates Robert had a son named William. A William Bratton was mentioned, however, in at least two historical documents involving the areas in or near Brattons Run in Virginia, *The History of Rockbridge County*, and *Chronicles of the Scotch-Irish Settlement in Virginia*.

The History of Rockbridge County mentions a William Bratton who was a brother of the prominent Robert Bratton discussed in the preceding paragraph, but it is unclear as to whether he ever lived in Virginia. In one of its entries, the history documents that "Robert Bratton, who married the widow of Alexander Dunlap, Sr., was one of four brothers. Samuel Bratton remained in Mifflin County, Pennsylvania; James Bratton, who married Dorothy Fleming, settled near Christiansburg. Three sons of another brother, William Bratton, went to South Carolina."[11] There is no mention in this history that Robert's brother, William, actually lived in Augusta County—he may have remained in Pennsylvania—but he did apparently have three sons who went to South Carolina, so perhaps one of them was our William. Our William did, according to what is believed, live with or near brothers who were with him after he arrived in what is now South Carolina, so there may be a connection there.

The second historical document that mentions a William Bratton, *Chronicles of the Scotch-Irish Settlement in Virginia*, refers to him twice, once in 1795 and again in 1800,[12] again without providing much identifying information.

Yet another historical source, *Waddell's Annals of Augusta County, Virginia from 1726 to 1871*, mentions a William Bratton in a well-documented story about an Indian attack in 1756 on Fort Vause, a local fort near the Roanoke River in Virginia. William Bratton was listed as someone who was captured during the attack and later escaped or was "returned."[13] This William could also have been our William's father. However, there is also the possibility it could have been our William, too, although he would have been only fourteen or fifteen years old at the time.

≈ ≈ ≈

William's daughter-in-law, Harriet Rainey Bratton, and her son, Dr. J. Rufus Bratton, were interviewed in the 1800s about William's background, and their interviews provided information on his wife as well. Harriet Bratton said that William came from *County Antrim* in Northern Ireland and married Martha Robertson in *Virginia* before moving to York County.[14] Dr. Rufus Bratton said William was born in *County Armagh*, Northern Ireland, lived in Pennsylvania before moving to North Carolina, and then moved to South Carolina. Rufus added that Martha Robertson was from Ireland, was born at sea, and that William married her in *Rowan County*, North Carolina.[15] Various online sources also list her maiden name as Roberson instead of Robertson.

Research continues by genealogists, so at some point we may know all of the answers to William's exact birthplace and his parentage. At this point, however, we will switch gears and focus on William's move to South Carolina.

Into the Carolina Backcountry

Prior to the 1700s, most residents of South Carolina had settled in the coastal areas, as the inland and northern areas of the colony known as the backcountry were largely controlled by Indians and were quite wild and unsettled. Settlement was encouraged by the British Crown after it took control of South Carolina in 1729. Settlers were offered financial and other incentives, and the Crown hoped to use the settlers as a buffer to protect the coastal planter community from Indian attacks.

As the French and Indian War began in earnest in 1754, many Scots-Irish who had settled in Pennsylvania and Virginia took the Great Wagon Road down to North and South Carolina. They emigrated to the Carolinas in droves from the late 1730s to the 1760s. It is likely that William took this road, as it was a well-established route by the time he arrived in what was then a part of North Carolina in the 1760s.

If William lived in Virginia before moving to the southwestern part of North Carolina, his move may have been a result of the increasing pressure from Indian attacks on the Virginia frontier. The French and Indian War, also called the Seven Years' War (1754–1763), was officially over by then, but Indian attacks continued. Other reasons for the move were probably the availability of colonial land grants and the presence of Scots-Irish Presbyterians who had already settled there. The Scots-Irish were very clannish and tended to live together in communal, family-related groups known as clachans, much the same as in Ulster, Northern Ireland, so the Brattons would have been welcomed to the area.

William Bratton, his young wife, Martha, and their first child, Elsie (who was born in 1766), arrived in North Carolina by 1766 at the latest. The exact time of their arrival is unclear, but records show that William bought property in the area in 1766.[16] The area where William bought property was then a part of North Carolina but would become a part of South Carolina in 1772, when the boundary between the two colonies

Ulster Counties,
Northern Ireland
(shaded area), where
many Brattons lived
before coming to the
colonies.

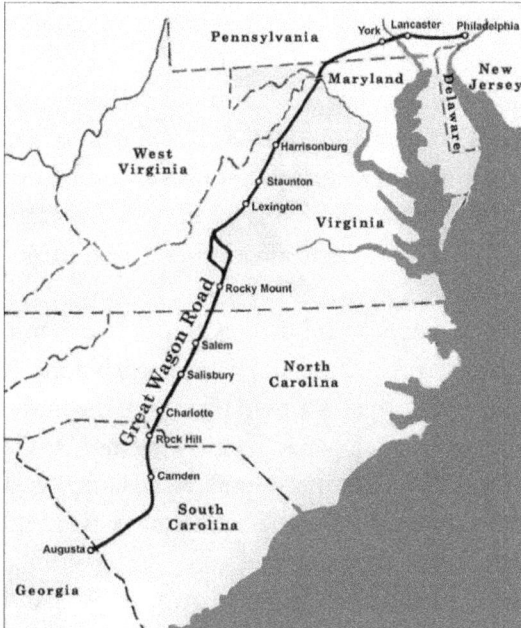

The Great Wagon Road.
Courtesy of J. D. Lewis.
A route many Scots-
Irish took on their way
south after immigrating
from Ireland.

in this area was finally established. The young couple originally settled in an area called the Waxhaws on the east side of the Catawba River.[17]

The Waxhaws were named after a Native American tribe that had been decimated by war and disease, so the tribe was not much of a threat, and the land was rolling but not rugged, with good soil. Scots-Irish families had settled it in the 1750s and founded the first Presbyterian Church in South Carolina. Andrew Jackson, seventh President of the United States, was born there,[18] and his family may well have met the Brattons.

Also living in the Waxhaws were four men and one woman thought to be William's brothers and his sister, along with their spouses and children. William's brothers were John, Robert, Thomas, and Hugh Bratton. His sister was Jean, and her husband's name was Samuel Guy. "Hugh and William were apparently the youngest of the siblings, while the other three brothers and their sister were older."[19] We do not know if William and Martha arrived with William's brothers and sister or if William's siblings were already there, but the presence of siblings and the Scots-Irish community would have made the Waxhaws a good choice.

In May 1763, John Bratton, who was probably William's oldest brother, purchased 200 acres in the Waxhaws on Flat Creek, and it is likely that all the Bratton siblings were already living on John's homestead. District and colony lines were being redrawn repeatedly with the influx of new settlers, and in 1764 the Flat Creek area was incorporated into South Carolina. In 1766 William and Martha moved west of the Catawba River to an area near the small settlement of McConnells in what is now York County, South Carolina.[20] They bought property along Fishing Creek or nearby, where a large amount of creek bottom was available for small farmers.

The journal of an itinerant Anglican minister, Charles Woodson, who traveled the backcountry from 1766 until 1773, reflects his shock at conditions in the Waxhaws and provides a vivid picture of life in the area and of the Carolina backcountry in general. Fair warning: While Mr. Woodson seemed to be a dedicated, honest minister, he had passed much of his life in his native England and in Charleston, which had modeled itself after London, and he had many biases. The largest groups of non-English whites lived in the backcountry—many Germans and

Scots-Irish—and he especially disliked most Scots-Irish Presbyterians. An entry from his journal, transcribed as he wrote it, describes the country and his feelings towards the Scots-Irish:

> This is a very fruitful fine Spot, thro' which the dividing Line between North and South Carolina runs—the Heads of the P. D. River, Lynch's Creek, and many other creeks take their rise in this Quarter—so that a finer Body of Land is no where to be seen—But it is occupied by a Set of the most lowest vile Crew breathing—Scotch-Irish Presbyterians from the North of Ireland.[21]

In all fairness to the Brattons, Mr. Woodson did note that the Presbyterian minister at the Waxhaws' church was a good man, and that on February 24, 1767, when Mr. Woodson preached at Fishing Creek, he found it "settled chiefly by Presbyterians, but several worthy Church People among them."[22] Mr. Woodson complained about the Presbyterians throughout his journal, writing that he could not file official complaints as all of the Magistrates were Presbyterians. One of his complaints was that Presbyterians liked to drink whiskey and homemade brandy and that they, along with other members of the backcountry, often disrupted his services.[23]

Many of the backcountry inhabitants didn't like him, either. Backcountry folks were very independent, and the Scots-Irish clung to their own religion. Many resented any pressure to conform to England's attempts to "civilize" them by converting them to the Anglican Church, the official church of the Province of South Carolina. In addition, there was an ongoing period of religious fervor that swept through much of the country during that time, the Great Awakening; backcountry folks most likely saw a number of traveling preachers and probably took few of them seriously.

South Carolina men liked to drink, as Mr. Woodson noted, and they weren't going to give that up no matter what they heard from a pulpit. The habit was widespread among the men, but the women did not usually drink much, and by law it was illegal to serve slaves without the permission of their masters.[24] Many believed that alcohol was good medicine, a good way to blow off steam and to lubricate during social events. It was thought that only the weak of mind or spirit would become "alcoholics," a term not even in use during that time. It would be surprising if William had not felt the same way.

On a more serious note, Mr. Woodson took pity on the plight of local Indians (Hooker, *The Carolina Backcountry*, 121), helped deliver a baby (53) when no one else was available, and deplored the lack of medical care, which was basically nonexistent except for folk medicine. He was also greatly concerned about the lack of public education and the plight of the poor, and unsuccessfully petitioned the legislature in hopes of finding a solution:

> The Back Part of S.C. not being laid out into Parishes, and no provision made for the Poor, The Country in General was coer'd with Swarms of Orphans, and other Pauper vagrant vagabond Children to the Great Increase of all Manner of Vice and Wickedness. I therefore excited the People to petition the legislature for the Establishment of some Public Schools, where these children might be taught the Principles of Religion, and fitted to become Useful Members of Society.[25]

While Mr. Woodson was discovering, lamenting, and battling the backcountry conditions, William Bratton's family was making the most of them, determined to secure their fresh start. Their circumstances were not as dire as those of many backcountry people; they already knew how to hunt, fish, farm, and fight, and they valued education—as you will see later—so they probably had some "book learning," too. They also had a strong Scots-Irish family and community for support.

Brattonsville Begins

By 1771 the Bratton clan all had property in the Fishing Creek area. William's brother, Thomas, bought his property there in 1766, and Thomas's land grant shows that Robert was already living nearby, as were William's sister Jean and her husband. On August 11, six days after Thomas bought his property, , William bought his property. Hugh Bratton bought property adjacent to William's property sometime before 1967. Finally, the last of the brothers, John Bratton, purchased property in the Flat Creek area in 1771,[26] so by then the entire family was practically within walking distance of each other.

William was already living on the land when he bought it, and there were some buildings on the property, so no one knows when he and Martha began to live in the main house, the house now referred to as The Colonel William and Martha Bratton House. They may have been living in a small backwoods log cabin on their property while their main house was being built. Backwoods cabins were small, single-room buildings with a dirt floor and a chimney, and they were dark, with no windows.

No matter what their living circumstances, family nearby was especially good news as the Bratton babies began to arrive. Martha and William's first child, Elisa, was born in September of 1766, when Martha was only about sixteen years old, and by 1771 she and William had two more girls. Women in the eighteenth century often had back-to-back babies, becoming pregnant as soon as they quit nursing. William's siblings were doubtlessly having their babies, too, so the clan was busy caring for little ones in addition to building adjoining homesteads.

The seeds of what would later be called Brattonsville were being planted and were growing, along with the community.

The New Acquisition

When property boundaries were finalized in 1772 and the Bratton homestead became part of South Carolina, it became part of what was called The New Acquisition until after the Revolutionary War. Camden was the center of the district and was about seventy-five miles from York County, a long way to go on horseback for a court hearing. Some official business, such as the recording of deeds, required a trip all the way to Charleston. The colony of South Carolina was fortunate, though, in that it had gained a territory that had become well-populated, primarily with Scots-Irish people.

The backcountry was changing with the formation of communities. It was no longer as empty or as wild, although it still lacked law and order. Local militias were formed in the New Acquisition and elsewhere in the backcountry to protect against Indian raids and bandits. The American

Colonel William and Martha Bratton house, at Historic Brattonsville near McConnells, SC. Photo by author, 2015.

Interior of a backcountry cabin, Historic Brattonsville. Photo by author, 2015.

Revolution was gearing up, but most backcountry residents were still more focused on surviving, expanding, and protecting their property.

The settlers, as indicated earlier, were communal and clannish, and their meetinghouses—the forerunners of their congregations—became the focal point of backcountry society. The Anglican Church of England wanted to convert everyone in the province, but not many Anglicans ventured out to the backcountry, and the residents there were inclined to follow the beliefs they had brought with them. The establishment of the Bethesda Presbyterian Church in 1769, just a few miles from the Bratton clan's properties, brought added cohesion and support to the community, and the Brattons were founding members. Rev. John Simpson of Fishing Creek was their first minister and became a close friend; his son would marry one of William and Martha's daughters.[27]

William and his brothers would have stayed busy clearing, planting, and tending the land, and hunting and raising hound dogs, horses, hogs, and other livestock. They were also charged with protecting their homes and property. Martha would have been busy with women's work, which included not only caring for children but also working in the fields, washing, mending, sewing, cooking, nursing the ill, and many other chores.

Clothing was simple and loose. Men wore frocks and trousers. Women typically wore a shift, a stay for back support, and a short petticoat. Women covered their heads, probably to keep their hair clean and out of the way while doing chores. Infants and toddlers wore gowns. The settlers didn't exactly have spare clothes, and decent shoes were prized and well cared for.

Chores extended from dawn to dusk and then continued by firelight or candlelight. Everyone had daily chores to do. Even small children were expected to help as soon as they learned how to walk. Boys learned how to hunt, fish, build, and repair, and they worked in the fields or gardens at a young age. Girls learned women's work, including how to use a spinning wheel and to mend clothes—an endless task. Older children had to watch the younger children because all the adults were busy working.

It was hot and humid in the summertime, sometimes swelteringly so. Baths would have been a major ordeal, heating water in tubs over a fire and using homemade soap. Let's hope they had some good folk remedies for fleas and ticks as well. And let's not forget folk remedies for just about anything else that ailed them. If there were any doctors available, they would have been scarce, and someone would have to "fetch" them via foot, horseback, or wagon, or to take the sick person to a doctor's home for treatment.

The Bratton Slaves

The Brattons may or may not have started out with slaves, as written records of slavery were spotty in those days, and slavery wasn't nearly as prevalent in the backcounty as it was along Carolina's coastal areas. It is clear, though, that William Bratton owned at least one slave at the time of the American Revolution, as we have a well-known story about him. Watt, as he was known, was a trusted family slave who helped save the day in a famous battle you will hear all about soon.

If William and Martha had it rough in the early years, their slaves had it even rougher. Slaves were considered chattel—personal property—and were only provided with the barest of necessities. The quality of their lives varied with their circumstances:

Following is a description of slavery in the backcountry before the Civil War:

> Contrary to the overwhelming image of the grand Southern plantation worked by hundreds of slaves, most agricultural units in the South up until about two decades before the Civil War were small farms with twenty to thirty slaves each. The conditions of slaves under these circumstances were most easily grouped into the experiences of field slaves and house slaves. The vast majority of plantation slaves labored in the fields ... . Enslaved people in all regions and time periods often did not have enough to eat; some resorted to stealing food from the master. House slaves could slip food from leftovers in the kitchen but had to be very careful not to get caught, for harsh punishments awaited such an offense.

Clothing, distributed by the master, usually once a year and often at Christmastime, was apportioned according to sex and age as well as to the labor performed by its wearer. Children, for instance, often went unclothed entirely until they reached adolescence .... House slaves tended to be dressed with more modesty, sometimes in the hand-me-downs of masters and mistresses. The relationships of slaves with one another, with their masters, with overseers and free persons, were all to a certain extent shaped by the unique circumstances of life experienced by each slave. House slaves, for example, sometimes came to identify with their masters' interests over those of fellow slaves.[28]

We do not know the details of how the first Bratton slaves lived, but slaves in colonial times usually resided in one-room houses with dirt floors. While they had to get permission from their owners to marry, slave marriages were encouraged as this would increase the slave population. Slaves had no legal rights for many years and could be punished or even executed at will by their owners. Some found solace in the religion they brought with them, and the Brattons may well have heard them singing religious chants or hymns at night.

Seeds of Discontent in the Backcountry

While the Bratton family was building a plantation in what would later become part of York County, South Carolina, the American Revolution was gathering steam and coming to the Carolinas. To understand the Bratton role is to also understand a bit more about the backcountry, its rising planter class, and backcountry settlers' feelings towards England and the coastal areas of Carolina.

By the eve of the Revolution, South Carolina's extensive backcountry was no longer an unoccupied frontier; it contained about thirty-five thousand settlers, three-fourths of the South Carolina's white population. South Carolina's colonial government was based in the coastal region, though, and by 1768 it held about eighty-six percent of the colony's taxable wealth and ninety percent of its slaves.[29] Settlers like the Brattons were buying up land and increasing their slave population.

They were also operating gins, growing and selling crops, and beginning to trade throughout various districts.

As subjects of the Crown in a Royal Colony, the Province of South Carolina elected their own legislature and assembly, and had a court system and a governor. However, the governor was usually appointed by the British government and held executive power. Unfortunately for the backcountry, they were underrepresented in the assembly, unhappy with a tax rate that favored landowners from the wealthy rice-produc-ing parishes, and "were almost entirely without avenues to colony wide power."[30] They even had to ride all the way to Charleston for court hearings until 1769, when seven circuit court districts were established in South Carolina with courthouses for each district.

"No taxation without representation" was a slogan heard throughout the country. It summarized one of the major grievances the thirteen colonies had against England, but it affected the backcountry even more than the lowcountry of the Carolina coast. For the backcountry, this slogan applied not only to England but also to Charleston to a great extent. Charleston residents had always considered backcountry folks uncivilized and wanted to maintain control in terms of money and power, so they passed legislation that primarily benefited themselves. The French and Indian War had brought a certain peace to the country but it also brought much debt for England, and England thought it only just that the colonies pay for the British soldiers sent to America to help protect them from Indians.

So, the backcountry had basically been left to fend for itself—to protect itself from horse thieves, squatters, and murderers. Some of those who stole from or terrorized backcountry settlers had been left destitute and desperate due to Indian raids and other hardships of the backcountry; they were just struggling to survive. Others took advan-tage of the situation: looting, shooting, and causing harm whenever and however they could. As a result of the lawless conditions, local populations formed militias for self-protection and held regular drills.

Records have not been found that show William Bratton was a member of the militia before the American Revolution, but he would have been counted as one anyway as an adult male in the community.[31] Planters like William "were oriented towards slave acquisition and commercial agriculture. Justices of the peace and militia officers—the primary sources of civil authority—were drawn from their ranks ... ."[32] William Bratton fit the bill on all counts.

> Militia musters were held at least six times a year, and meetings of local justices became the occasion of neighborhood get-togethers. Charles Woodson disapproved of the rowdy behavior associated with these events, but his description shows the necessities of exchange and administration fostered a degree of community order while permitting justices and officers to display their authority.[33]

The Revolution Comes to South Carolina

The Province of South Carolina finally had enough of the British government and sent five delegates to the First Continental Congress in Philadelphia in 1775. The defacto government of South Carolina was formed, and the First Provincial Congress was elected and convened in Charleston. A Council of Safety was created to direct local communities, and part of the Council's responsibility was to command an army for the defense of the Province.

> In June 1775 the South Carolina Provincial Congress ordered each of its twelve districts to raise a regiment of foot soldiers for the defense of the province, and this order was soon followed by a request from the Continental Congress for three regiments of provincial troops. The New Acquisition Militia (NAM) was organized under the command of Colonel Thomas Neel, and its original officers included Samuel Watson, William Byers, Alexander Love, Thomas Fitzpatrick, Robert McAfee, Francis (Frank) Ross, and William Bratton.[34]

William Bratton was elected to command the militia company from the Bethesda congregation. Two of his brothers, Hugh and John, served with him. Each militia regiment was drawn from communities, and William was an obviously good choice. He was already well known to the community, not only as a church member, community member, and planter but also as a civic-minded leader with appointments as a road overseer and an officer of the court.[35] Military positions did not necessarily depend on experience but on popularity; as the war went on, William was consistently elected and re-elected by his men to fight against the Tories—as the King's men or British regulars were often called—and the American Loyalists, who were loyal to English rule. And do not forget the Indians, who were sometimes pro-British and sometimes pro-American. The Americans who fought against English rules were called Patriots, Whigs, or simply rebels. We will use the terms Tories, Loyalists, and Patriots for the sake of clarity.

Backcountry folks weren't exactly interested in joining the American Revolution at first, considering it more of an issue between the rich planters of Charleston and England and the northern colonies. After all, they had been despised and ignored for the most part, and had learned to take care of themselves. They hadn't exactly seen the King's men rushing in to help them when criminals were terrorizing them. However, many were loyal to the King or fearful of England's power, and the American Revolution would see family members and neighbors turning against each other, sometimes switching their loyalties back and forth. William Bratton was conservative but by all indications, he always remained loyal to the idea of independence from England.

During the Revolutionary War, Bratton fought on horseback and on foot, most likely using a musket, knives, and even a tomahawk, and may have even taken a few scalps himself. Many backcountry men had learned how to fight like Indians and how to melt away into the woods. Colonel Bratton also carried his own ammunition such as shot molds, tinder lighters, and cartridge boxes. Food and supplies were often scarce, the weather could be freezing or scorching, and he was doubtlessly worried constantly about his family at home.

William Bratton either fought or was indirectly involved with twenty-three battles.[36] I do not have specifics for all of them—some may be skirmishes noted by men who served under him and not major battles—but I will share the highlights of what I did find.

Military Service and Battles: 1775–1779

William fought with the New Acquisition Militia in most of its early campaigns, including:

> [He fought with] an expedition into the Cherokee Territory in 1775 to put down a Loyalist revolt (known afterwards as the 'Snow Campaign' due to the bad weather) ... and in an even larger campaign against the hostile Cherokee Indians in the summer and fall of 1776 that took the men from western South Carolina far into the mountains of North Carolina."[37]

The Snow Campaign occurred after Cherokee Indians started to attack backcountry settlers on Carolina's western frontier. The Cherokees had sided with the British, receiving supplies from British posts. The Indians were elusive, but the Patriots had the advantage in firepower and went after the Indians' towns and crops, forcing them to stay and defend them.[38]

The British army moved north after the defeat of Charleston in 1776, and a period of relative calm settled over the backcountry. At the end of 1776, William was a captain in the New Acquisition Regiment. He had also been appointed justice of the peace for the district,[39] so his influence and prestige were growing. William Bratton was not a large man. He was only about five feet eight inches with a small frame and a narrow face but he stood tall in the eyes of the community. His wife, Martha, was also highly respected in the community for her intelligence, her willingness to work hard, and her healing ability. William and Martha had four children at that point, including a son, William A. Bratton, who was born in 1773.

The Brattons, other backcountry residents, and South Carolina enjoyed almost three years free of British rule and authority from 1776 to 1779, so William had time to enjoy his growing family. That changed with Britain's new strategy to shift the war to the South, placing South Carolina in the path of invasion in 1779.

Captain Bratton participated in or fought in three battles in 1779, the first two almost back-to-back in Georgia. The backcountry militia was called out for a campaign to relieve Augusta, Georgia, which had fallen to the British.

> That campaign culminated in the disastrous Battle of Briar Creek in Screven County .... The American army under Brig. Gen John Ashe was attacked by a British army from Florida and soundly defeated. The men of the New Acquisition headed north towards Augusta, and on March 29 they overtook a party of Tory militia and Cherokee Indians near Rocky Comfort Creek in Richmond County .... A fierce hand-to-hand battle ensued, and Major Ross was mortally wounded by a tomahawk. William Bratton as senior captain was promoted to major and assumed command of the detachment.[40]

The third battle was in June 1779, at Stono Ferry in Charleston County, a British outpost where several South Carolina militias had been sent to defend Charleston against a new British invasion. The Americans attacked but were defeated, with heavy casualties,[41] and Colonel Thomas Neel, William's immediate superior, was killed. Once again, William Bratton was promoted due to a battlefield casualty, this time to lieutenant colonel.

William went home, and almost a year went by before he fought again. His fifth child, another daughter, was born in August 1779. Picture a busy household of four girls and one boy, all under twelve years old: Elisa, Jane, Martha, William, and Elizabeth.

Military Service and Battles: 1780–1781

On May 12, 1780, the Continental Army surrendered to the British in Charleston. The British stepped up their efforts to subdue the back-country, set up new outposts, and demanded that backcountry men take new loyalty oaths to British rule. Patriots, if they accepted the oaths, would also be given pardons for past offenses. If they refused, they were threatened, brutalized, or worse. Many Americans thought the war was over; they took the oath and accepted Royal protection. However, many more refused the oaths and fought. In York County, some rode to North Carolina to escape or to regroup as the British pursued them. In the summer of 1780, the climate in the backcountry was once again heating up, in more ways than one.

The British presence seemed to be everywhere, and Colonel Bratton proposed that the men of the militia retreat to North Carolina while awaiting reinforcements that were coming from Virginia. There was dissent among the troops, some of whom wanted to stay and fight what Colonel Bratton thought was a temporarily hopeless position. He resigned his commission, and the militiamen who stayed reorganized under new leaders. They failed miserably, and then decided he had been right all along. Bratton helped to raise another battalion of militia and began to fight again.[42] As word spread of British cruelty, many who had been previously loyal to English rule changed their minds and became Patriots.

Between June 1780 and August 1781, William fought in at least three times as many battles as he had fought since the war began. We will hit the highlights of most, focusing on a famous battle that took place near his plantation and made his slave, Watt, and his wife, Martha, famous in York County.

The first three battles William participated in took place between June 8 and June 20 and are referred to as the battles of Mobley's Meeting House, Hill's Iron Works, and Ramsour's Mill.

The Battle of Mobley's Meeting House in Fairfield County was Lt. Col. William Bratton's first battle in 1780. Tories who had been plundering the area set up camp at the meeting house. Colonel Bratton raised volunteers from the Bethesda neighborhood and set off with other local militiamen. The next morning, the Patriots surrounded the meetinghouse on three sides (the fourth side was a steep bluff), and attacked at sunrise. The fight only lasted a few minutes, and the Tories were killed or captured, with no casualties on the Patriot side. To the surprise of the Patriots, more Tories were killed trying to escape down the bluff than by American rifles.[43]

The second battles was at Hill's Iron Works in York County and Ramsour's Mill in Lincoln County. The ironworks was a key producer of ammunition, guns, and agricultural implements that people in the border area between the two Carolinas heavily depended on,[44] but the

Patriots were outnumbered by Captain Christian Huck's forces, who burned and plundered it. Huck was especially hated by the Patriots due to his cruelty.

> He had been sent into that area to cow the backcountry men into not interfering with the administration of loyalty oaths—or the king's business in general. But Huck and his men had also managed here and there to help themselves to property, or to use physical abuse on the farmers, planters, and their families.[45]

After the defeat at Hill's Iron Works, Colonel Bratton left for Tuckasegee Ford, near Charlotte, where he and other militiamen formed a brigade and elected Thomas Sumter, "The Gamecock," their leader.[46]

The battle on June 20 at Ramsour's Mill was long and vicious, involving much hand-to-hand combat. Both sides suffered many losses, but the Patriots prevailed.

≈ ≈ ≈

Colonel Bratton's next battle took place near his plantation on July 12, 1780, the battle that also made Watt and Martha famous. It is called the Battle of Huck's Defeat or the Battle of Williamson's Plantation. About seventy-five militia members of three regiments were present, including those from Bratton's Regiment, Neel's Regiment, and Lacey's Regiment.

The night before the Battle of Huck's Defeat, Captain Huck arrived at Colonel Bratton's home, only to find that he was gone. One of his men arrived before he did, and a confrontation ensued with Martha Bratton about her husband's whereabouts.

Following is what Colonel Bratton's oldest son, William Bratton Jr., remembered from that day:

> At last they were seen coming up the road, a long line of 'Red Coats' followed by a great multitude of 'Tories,'" Dr. Bratton recalled. Huck and the dragoons apparently brought up the rear of the column. A small squad of soldiers under Lieutenant Adamson was the first to arrive at the Bratton home. Martha met them on her porch, or "piazza" as Dr. Bratton referred to it,

and asked what they wanted. Adamson stated that they were looking for her husband, Colonel Bratton, and asked where he was. When Martha informed him that she did not know her husband's whereabouts, a "red-headed Irishman" named Henry "swore that he would make her know.

Seizing a sickle that was hanging on a peg in the Piazza, he placed it in a position around her neck and drawing his sword swore that, "If she did not immediately tell where her Husband was that he would cut her head off and split it." Young William, clinging to his mother's dress, was "transfixed with horror and fright" as his mother calmly replied, "I told the simple truth and could not tell if I would, but I now add that I would not if I could." However, before Henry could carry out his threat, Adamson struck him hard with the side of his sword and kicked him "headlong down the steps." Adamson then turned to Martha, apologized for Henry's behavior and assured her of his protection.

Following Adamson's intervention, the Loyalist soldiers waited on Huck's arrival, which according to Dr. Bratton "was not long after." Huck stepped up to the door and asked for an interview with Mrs. Bratton, which she granted. At first, Huck was "very courteous and polite," and when William approached him Huck sat the boy on his knee and treated him kindly, even allowing him to play with his watch and seals. Huck told Martha that he was authorized to offer her husband a commission in the royal militia commensurate with his current rank in the rebel forces, and urged her to use her influence to persuade Bratton to accept the offer. Martha replied that "she had no influence with her Husband in such matters," but Huck continued to press her, extolling the advantages that a British commission would bring to Bratton and his family.

At this point, Martha told Huck, "It is useless to prolong the interview if that is its purpose. My husband is in Sumter's Army and I would rather see him die there, true to his Country and cause, than have him live a traitor in yours." Huck then behaved very badly," Dr. Bratton recalled. "[He] sprang up from his chair and stamped about the room swearing fearful oaths of vengeance against the Rebels, and my Father particularly. The suddenness of his movement threw me from his knee on my face on the hearth, and the result of my misplaced confidence will attend me to my grave in the shape of a broken nose."

Captain Huck then ordered Martha to prepare supper for him and his officers, which she did. In addition to Mrs. Bratton and young William, the family at that time included Elisa or "Elsie," age thirteen; Jane, age twelve; Martha, age nine; and Elizabeth, age one.[47]

Martha was surely trying to buy some time in hopes that her husband would soon appear, along with many militiamen. She had sent her trusted slave, Watt, to warn Sumter's army of the approaching British troops. Imagine how terrified everyone was, especially Martha and Watt. Slaves often ran away, and an added incentive was their freedom, promised by the Tories, so Watt must have had Martha's full confidence. On the other hand, Captain Huck was a vicious man, and allegedly kept runaway or "rescued" slaves as personal servants or killed them. In any event, Watt did Martha's bidding, some credit him with saving the day, and he remained with the Brattons until he died. Slaves were usually buried in unmarked graves, but Watt's burial—along with that of his wife—received a special commemoration.

In the Bratton slave cemetery a single stone inscribed by a stone carver from Charleston, marks Watt and his wife Polly's graves. The stone reads: Sacred to the Memory of WATT Who died Dec. 1837 During the War he served his master Col. W. Bratton Faithfully and his children With the same fidelity Until his death.

Watt's Mission, painting by Dan Nance. Courtesy of Culture & Heritage Museums of York County, SC. Martha is sending the family's trusted slave, Watt, to warn Sumter's army of the approaching British troops.

Aurora's Council, painting by Dan Nance. Courtesy of Culture & Heritage Museums of York County, SC. Patriot military officers make plans to attack the British troops at Williamson's plantation. Colonel Bratton is near the middle, pointing towards the road leading to the plantation.

Also Polly his wife who died July 1838 Who served the
same family With equal faithfulness.[48]

William Bratton Jr. helped prepare a booklet in 1839 for a commemoration of the battle. It may contain some exaggerations but it also sheds
more light on the confrontation between Captain Huck and Martha,
and on the battle itself. According to the booklet, Huck and his officers
moved their troops to the neighboring home of James Williamson,
but their sentries and men were complacent. Colonel Bratton, who
was in Mecklenburg County, North Carolina, arrived that night with
seventy-five men, principally his neighbors. They concealed their horses
in a swamp, and attacked at dawn. Huck and his officers were in bed,
woken by the sounds of American guns. Huck mounted his horse and
attempted to rally his men but was quickly killed, and his men threw
down their arms and surrendered.[49]

According to a book written in 1848 by Elizabeth Ellett, *The Women
of the American Revolution*, Martha was afraid of danger from gunshots
while the conflict during the day of the battle was raging around her and
the children, , so she forced her little son to sit in the chimney, much
against his will. While he was there, a ball struck against the opposite
jam, and was taken by him as a trophy.[50]

William had been worried about his family being in the midst of
battle, not knowing at first that Huck had gone to Williamson's plantation
after stopping first at his house, and he asked the other two Regimental
commanders to parlay with the British to avoid a fight. That idea was
immediately rejected, so William then asked if they could fire warning
shots to draw the British away from his home. He was finally convinced
that neither were good options for winning the battle.[51] It seems that
the great Colonel Bratton was quite human, after all.

The next day, Martha and neighbors tended to the wounded from
both sides, and according to Elizabeth Ellet's book, Martha rescued one
of the wounded prisoners the Patriots wanted put to death—the same
lieutenant who had saved her from a reaping hook when she was being
interrogated at her house the night before.[52]

The painting on the previous page is believed to be a fairly accurate
representation of Martha Bratton, who was sending Watt, the Bratton
family's trusted slave, to warn her husband that British troops were

advancing toward their home early on July 11, 1780. The painting beneath, also believed to include a likeness of Colonel Bratton, portrays Patriot militia officers making plans to attack the British troops at Williamson's plantation under a bright aurora borealis early on the morning of July 12, 1780. Historical records, according to Michael Scoggins, who shared the images and related information via email July 23, 2015, indicate that "a rare and spectacular occurrence of the aurora borealis" occurred on the nights of July 11 and 12, 1780.

The Battle of Huck's Defeat was an enormous morale booster for the Patriots, as it was the first time they had defeated the British regular troops; word spread quickly throughout the backcountry, and men were eager to fight again. Two regiments of militia from the New Acquisition were formed under Sumter's command, one led by Colonel Hill and the other by Colonel Bratton.[53]

≈ ≈ ≈

Colonel Bratton participated in six more battles in 1780. The first two battles were at Rocky Mount and Hanging Rock, two British outposts situated close to one another. Rocky Mount, overlooking the Catawba River in Fairfield County, was attacked and won by General Sumter's forces in late July.[54] The next battle was a few days later at Hanging Rock in Lancaster County but it ended in defeat for the Patriots during a torrential rainstorm.

The Battle of Fishing Creek on August 18, a couple of weeks later, was another victory for the British. Sumter's army was making camp and feeling safe. It had been an extremely hot day with many bathing in the river, eating, or sleeping, and the men were caught off guard and panicked when Colonel Tarleton's forces attacked. Because of this, it was a battle that also became known as Sumter's Surprise.

On September 26, Sumter's brigade was at Bigger's Ferry on the Catawba River in York County being pursued by a detachment of British dragoons headed by Lord Rawdon. Fire was exchanged, but the British left, heading for Charlotte, and Sumter's militia moved north.[55]

Colonel Bratton next encountered the British at Fishdam's Ford in Chester County on November 9, another attempted surprise attack by the British. The British commander, Major James Wemyss, was wounded and captured, the skirmish only lasted about twenty minutes, and a victory by the Patriots was achieved despite the surprise. Colonel Bratton, however, did not arrive before the victory as it was far from his camp and he could not get there in time.[56]

The next battle Colonel Bratton fought in was a solid victory. Sumter's army had expected an attack from British Colonel Tarleton on November 20 at Blackstock's farm but fortified themselves well and had very few casualties compared with numerous casualties for the British.[57]

Colonel Bratton is confirmed as leading his men through the next seven battles:

+ Fort Granby, February 19–21, 1781
+ Fort Motte, February 24, 1781
+ Fort Watson, February 27–28, 1781
+ Radcliff's Bridge, March 6, 1781
+ Four Hole Swamp, April 7, 1781
+ Biggin's Bridge and Biggin's Church, July 16, 1781
+ Quinby's Bridge and Shubrick's Plantation, July 17, 1781[58]

The last battle that Colonel Bratton is believed to have participated in was the Battle of Eutaw Springs on September 8, 1781. It took place about fifty miles north of Charleston, and was the last important battle for the Carolinas. The Patriots were victorious, but the battle lasted three hours "in the scorching temperatures of early September. Both sides had fought hard, and casualties were high. The killed and wounded for the Americans amounted to more than 600 men out of approximately 2,000 engaged."[59]

"South Carolina played a decisive role in the winning of the American Revolution ... more pitched battles, clashes, and actions involving guerrilla forces were fought in South Carolina than in any other state of the original thirteen during the war."[60]

Home from the War

Colonel Bratton, at the age of thirty-nine, went home from war for the last time after the great Patriot victory at Eutaw Springs. Colonel Bratton had seen hundreds die during battle and was away from home much of the time. When he wasn't fighting, he was traveling, guarding, recruiting, planning, and sometimes organizing his own militiamen.

He had fought alongside some of his brothers, and at least one of them—his older brother, John—did not make it out of the war alive. John "died early in 1776, probably as a result of sickness incurred during the Snow Campaign."[61] The home of Colonel Bratton's friend, Rev. John Simpson, was burned, leaving his wife and children homeless. Many other friends and neighbors had family members killed, their homes burned or damaged and their crops and supplies plundered.

"The backcountry bore the scars of a civil war more brutal than anything expected. The heritage of their war, their hostility, and their interest in revenge were more long lasting."[62] Lawlessness continued in the backcountry, and in 1784 Colonel Bratton complained in a letter to Governor Guerard that thieves were "robbing ... travelers in open daylight upon the highway," and that it was "out of the power of the law to suppress them."[63]

Colonel Bratton was not as unfortunate as several members of York County, but as a natural leader and responsible citizen, he became more and more involved as a change agent himself through politics and other civic activities. In 1785 he was elected to the South Carolina General Assembly—a way, perhaps, to make more of a difference in backcountry conditions for his family and others. Colonel Bratton also distinguished himself with a civil service record that continued through 1797. Before describing his civil service record, however, let's take another look at Brattonsville and his York County life, focusing first on the Colonel's wife, Martha, and their children.

Martha and the Children

Martha had been left alone for months at a time, although there were growing Bratton families nearby who were sure to lend a hand when needed—especially during planting and harvesting season. Women's roles in the American Revolution are not well represented, as many were considered less intelligent and even morally inferior to men, but there have been a few books written about heroines of the Revolutionary War and of their lives. Some of these women visited their husbands on the outskirts of battle, and there were even camp followers on both sides of the Revolution to tend to the needs of its soldiers. Others, like Martha, sent or carried messages to troops to warn them of the enemy's strategy or location. We can also be quite sure that Martha knew how to shoot a musket and to defend herself in other ways.

Martha, considering her reputation and intelligence, was probably a good manager of people and property, too, a very good thing since her husband had been away so much during the Revolutionary War. Women of that era were not usually in charge of managing plantations or doing other men's work, but social norms break down during wartime, and women in the backcountry did not necessarily fit the norm, anyway.

One of Martha's many responsibilities would have been caring for the sick, as most of the healthcare was provided in the home:

> Early settlers in the Carolina Piedmont relied heavily on home treatments of diseases and injuries. Family traditions, social customs and superstition often shaped accepted medical practices in the eighteenth and nineteenth centuries. Home remedies and treatments were handed down from generation to generation in families, shared from neighbor to neighbor, and learned from home medical guides and newspapers. Medicinal recipes usually featured mixtures of garden herbs, local wild plants, and roots, and purchased narcotic drugs and chemicals.[64]

Life expectancy in the eighteenth century was about thirty-five years, including the high number of children who died during childbirth or childhood. A testament to Martha's skills as a healer is the fact that so many of her children—at least, all that we have a record of—lived to adulthood, something quite unusual in those days. She may have had births we have no record of, however. According to the Bethesda Presbyterian Church Cemetery interment records and her tombstone, three unidentified female infants are buried with Martha.[65] Gravestones were very expensive, and it wasn't unusual for more than one person to be buried in the same place. Logic would suggest that the infants on Martha's tombstone were her daughters.

The education of her children would have been another responsibility for Martha. Education in the Carolina colonies usually took place at home unless parents could afford to educate their children through private schools or tutors. We do not know much about the state of education in the Bratton home, but the Scots-Irish Presbyterians placed great importance upon education, and the Bratton boys probably received at least the basics of reading, writing, and arithmetic. Education in terms of *book learning* was not seen as important for girls; if they were taught to read, it was primarily so they could read the Bible and other religious texts. A testament to the importance of education and healthcare for the Brattons is the fact that two of their sons became physicians, and that—as Brattonsville grew—a school for the family and for other children in the community was eventually established at Brattonsville.

Martha and William had their sixth child, Agnes, in 1785—another baby girl. Their seventh and last child was born in 1789, a second son they named John Simpson Bratton. At the age of thirty-nine, Martha's child bearing was over. Her children were born over a twenty-three-year span of time, and at least some of the older children were married and having children of their own when Martha had her last child—not an unusual situation for those days.

While Martha was taking care of home and hearth and having babies, her husband was busy expanding the plantation's business. According to the Historic Brattonsville website (chmuseums.org), Colonel Bratton obtained a license to operate a tavern in 1786, so that brought more prosperity to the family. By 1790 he owned twelve slaves, making him one of the largest slave owners in the region. He also acquired a cotton gin at some point, taking advantage of the revival of the cotton market after the invention of the cotton gin in 1793.[66] Colonel Bratton, as he was known after distinguishing himself in the American Revolution, also continued his long, twenty-eight history of civil service, which had begun when he was appointed as a road overseer.

Civil Service

As a civil servant, Colonel Bratton had power, prestige, and credibility. Before the war, he had been a road overseer, a justice of the peace, and a tax inquirer and collector.[67] After the war, he was also held in high esteem as a Revolutionary War hero. When South Carolina reorganized its county court system in 1785, he became one of the original justices and magistrates from York County, and, as previously mentioned, was also elected to the South Carolina General Assembly in 1785.[68]

Colonel Bratton represented the Camden district in the General Assembly's House of Representatives during the Sixth, Seventh, and Eighth General Assemblies from 1785 to 1795. The General Assembly was dominated "by army officers, many of them veterans of the Civil War," and "it was the first legislature in South Carolina's history in which a majority of legislators came from outside Charleston's District."[69]

The backcountry finally had the representation it had wanted for so many years, and laws were passed that began to meet its residents' needs. Some of the laws passed would seem harsh by today's standards. A vagrancy law, for example, was passed in 1785 that provided "for the erection of shipping posts, stocks, and pillories in every county."[70] The passage of similar laws, along with others that punished and deterred people from even more serious offenses, did, however, help curb the lawlessness of the backcountry, and more equitable representation provided the population with advantages they had never known during the colonial period.

In 1790 Colonel Bratton was the York County delegate to the South Carolina Constitutional Convention. He was then elected a senator three consecutive times, serving from 1791 to late 1794. South Carolina and the rest of the states were going through many growing pains as their new nation developed, and Colonel Bratton became a part of this process. An important issue was dealing with the huge cost of the Revolution, including back pay for its soldiers, supplies, and items lost in battle such as horses and guns. This was one of Colonel Bratton's most important duties from 1785 to 1790,[71] and it was an especially difficult task during 1786 when many Americans were suffering from a post-war economic depression.

In addition to his service as a representative and as a senator, Colonel Bratton held a couple of other important positions between 1786 and 1791. He was Commissioner of Aero Iron Works in 1786, the ironworks that was located in York County and had been burned by the infamous Captain Huck in 1781.[72] He was also commissioner to superintend the building of jails and courthouses in the Pinckney District in 1791.

When he was elected Sheriff of the Pinckney Legal District in 1795, a newly created district that included York County, Colonel Bratton resigned as Senator. He served as sheriff for three terms (1795–1798.[73]

"County's First Court."
Article from the *Yorkville Enquirer* describing the court and listing Colonel Bratton as one of three Judges. The other two articles, "Looking Backward," provide interesting commentary on the times. From the York County Library Digital Collections.

COUNTY'S FIRST COURT

Yorkville Enquirer

Records Show Initial Tribunal Was Held Here in Year 1786.

THREE JUDGES WERE ON THE BENCH

Names Familiar To York County For Ages Included In List Of Those Serving On Both Grand and Petit Juries At The Start.

Owing to the number of former residents spending a few days in Yorkville and York county in connection with the Kings Mountain Sesqui-Centennial, a little of the early history of York county may have more than an ordinary appeal. Especially interested, of course, will be those people in various sections of the county who are direct descendants from the early settlers mentioned in connection with the first court ever held in York county.

Some facts concerning the first court held in 1786 follow:

Grand Jury—Robert Johnston, Sr., foreman; Robert Leeper, Sr., Robert Adams, John Faires, Sr., James Faires, Matthew Bigger, Thomas Black, Sr., John Anderson, James Wilson, B. C. Sam'l Moore, Warren Beaufort, Joseph Lowry, William Minter, Col. Fred'k Hambright, William Copelass, Sr., Capt. Wm. Byers, John Venable, James Ross, Capt. John Chambers, Philip Sandifer.

Petit Jury—William Davis, Joseph McKenzie, Thomas Patton, James Bigger, Jr., Joseph Waddle, Alex McWhorter, Archibald Barron, Nathan Henderson, John McConnell, John Swan, John Polk, Sr., James Greer, Samuel Rainey, James Mitchell, John Carson, John Jordan, John Dickey, James Hillhouse, Robert Kirkpatrick, David Dickey, Alex Barron, James Hope, John Moore, William Smith, Abraham Greer, Isaac Sellars, William Blair, Robert Brown, John Wilson, William Carson, Sr., Francis Gilmore, Robert Patterson.

Judges—Col. William Bratton, John Drennan, Esq., David Leech, James Wilson, Col. William Hill.

October court of 1787:

Grand Jury—Col. Samuel Watson, foreman; David Johnston, Robert Leeper, Jr., John Kerr, James Moore, John McConnell, Joseph Feemster, James Jamison, James Martin, Adams Meek, Archibald Barron, Richard Wilson, John Finley.

Colonial Commander of the district between Broad River and Catawba—Col. Thomas Neel.

Officers at outbreak of the war who served until 1779—Col. Thomas Neel, Lt. Col. Ezekiel Polk.

Col. Neel killed at Stono, June 29th, 1779.

After Stono—Col. William Bratton, Col. Samuel Watson, Col. Andrew Neal, Col. William Hill.

Col. Andrew Neel killed at Rocky Mount.

After Rocky Mount and until close of the Revolution—Col. William Hill, Col. William Bratton, Col. Samuel Watson.

Incomplete list of officers of lower rank: Lt. Col. James Hawthorn, Major Ross, Major Hal Dickson, Capt. Malcolm Henry, Capt. William Henry, Capt. Thomas Spratt, Capt. Joseph Howe, Capt. Jacob Barnet, Capt. Thomas Neel, Jr., Capt. William Byers, Capt. John Chambers.

Early court records reveal that the first will be recorded in York County was that of James Powell, dated 1800.

Evening Herald

Looking Backward

York County court records prior to 1800 describe a case in which one man bit off the ear of another man. This crime was considered one of the lowest and instead of suing for damages the plaintiff made an agreement whereby the defendant confessed his crime in court. Thereafter the defendant and his family were shunned.

Evening Herald, Rock Hill

Tuesday, Nov. 15, 1955

Looking Backward

Nov. 14, 1925

Featherbeds were a rarity and straw was a luxury with many residents of York County after the Revolutionary War, minutes of the court records 130 years ago reveal.

Evening Herald, Rock Hill

Monday, Nov. 14, 1955

Papers of Dr. David A. Bigger. Kindness of Mrs. Bigger. July 16, 1954

Colonel Bratton's last form of civil service took place in 1797, when he showed his commitment to education by becoming a trustee " to establish and incorporate a college in the Pinckney District,"[74] Alexandria College. By 1798 Colonel Bratton's civil service had ended, and he was fifty-five years old. It was time for him to go home and stay, devoting the remainder of his years to his plantation and family.

Will and Estate

By 1813, Colonel Bratton's plantation had grown to be one of the largest in the county, and his slave population followed suit. By the time of his death in 1815, he owned twenty-three slaves.[75]

Colonel Bratton had lived through the American Revolution and four Presidents of the United States of America. His country was full of young people with large families. The average age for its white population was around sixteen, and the average number of children born was eight. Colonel Bratton was seventy years old and had lived a long time for that day and age. He was growing weaker and needed to make plans for the disposition of his property. In 1813 Colonel Bratton decided to complete his will.

All but two of Colonel Bratton's children were married at the time: his youngest daughter, Mary, and his youngest son, John. Men usually passed their land on to sons in those days, providing for their wives and daughters with gifts of property and with the right for their widows and unmarried daughters to live on the land and to be supported by the estate. Colonel Bratton's will followed this pattern.

His wife, Martha, was given the use of the plantation property for the remainder of her days, along with several slaves and other items of personal property. His unmarried daughter, Mary, was given two hundred acres, furniture, slaves, her choice of one horse, and permission to live on the main plantation as long as she remained unmarried. Colonel Bratton's four married daughters were given two to five slaves each. His oldest son, William, had moved to Winnsboro and already had his own home; William received one Negro boy. Colonel Bratton's youngest son, John, received gifts of at least four slaves and property such as guns and tools, and he would eventually inherit the plantation.[76]

My transcription of the Colonel Bratton's Will is typed as it was written and copied from the Department of Archives and History in Columbia, South Carolina.[77] Incorrect capitalization, punctuation, and spelling errors were common in those days, and I have left all of those errors in the will for purposes of authenticity. However, I did separate the items of the will into separate paragraphs for ease of reading.

WILL OF
WILLIAM BRATTON
SOUTH CAROLINA

South Carolina

In the name of God Amen. I William Bratton of York District in the state aforesaid being weak of Body but of sound and disposing mind and memory do make and ordain this my last Will and Testament in manner and form Following First I give to my wife Martha Bratton the following Negroes that is to say June, Lydia Peter, Netty, Nelson July, Cloe Ben Kitty Harry, Watt; Polly Harriott, Butler Limus Jack Winney Jim June Archey Patt Isey and Moses and all my beds and bed furniture my whole stock of horses Cattle sheep and Hogs, my waggon and Geers, My Riding Chair and Harness, also all my household and kitchen furniture, also all my plantation tools her saddle and bridle, my loom and its appurtenances my smith tools my cotton machine and all the salt and provisions of any kind that I may die possessed of to have and to hold all the aforesaid Negroes goods and Chattels to my said wife for and during the term of her natural life

Item--I also give and bequeath to my said wife Martha Bratton the use of My plantation whereon I now live together with the tract of two hundred acres of land I purchased of Henry Good for and during the term of her natural life

Item from and immediately after the decease of my said wife I give--and devise the said tract of two hundred acres of land I purchased of Henry Good to my daughter Mary Bratton together with my bed and bed furniture my riding Chair and Harness, her saddle and Bridle and her choice of one horse out of my stock of horses my household and kitchen furniture unto my said daughter Mary Bratton her Heir and assigns forever

Item from and immediately after the decease of my said wife I give and devise the said plantation whereon I now reside together with all and singular the aforesaid Stock of Cattle sheep Hogs and Horses, (except the choice of one horse out of my stock which has been before bequeathed to my daughter Mary Bratton my waggon and geers plantation tools Loom and appurtenances unto my son John S Bratton to have and to hold the said Land, good and Chattels to my said son John S Bratton his heirs and assigns forever

Item I give and bequeath to my said daughter Mary Bratton the following Negroes that is to say Jack Winney, Izey Limus Harriott and her increase, and it is my Will and desire that my said daughter Mary Bratton shall have her maintenance and support on and from the plantation whereon I now reside so long as she remains single and unmarried

Item I give and bequeath to my said son John S. Bratton the following Negroes to wit, Watt Polly Jim & Nelson also my rifle gun, my sword and Pistols and Cotton Machine & Smith tools––

Item–I give to my daughter Jean Simpson two negroes to wit June and Lydia

Item––I give to my daughter Martha Foster five negroes (Viz) Patt July Cloe Ben and Kitty

Item––I give to my daughter Ealie Sadler two negroes (Viz) Peter and Betty

Item––I give to my daughter Agnus McCaw two Negroes to wit––archy and Luce

Item I give to my daughter Elizabeth Irwin two negroes (Viz) Butler and Moses,

Item I give to my son William Bratton my negroe Boy Harry––

Item It is my will and desire that my crop of Cotton that is or may be on hand at the time of my death may be immediately sent to market and sold and also that the residue of my personal property not herein bequeathed be sold at public sale and that the money arising from the sale of my said crop of cotton and the residue of my personal Estate be applied to the payment of my just debts and if any monies remain after the payment of my just debts I give and bequeath to my wife Martha Bratton

Item it is further my will and desire that all my negroes shall continue and remain on my plantation and continue to work the same in the usual manner that I have been in the practice of doing until a crop or crops shall be raised sufficient to pay and satisfy all just demands against my Estate at my death or at the death of my wife should she survive me, and that none of the Legacies herein given or devised shall be demandable or payable until all just debts or demands against my Estate be paid Lastly I do hereby appoint my wife Martha Bratton Executrix and Doctor William Bratton and Doctor James Simpson, Executors of this my last will and testament hereby revoking all wills by me heretofore made, and declaring this to be my last will and testament in witness whereof I have hereunto set my hand and Seal this 27 day of December in the year of our Lord one thousand eight hundred and thirteen——————

Signed Sealed Published) Wm. Bratton (Seal)
Pronounced & Declared)
in presence of   )
Nathaniel Moore
Thos. Moore
Eli Moore

Colonel Bratton's estate was inventoried and appraised in 1815, and it totaled $8247.75. That amount is between $105, 000 and $127,000 in today's money. When you consider that the plantation was practically self-sustaining with slave labor, it would have been worth much more. Among the items inventoried were plantation supplies you would expect, such as horses, cattle, sheep and hogs, plantation utensils and tools. Three groups of items were listed as worth over $400 but the most expensive item was worth over ten times that amount: "Negroes," valued at $6,505.[78]

William Bratton's Legacy

Colonel William Bratton died on February 9, 1815, at the age of seventy-three. Martha Bratton followed less than a year later, on January 16, 1816, when she was sixty-six years old. Both were buried at the Bethesda Presbyterian Church Cemetery, where many Bratton family members are buried. William Bratton's legacy lives on through people and places that express his values and honor his memory. Among those are his children, of course, and the establishment of Historic Brattonsville, now a "living history" plantation and battlefield.

The Bratton Heirs

The Brattons raised eight children to adulthood, quite a feat in those days. It is beyond the scope of this book to capture all of their lives, although some are quite fascinating, so a brief summary of each is provided.

1. Elsie Bratton (1766–1825) married David Sadler, who fought with Colonel Bratton at the battle of Huck's

Defeat. According to family lore, David Sadler asked Colonel Bratton for Elsie's hand in marriage after the Revolutionary War ended, but he refused and locked Elsie in her room in the second story of their log home. With the help of Watt (a Bratton slave), she escaped out of her window and down a ladder, and David carried her away on the back of his horse. They returned about three weeks after their elopement to ask for the Colonel's blessing, received it, and went on to have twelve children.[79]

2. Jane Bratton (1768) married Dr. James Simpson, who was the son of Bratton family friend and minister John Simpson. Jane and her husband moved to Anderson County with her father-in-law, her sister, Elsie, and Elsie's husband. Her date of death was not found.

3. Martha Bratton (1771–1813) married Rev. John Foster.

4. Dr. William Bratton Jr. (1773–1850) moved to Winnsboro and married Christina Winn, oldest daughter of Colonel Richard Winn. They had one child, and then Christina died in 1817. He married Isabella Means, and they had two children, one who became the famous Civil War general you will read about in this book's next chapter.

5. Elizabeth Bratton (1779–1840) married William Jaor Ross Erwin.

6. Agnes Bratton (1785–1840) married Robert McCaw.

7. Mary Bratton's date of birth is uncertain. Mary married George Steele, and she died in 1838.

8. John S. Bratton (1789–1874), the first heir of Brattonsville, married Harriet Rainey, who outlived him by over thirty years and ran the plantation until her death in 1874.

Both of Colonel Bratton's sons became physicians, and there have been Bratton physicians in every generation since then. William and

John, according to family tradition, "trained in the medical profession under Dr. James Simpson,"[80] the son of Rev. John Simpson and the husband of Jane Bratton, William and John's sister. Three of John's sons studied medicine, followed by one of their sons and several other Brattons throughout the entire family history.

Historic Brattonsville

Much has been written in great detail about Brattonsville since the Revolutionary War days, and an entire book could be written on the subject. Historic Brattonsville, as it is now referred to, is listed on the National Register of Historic Places and became open to the public in 1971. It was leased to the York County Historical Commission in 1969, and was badly in need of restoration. The last Bratton family member to occupy it, the family of Virginia Bratton, moved to Yorkville in 1914.

6—Evening Herald, Sat., March 22, 1975

Auxiliary honors pioneer doctors

By ANN WILKERSON
Evening Herald staff writer

DR. JAMES RUFUS BRATTON
Began practice in Yorkville in 1845

DR. JAMES RUFUS BRATTON
Has practiced in Rock Hill since 1940

DR. RUFUS ANDRAL BRATTON
Died in 1942 at the age of 82

DR. JAMES RUFUS BRATTON JR.
He is fifth-generation doctor

"Auxiliary Honors Pioneer Doctors." Article by the *Evening Herald*, March 22, 1975. From the York County Library Digital Collections.

Historic Brattonsville is a 778 acre site that includes a visitors' center and bookstore, over thirty colonial and antebellum structures, a Revolutionary War battlefield site, trails, and heritage breed farm animals. Among the structures are what is thought to be the original home of Colonel and Martha Bratton; The Homestead, an opulent, formal two-story house built by Dr. John S. Bratton, the son of Colonel Bratton; and the Brick House, which served as a residence, country store, and post office for many years. There are also a gin, slave houses, and various outbuildings.

For a concise, yet fascinating summary of what happened to Brattonsville and some of its family members after Colonel Bratton and Martha died, please refer to appendix B in this book, which contains an article written by Joseph H. Rainey, curator. The article contains interesting facts about the school and store established at Brattonsville, the War Between the States, and the hardships of Reconstruction in York County. It also contains a story about one of Colonel Bratton's sons, Dr. J. Rufus Bratton; Rufus was allegedly involved in the lynching of a black militia leader after the Civil War, and escaped federal authorities by fleeing to Canada.[81]

Before leaving the subject of Brattonsville, it is important to once more address an issue that Historic Brattonsville and this author recognize as very important and sensitive: the Bratton family slaves. Slavery was a part of the Bratton family legacy through the Civil War. However terrible, slavery was a real, everyday part of the social fabric that made up white society for a long time—and one of the main reasons that the Brattons and other planters prospered. When Dr. John S. Bratton, son of Colonel Bratton, died in 1843, he "had the largest plantation in the county ... and was also the largest slaveholder, owning around 143 slaves."[82] Owning slaves, however, does not mean that the Brattons were inherently evil anymore than not owning slaves would have made them inherently good; it was a fact of life and accepted as such by the majority of Southern white Americans.

Historic Brattonsville holds periodic reenactments of life in the eighteenth and nineteenth centuries that include the descendants of the Brattonsville slaves who provide African-American interpretation. There are even occasions where people are allowed to spend the night in slave houses, wearing shackles to experience to some extent what it would have been like to live as a slave. A link on the Historic Brattonsville website is devoted to African American history and stories of the Bratton slaves.[83] There are also hundreds of Brattonsville slave descendants who have traced their lineage to a white Bratton male. Strauss Moore Shiple, who has worked with family for years to find cousins who came from the Bratton line, said in a 2008 interview on the subject, "What is now called Brattonsville is an important part of York County's history, and what we want to do is show that our side of the family, all descended from that same Bratton family, have a place in that history, too."[84]

Historic Brattonsville's recognition of this part of the Bratton legacy, along with its reenactments and living history site makes it well worth the trip. One of the homes in Historic Brattonsville was even used as a location in the 2000 movie, *The Patriot*, starring Mel Gibson.

Summary and Conclusions

During his seventy-plus years, William Bratton emigrated from Ireland to the British colonies of North America and eventually settled with other Scots-Irish in the wild backcountry of South Carolina. He joined the backcountry militia, at first to protect his family from local lawlessness, and then to fight Indians, Tories, and Loyalists as a Patriot. He became a Revolutionary War hero.

Colonel Bratton, as he was known after the war, was involved in civil service with his community beginning in his thirties. After the war, he helped shape the new United States of America while serving as a district representative and a state senator. He held several other service positions, and was even a trustee of a local college.

While Colonel Bratton was planting, protecting, and serving, he and his talented wife, Martha, also a hero of the Revolution, were also busy raising a large family of eight children and becoming one of the wealthiest and most prominent families of York County, South Carolina. Two of their sons became physicians, beginning a long family tradition that continues today, and one of them managed the family plantation so well that it became the largest in the county. Brattonsville is now a living history site in York County, South Carolina, that provides reenactments of life in colonial times.

By all accounts, William Bratton was a strong leader and a loving father who served his country with courage and honor. His obituary, published in the Charleston City Gazette on February 28, 1815, is an excellent tribute that says it best.

> *Col. William Bratton* - Died on the 9th of Feb. 1815, in York District in the 72nd year of his age. He was one of the old Revolutionary characters worthy to be remembered. He was one of the heroes of '76, who bravely defended the rights of our country, and was instrumental in procuring for us the blessing of freedom and independence. He was a fine patriot, and had naturally a strong love for independence. Under a well-regulated government, he was a good citizen but could not tamely submit to the encroachments of any man or body of men, on his perfect rights. His services were zealously devoted to his country through the Revolutionary war, and for many years afterwards in the Legislature. Through a long and active life he generally enjoyed good health, possessing a good constitution and a firm mind, judicious and intrepid in the execution of his plans. At length he was taken with a lingering disease, which terminated his existence. It may be truly said of him that he was a strictly honest, virtuous, good man. He was exemplary in his integrity, benevolent and friendly in his disposition, ever ready to relieve the distressed and help the needy. He has left a widow and a numerous family, besides a large circle of friends and acquaintances to lament his loss.[85]

Our next chapter skips a generation, taking us to one of Colonel Bratton's grandsons, John Bratton, who became a well-known hero in the War Between the States. Like his grandfather, he was also a farmer, a politician, and more, and exemplified the determination and skills needed to help his family survive a war and to serve his young country with honor.

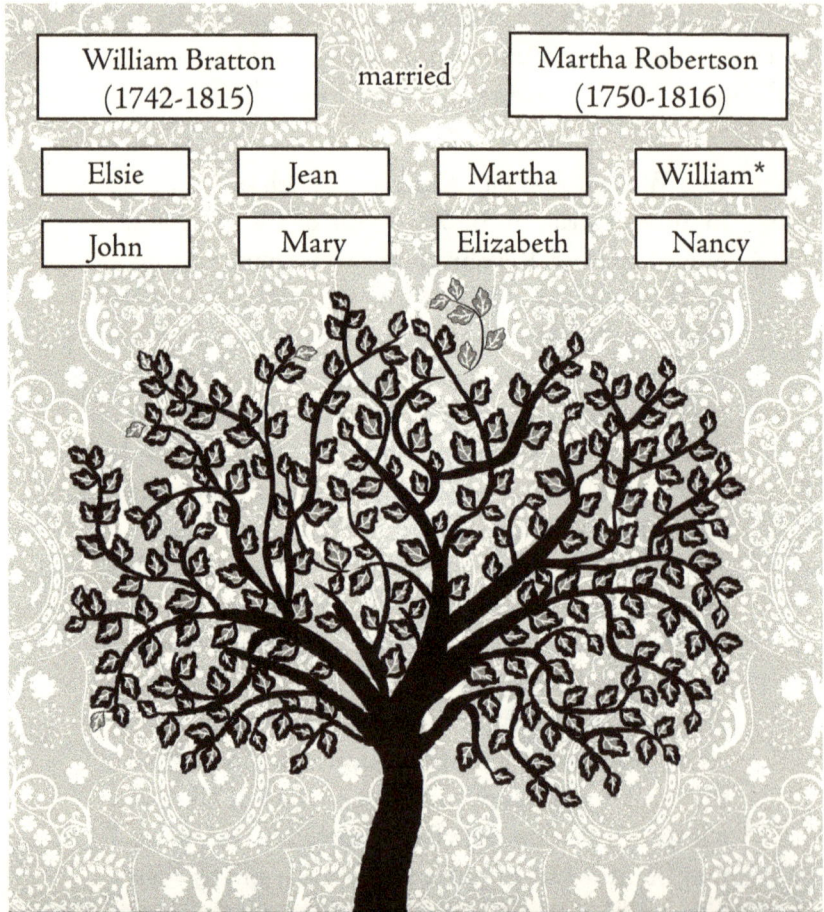

William Bratton
(1742-1815)

married

Martha Robertson
(1750-1816)

Elsie

Jean

Martha

William*

John

Mary

Elizabeth

Nancy

*William A. Bratton
(1773-1850)

married

Isabella J. Means
(1789-1858)

John Bratton
(1831–1898)

CHAPTER TWO

General John Bratton
Old Reliable

———★———

T HEY AFFECTIONATELY CALLED HIM "Old Reliable" after his service in the American Civil War. As a man of education and South Carolina's planter class, John Bratton was also known for his personal honor, courage, and sense of duty. He rose from a private to a brigadier general during the Civil War, where his behavior was even honored and acknowledged by the enemy.

John Bratton was pulled into politics at the beginning of the Civil War and became even more politically active after the war ended. He served in several capacities, but all he really wanted to do was ride his horses and manage his plantations in the sweet Carolina sunshine. However, as a gentleman farmer and physician from Winnsboro, South Carolina, with a family heritage of service and honor, John Bratton could not resist the call of duty. Like his grandfather, Colonel William Bratton, and his father, of whom you will hear more shortly, John always responded to the call of duty. He helped to navigate his state and country through the miseries of the Reconstruction era in the South and was an influential part of South Carolina's Conservative regime when Reconstruction ended.

General Bratton, as he was referred to after the Civil War, was finally able to return to farming full-time around 1890, when he retired from politics. He died eight years later. John saw more misery during his lifetime than many people see in two, yet the General died with his good nature intact and a grateful heart, and with accolades from all who knew him.

Growing up in Winnsboro

John Bratton was born in Winnsboro, South Carolina, on March 7, 1831. Winnsboro is located in beautiful Fairfield County in the Piedmont of South Carolina, and sits between the Broad River on the west and the Wateree River on the east. When John was growing up, it was a blend of Scots-Irish and highly cultured French Huguenots from Charleston and the coastal regions, and it was sometimes referred to as "the Charleston of the upcountry."

Winnsboro was chartered in 1785, and became one of the biggest producers of cotton in the upland after the invention of the cotton gin in 1793. The majority of the population consisted of the African American slaves needed to work in the cotton fields.

Winnsboro was also known for its quality of education and its high number of religious communicants.

"Mt. Zion in Winnsboro was one of the first schools to be chartered in the South Carolina Upcountry in 1777, started in Charleston by a benevolent group who saw need to improve cultural and educational conditions in the frontier area."[1] It began as an elementary school and became a college in 1785, and families from all over the state sent their children to school there. In 1848 a boarding school for the education of young ladies, the Winnsboro Female Institute, became a counterpart to Mt. Zion College, and girls were sent there to master the skills required of ladies of social standing.

While attending school, the children also went to church on a regular basis. "No part of the state is said to have had more religious communicants than Fairfield."[2] Mobley's Meeting House, six miles west of present-day Winnsboro, was begun by Presbyterians but was used by all denominations. It was also the site of a famous Revolutionary War battle in 1780 led by Colonel William Bratton, John's grandfather.

Parents and Siblings

John Bratton's father was William Bratton, a well-to-do and widely respected physician and planter and the son of Revolutionary War hero Colonel William Bratton. Dr. William Bratton was one of the "first pupils and graduates of Mt. Zion College of Winnsboro and later received training under the tutelage of Dr. [Benjamin] Rush,"[3] an eminent and popular physician, civic leader, and humanitarian in Philadelphia. Dr. Bratton also served during the War of 1812; represented the Fairfield District in the 24th and 25th South Carolina General Assemblies; was a member of the licensing board of physicians at Columbia in 1817; and was commissioner of public buildings in the Fairfield District in 1831.[4]

Dr. Bratton moved to Winnsboro around 1805, when he married his first wife, Christina Winn. Christina was the daughter of Maj. Gen. Richard Winn, who served with Colonel Bratton during the Revolutionary War at Huck's Defeat. Winn was also was one of the founders of Winnsboro, and the town was named in his honor. In 1805 he gave Dr. Bratton a wedding gift in honor of his daughter, Christina: one hundred acres of land adjoining the town of Winnsboro[5] and a house named Wynne Dee.

Dr. Bratton and Christina had four children,[6] but all of them died at a young age. I have not been able to locate the name and burial place for one of the children, but three are buried at the Sion Presbyterian Cemetery in Winnsboro: William M. Bratton (1801–1806); Nancy Bratton (1804–1805); and Sarah Elizabeth Bratton (1813–1815). Christina died a couple of years later in 1817 and is also buried at the Sion Presbyterian Cemetery.

Dr. Bratton's second marriage was to the woman who would become John Bratton's mother, Isabella Jane Means Judge (1824–1905). Isabella was the widow of Rev. Hilliard Judge, a Methodist minister, and had three sons by Reverend Judge: John Means Judge, born in 1814; James Lawrence Judge, born in 1816; and Hilliard M. Judge, born in 1818.[7]

Dr. Bratton and Isabella had four children, two girls and two boys. Their first child, Isabella "Belle" Means Bratton, was born in 1824 and was soon followed by another daughter born in 1825, Mary Means Bratton. A son, William M. Bratton (he was given the same name as the firstborn son of Dr. Bratton and his first wife, Christina), was born in 1826, followed by John M. Bratton, who was born at Wynne Dee, the family residence. John's middle initial comes from his mother, who referred to him as "John M. Bratton" in her will,[8] but he rarely, if ever, signed his name as anything other than John Bratton.

John Bratton was the last child born to Dr. William and Isabella Bratton, and doubtlessly benefited from the attention bestowed on the youngest of seven surviving children. John's father was said to be a very kind and benevolent physician, so John was probably quite well-treated by both his family and by their community.

Childhood and Education

Although we have few specifics, John probably had a great time growing up in Winnsboro. His father could more than afford to provide for all of his family's needs as a physician who was also a planter. He owned 100 slaves in 1830 and 176 slaves in 1840, a clear reflection of prosperity.[9] In addition, Fairfield County, with its rolling hills and fertile valleys, was considered a picturesque, healthy place to live. John lived on a thriving plantation where he ate well, learned to ride horses, and had a large family. When John was three years old, he may have witnessed one of the most spectacular meteor showers in history, a three-day event that was referred to as "the night the stars fell," when many thought judgment day was at hand and fell to their knees in prayer or ran to churches.

John was probably aware that Andrew Jackson, who fought with John's paternal grandfather in the American Revolution, was president of the United States from the time of his birth until John was about six years old. He may have also heard of the Panic of 1837, a financial crisis that resulted in a recession lasting several years that some blamed on President Jackson. The Great Fire of Charleston, in which half of Charleston burned, was also a likely topic of much conversation in Winnsboro. There were other foul winds blowing, too, that were an indicator of things to come: South Carolina, upset about a tariff it felt was unfair, threatened to secede in 1832. Slaves in some places were revolting. A few years before John's birth, Denmark Vesey, a freed slave, planned an unsuccessful attack on Charleston. In the year John was born, an enslaved preacher named Nat Turner led nearly eighty slaves in a violent rebellion, killing at least fifty-seven whites. As a child, though, John was probably more interested in plantation life, and would have been clueless about what was to come.

John would have begun his education at home, instructed by family members or a tutor. State funded education was becoming more prevalent, but most Southerners believed education was a private matter that should begin in the home, and that it should include at least some

The Market House and Town Clock, Congress and Washington Streets, Winnsboro, SC. Built around 1833, it is the oldest continually used clock in America. This historic building and the one below would have been familiar sights to John Bratton. From the Historic American Buildings Survey, Fred D. Nichols, photographer, April 1940.

Winnsboro, SC, County Courthouse, built around 1832. It was designed by Robert Mills, architect of the Washington Monument. Courtesy of Fairfield County Museum, Winnsboro, SC.

religious education. Military academies like the Mt. Zion Institute in Winnsboro, which was where John went, were the typical educational institutions for male children of the elite. John may have been indulged at home but that was not the case at school, where discipline was sometimes quite harsh. While attending Mt. Zion, John was described as "quiet, cultured, self-possessed, unostentatious, efficient, without fear and without reproach, and not self-seeking,"[10] some of the leadership qualities that would be reflected throughout his life.

After Mt. Zion, John was educated at South Carolina College in Columbia. While there, he was a member of the Euphradian Society (also known as Phi Alpha Epsilon) and he graduated in 1850.[11] South Carolina College had an internationally renowned faculty and was considered the best college in South Carolina at the time.

John then attended South Carolina Medical College at Charleston, where his thesis was titled "Fecundation" (studies of fertility and pregnancy). After graduation, he attended medical lectures in Charleston and New Orleans.[12] John graduated as a physician in 1853 and began his practice in Fairfield County at the age of twenty-two.

Antebellum Prosperity

Medicine and Marriage

Medicine went through a lot of changes while John was attending medical school but it did not really progress much until after the Civil War. Back then physicians were not even licensed. "The American Medical Association (AMA) was created in 1846 to raise professional standards for doctors, [although] the organization made little progress influencing medical practices during its first half century."[13] When John entered medical school, physicians still bled and purged, believing that toxins and infections in the body were drawn out that way, and they used only a small number of medicines.

Physicians—all males—did not closely examine women, as it was considered improper. "The parochial, anti-scientific, and highly commercial atmosphere that prevailed in the nineteenth century was a major factor in retarding American medicine and contributing to the decline of the profession."[14] Both John and his father had among the best medical educations available at the time, but many people were still afraid—with good cause—that the cure would be worse than the disease. They would go to doctors as a last resort. Many people died from surgery, as sepsis was not well understood. Many others suffered from mercury poisoning from traditional medicines.

Although John had followed in the footsteps of his father to become a physician and he continued to practice medicine until the Civil War, his heart was on the farm. We do not know if farming had always been John's preference or if he found the reality of practicing medicine too disheartening, but his medical practice only lasted a few years. His father, Dr. William Bratton, had died in 1850, and when John's mother, Isabella Bratton, died in 1858, he inherited Wynne Dee and several acres of land, and farming became his focus. Mrs. Bratton had willed the house and land to him in 1857,[15] so John may have planned accordingly. "According to the 1860 Federal Census and slave schedules, he owned real estate worth $21,000 and seventy-six slaves in Fairfield District."[16]

≈ ≈ ≈

On September 1, 1859, John married Elizabeth Porcher DuBose,[17] an intelligent and educated young woman from an aristocratic background. Elizabeth's parents, Theodore Samuel DuBose and Jane Sinkler DuBose, were quite prominent in Winnsboro and were on the Register of Carolina French Huguenots. Mr. DuBose was born near Charleston and engaged in planting there until 1836 when he moved to Winnsboro where he also had large plantation interests. He was a nephew of General Francis Marion; also known as "The Swamp Fox," of Revolutionary War fame.[18] One of his sons, William Porcher DuBose, a graduate of the Citadel, became an Episcopal priest. After the Civil War, William also founded the School of Theology at the University of the South in Sewanee, Tennessee.

John was twenty-eight and Elizabeth was twenty-one when they married, and they had probably known each other for years due to their family connections. Elizabeth had been raised on nearby Roseland Plantation, one of several owned by her family. Both John and Elizabeth came from large families, which of course were quite common in those times. Elizabeth's parents had somewhere between eleven and fourteen children, but only seven of them made it to maturity. When John and

Elizabeth married, both of John's stepbrothers had moved to Atlanta and subsequently died there; his older brother, William, had moved to Alabama; and his sisters, Belle and Mary, were living nearby.

John and "Bettie," as he called her, would make their own large family—ten children in thirteen years. They quickly began their family, and their first child, William DuBose Bratton, was born on June 23, 1860, almost nine months to the day after they were married. Bettie was of the Episcopal faith and at some point, John Bratton became an Episcopalian, although we will see in one of his letters to Elizabeth that he did not always take religion as seriously as she did.

Plantation Life

Much has been written about antebellum life on Southern plantations, and one can imagine a large home full of house servants, numerous

Elizabeth Porcher DuBose Bratton. Courtesy of Lucy B. Doak, Bratton descendant, Raleigh, NC.

outbuildings such as barns, animal pens, cotton gins, smokehouses, tool sheds, slave quarters and more.

The life of a plantation mistress was definitely not all peaches and cream. Women were legally dependent on their husbands, with no control over property or children. They were responsible from sunup to sundown for running the household. They had to keep the silver and other valuables locked up, make sure the slaves, or "servants" as the Brattons referred to them, were behaving, and provide for the health, education, and morals of their children. Plantation mistresses were also expected to turn a blind eye to any sexual escapades or other misdeeds of their husbands or other male relatives.

Death during childbirth was common and healthcare was poor, even with a husband who was a physician, and women often spent much time nursing sick children and relatives. They were also often responsible for the health of their slaves.

Men also had role expectations, of course, and were expected to be of good moral character, good "masters," leaders, and providers for their family. They were expected to work with their overseers on running the plantation, to make purchasing decisions and all other major financial decisions, and to be socially prominent, chivalrous, and respectable. And they expected to be revered and honored by their families, at least in public. A man's honor was not to be taken lightly, and even Abraham Lincoln was challenged to a duel after calling a man a liar.

Without knowing more specifics of John and Bettie's life on their plantations, we cannot draw absolute conclusions but we can glean a picture or two from those who knew them or lived nearby. One type of perspective can be found in the oral histories of former slaves.

Slave Narratives

Slave Narratives: A Folk History of Slavery in the United States From Interviews with Former Slaves, 1936–1938, was a part of President Roosevelt's Federal Writer's Project, a federal government WPA project to fund written work and support writers during the Great Depression of the 1930s. I was quite fortunate in locating interviews with two of General Bratton's former slaves; an interview with a former slave whose husband rode with General Bratton and his "Red Shirts" after the Civil

War; and an interview with a former slave of General Bratton's good friends, the Gaillards. All of these interviews took place in Winnsboro between 1936 and 1938 and provide a few snapshots of what life in Winnsboro and on the plantation was like for the Brattons and their slaves before the Civil War changed their world forever.

Jim Henry and Phillip Evans were two former slaves who were born on the "Canaan place" as Phillip described it, about six miles northeast of Winnsboro. Jim was seventy-seven years old when he was interviewed and Phillip was eighty-five.

Jim Henry remembered General Bratton telling him that he (Jim Henry) came from " 'stinguished stock, dat he bought [his] father, James, from de Patrick Henry family in Virginia." Jim Henry said that during slavery, his family lived in "one of de nice log houses in de Bratton quarters," and slept in "pole beds, wid wheat straw ticks, and cotton pillows." The Brattons "was always sheep raisers, and us had woolen blankets and woolen clothes in de winter." Jim indicated that slave children were never made to work but were allowed to "run 'round in deir shirt-tails in summer time … and was as happy as de days was long." He said that when General Bratton was "off in de war," they had an overseer, who made "everybody," including Jim's mother, who was one of the seamstresses, go to the fields. Little children were watched by an old "mauma," and there were so many children, "twenty-five or thirty," that "they had to be fed out of doors." Jim said that there were actually two overseers, "Wade Rawls and a Mr. Timms." Jim Henry would have been between four and six years old at the end of the Civil War, and most of his "memories" came from his mother.[19]

Phillip Evans, born in 1852, would have been about thirteen years old at the end of the Civil War. His father was bought by General Bratton "from de sale of de Evans Estate," his grandfather "ketched in Africa and fetched to America on a big ship in an iron cage." Phillip said that he and his siblings were born on "de Canaan Bratton place," and that "General Bratton loved dat place; so him named it proud, like de Land of Canaan." He described "Marster General Bratton" as a "great sheep raiser," and talked about how a neighbor's hunting dogs would "pester de sheep" and sometimes got peppered by shotguns as a result.

He said his "mistress was Miss Bettie," and that she was "a DuBose,"[20] a well-known name in those parts.

Phillip echoed Jim Henry's statements about General Bratton not allowing slave children to work: "I just played 'round, helped feed de stock and pigs, bring in de fruit from de orchard and sich like." The "marster" was kind, and gave him small coins. Slaves were usually left to their own devices when it came to delivering their children, and Phillip helped to bring his brother, Richard, into the world by running for "de old granny on de place to come right away" when his mother was in "de pains."

Mr. Evan's family lived in a "nice plank house" during the slavery years. He said, "Us had a good master. Our livin' houses and vittles was better and healthier than they is now." They ate "peas, okra, Irish 'tators, mush, shorts, bread, and milk. Dere was 'bout five or six acres to de garden." Their shoes were made on the place and had wooden bottoms. His father was the foreman, the "only slave dat was give de honor to wear boots." Phillip also talked about how "Us went fishin' in de Melton Branch wid hooks," describing how good the "rock rollers, perch and catfish" tasted.

Phillip indicated that there were three overseers, and named two: "Mr. Wade Rawls" and "Mr. Osborne." He would not name the third overseer, as there had been "some trouble" between the overseer and one of his uncles. One of the overseers insulted Phillip's aunt, so her husband beat him. Phillip's uncle then ran off and hid until he was caught. The man's punishment was a whipping, according to Phillip, who said,

> They take him to de whippin' post of de town, tie his foots, make him put his hands in de stock, pulled off his shirt, pull down his britches and whip him terrible. Stealing was de main crime. De whippin's was put on de backs, and if you scowled, dat would git you a whippin' right dere and then.

Phillip also talked about two mulattoes on the plantation.

> Dere were just two mulattoes on de place. One was a daughter of my aunt. All de niggers was crazy 'bout her and wid de consent of my aunt, marster give her to some kinfolks in Arkansas. De other was name Rufus.[21]

Louisa Davis, former slave, was interviewed when she was 106 years old, so she would have been between twenty-seven and twenty-eight years old at the end of the Civil War. Ms. Davis had a different master in Fairfield County, Jim Lemon, but her husband, a foreman, knew General Bratton and rode with him and other "Red Shirts" in 1876. Her descriptions of slave life for those who lived on larger plantations would likely be very similar to those of former Bratton slaves, and she added a few more items of interest. Like the Bratton slaves, Louisa and her family were allowed to catch and eat fresh fish, were well clothed and well fed, and had "hogs a plenty, big flock of sheep, cotton gin, slaves to card, slaves to spin, and slaves to weave." Louisa added that they were allowed to rest on Sundays, and to dance to fiddlers, something she enjoyed tremendously. Her mother was a housemaid and her family got to eat the same food as her master's family, something she seemed quite thankful for, as the field slaves only got weekly rations at the smoke house. Louisa also stated that her master's family, Presbyterians, were "concerned 'bout our soul's salvation," and that she went to church.[22]

Louisa talked about slave patrollers, men who went after slaves or former slaves who weren't supposed to leave the plantation without permission. Her husband, Sam, lived on a different plantation, but Louisa was a self-described "goodlookin' woman," who said Sam wanted to see her more than allowed, so he "sneaked out" without permission: "Didn't Sam want to see me more than twice a week? Wouldn't he risk it widout de pass some time? Sure he did. De patrollers got after and run Sam many a time."[23]

Ned Walker was a former slave of the Gaillards, close friends of the Bratton family. His master was David Gaillard, who owned a plantation on Wateree Creek. Ned married "Sylvin Field, a gal on de General Bratton Canaan place." Ned spoke at length about his admiration for the Gaillards, citing similar living conditions as those of the Bratton slaves, and the fact that "De young white marsters break de law when they teach daddy to read and write." Ned was also grateful to his master because, after the Civil War, "Him fix it so de slaves stay altogether, on dat 1385 acres and buy de place, as common tenants, on de 'stallment plan."[24]

During the WPA's interviews with former slaves, they may have been asked if there were any mulattoes on the plantations where they lived.

Ned Walker's response (page 178) was, "No sir, us had no mulattoes on de place. Everybody decent and happy." Two mulattoes were mentioned in the interview with former slave Phillip Evans, who said they lived on one of John Bratton's plantations. Mulattoes, usually the progeny of a male member of the planter family and a slave woman, were a topic of gossip and speculation on plantations. Mulatto children were a common sight on many plantations, and sometimes their birth caused a problem between a planter and his wife and they were mistreated or even sold off. Sometimes, on other occasions, a mulatto received special treatment. We do not know if John Bratton fathered any children by black women, but it would not be an unusual occurrence in those days, and there may be at least one possibility that this occurred.

Elliot Bratton, a native New Yorker now living in Baltimore County, Maryland, is a black descendant of the Brattons, one of at least one hundred African-Americans who can trace their heritage back to the Brattons. Elliot believes he is a direct descendant of General John Bratton based on the word of his great-uncle, James M. Bratton (1887–1979). In

Wynne Dee, home of General John and Elizabeth Bratton, still stands. One of Winnsboro's most historic homes, it is built in an L-shape with a wide, one-story porch in the design of many upcountry homes of this period. Photo taken at Christmas, circa 2014. Courtesy of Penny Renwick, Winnsboro, SC.

an interview with Elliot's father and James's nephew, Noble C. Bratton Jr., James related that his father, Ruffus Bratton (born 1855, died circa 1913), was the son of General Bratton. Among the details found in the notes of this interview were that Ruffus Bratton and his younger half-brother, Theodore Bratton, were "best friends," that Theodore had taken up the study of law but made a career in the ministry, and that Theodore had a sister named Isabel, also referred to as Isabella, and a brother named William who had died on a ship. James, who said he observed interactions between Ruffus and his half-siblings, Theodore and Isabel, said that the latter was quite fond of Ruffus. Over the years, Elliot has researched Bratton genealogy and, in the process, confirmed some of these details.[25] (For details of his research, please refer to appendix D, written by Elliot Bratton.)

I found no information that Theodore Bratton studied law, but he did have a sister named Isabel and a brother named William who died after an accident on a ship.

General Bratton would have been unmarried, around twenty-four years old, and a practicing physician in Winnsboro when Ruffus (also spelled with one "f" in US Federal Census records) was born. According to Phillip Evans, former Bratton slave, there was a mulatto slave named Rufus living on General Bratton's plantation, a slave who might have been the General's son and a forebear of Elliot Bratton.

The War Between the States

The War Between the States, or the Civil War, as we will refer to it, was fought from 1861 to 1865 and was America's deadliest war in terms of how many people, soldiers and civilians included, perished. The United States of America, hereafter referred to as the Union, fought against the Confederacy, eleven Southern states that left the Union in 1860 and 1861.

A common misconception of the war, is that it revolved primarily around the moral issue of slavery. It is not quite that simple, however.

> The problem for Americans who, in the age of Lincoln,
> wanted slaves to be free was not simply that southerners
> wanted the opposite, but that they themselves cherished
> a conflicting value: they wanted the Constitution, which

protected slavery, to be honored, and the Union, which had fellowship with slaveholders, to be preserved. Thus they were committed to values that could not logically be reconciled.[26]

When the U. S. Constitution was ratified in 1788, slaves were present in all of the colonies. The Quakers and a few other individuals or groups opposed slavery during the Revolutionary era, and it was debated during the Constitutional Convention of 1787. Southern delegates would never have supported the Constitution unless provisions were included that protected slavery, however, and slaves were counted as 3/5 of a person for Congressional apportionment purposes. Slavery continued to be a divisive issue; northern states abolished slavery and Congress abolished international slave trading by 1807, but the abolitionist movement really did not start until the mid-nineteenth century. Even President Lincoln, an abolitionist, did not run on an anti-slavery platform. Instead, his platform involved halting the expansion of slavery into United States' territories.

The Southern Point of View

The catalyst for the Civil War was the expansion of slavery issue. The cause of the Civil War, from the South's point of view, was their belief that the North had repeatedly violated the Constitution, which protected states' rights, including those rights involving property (i.e., slaves). Southerners did not believe that the federal government had the power to stop the expansion of slavery into United States territories, and they felt that the federal government had already been encroaching steadily upon the states' rights in other ways too. Among other things, the federal government had nullified the Fugitive Slave Act (whereby runaway slaves were returned to their owners), had passed laws favoring northern manufacturing interests, and had created unrest in the Negro population. The South further believed that the Constitution gave them the right to secede, while the federal government held the opposite viewpoint.

The South wanted its way of life to remain unchanged, but the North had been changing rapidly since the American Revolution. The South remained predominantly agrarian, with slavery interwoven into its economy, while the North had become more industrialized and had a large pool of labor to draw from as emigration continued in force. The abolitionist movement was increasing, especially with the publication of literature like *Uncle Tom's Cabin* in 1852, an anti-slavery novel by Harriet Beecher Stowe. The South had fewer Electoral College votes than the North, and Abraham Lincoln was elected even though he was not on the ballot in ten southern states.

When Lincoln was elected president of the United States, the South felt that their rights would be further eroded and that slavery, the foundation of their economic system, would eventually be abolished. If the expansion of slavery was halted into new territories that then became states, the balance of power would shift even more to the North, and the Southern way of life, along with its economy, would be gone.

Talk of secession was rampant in South Carolina before Lincoln's election, but some thought that secession would not lead to war. An article in the *Yorkville Inquirer* on December 16, 1860 (page 63), expressed confidence that several states would secede, followed by reconstruction of the United States, and that France and Britain, dependent on the South for cotton, would side with the South. Others felt certain that secession would lead to war, although not many seemed to realize it would be the bloodiest war in American history. The odds were great against the South: There were twenty-one million people in the North compared with nine million in the South—about four million of those slaves—and the value of all Confederate goods was only a fraction of that in the North.

The Beginnings of War

Lincoln was elected president of the United States on November 6, 1860, and on December 20, 1860, South Carolina became the first southern state to secede from the Union. A fierce advocate of states' rights, South Carolina had threated secession in 1832 over what it perceived as an unfair tariff that was subsequently renegotiated.

Within three months of Lincoln's election, six more states seceded and in February 1861, the seceding states created the Confederate constitution. Jefferson Davis was elected president of the Confederacy, and its capitol was located in Richmond, Virginia.

"The New Confederacy."
The Yorkville Inquirer
(*Yorkville, SC*), December
16, 1860. From the
Library of Congress,
Chronicling America.

THE NEW CONFEDERACY.

The N. Y. *Herald's* Washington correspondent says: There is no use disguising what is before us. Cool and sagacious observers see no prospect of avoiding a rupture. By the 1st of February, South Carolina, Georgia, Alabama, Mississippi and Florida will be out of the Confederacy. By that time, they will have consummated such an understanding with France and Great Britain as will enable them even to set Federal coercion, should it be attempted, at defiance. They will insert in their Constitution a clause prohibiting the importation of Africans, which will tend to conciliate the border States, and in a short time every one of the latter, except Delaware, perhaps, will join the Southern Confederacy. This denouement is considered so certain, that already the minds of statesmen are almost exclusively turned to projecting the means and conditions of reconstruction.

After Lincoln was elected and southern states began to secede, war was anticipated. President Davis called for 100,000 volunteers to join the Confederate army, and was met with an enthusiastic response. Many felt that the war would be over in ninety days after one big battle.

In April 1861, the Civil War began after an attack by the Confederates on Fort Sumter in Charleston Harbor. A Union garrison had remained there after the South seceded, and the South claimed the fort as theirs since it resided on Confederate land. Confederate artillerymen had already fired on the fort when Federal warships tried to resupply it, but President Davis called a halt to that unless further attempts were made. President Lincoln decided to resupply the fort with unarmed vessels bringing food for the hungry men but would not surrender it because he felt that the states' secession was invalid. The Confederacy did not want to fire on unarmed ships and be blamed for stating the Civil War but they could not accept Federal troops on their land, so they gave the fort's commander a chance to surrender. When he refused, shots were fired; the outgunned commander soon surrendered, and Confederates took the fort without any bloodshed on either side.

Luke Austin wrote an excellent book in 2003 about John Bratton's civil war experiences, *General John Bratton: Sumter to Appomattox, in Letters to His Wife,* so this book will not attempt anything more than a summary, highlighting the basics and focusing on some of Bratton's hardships and concerns as he rose from private to brigadier general.

John Bratton was there when the first shots of the Civil War were fired in Charleston, South Carolina, and he probably heard some of the last shots fired before General Lee's army surrendered at Appomattox Court House in Virginia. Among the first to join the Confederacy, John Bratton fought in several battles and skirmishes, including the Peninsula Campaign, the Battle of Seven Pines—where he was wounded and expected to die—Chickamauga, and the Battle of the Wilderness, where he was promoted to brigadier general. Before the war's end, Bratton also fought in the Battle of Cold Harbor and the Battle of Darbytown Road, where he was wounded for the second time. For a complete list of his battles, please refer to appendix C.

Bratton's losses and struggles were great, but the respect of his men for him was even greater as he surrendered the largest brigade of Lee's army, a brigade that maintained its dignity and coherence even as other surrendered troops scattered to the four winds.

Civil War Service: 1861–1862

John Bratton enlisted as a private but was quickly elected to captain of the Fairfield Fencibles, one of two companies from Winnsboro.[27] Bratton spent most of his first year in the Confederate army preparing for battle, proving his skills as a leader and providing support services, but he was not involved in any major battles until May of 1862.

The Fairfield Fencibles Company was part of the Sixth Regiment South Carolina Volunteers under Colonel James H. Rion. The Fencibles were ordered to Charleston and Fort Sumter, where the Civil War began. They took no part in the action, but Captain Bratton "awoke at 4:30AM to the boom of the first canon shot from Fort Johnson,"[28] and witnessed the bombardment of Fort Sumter from the mainland. The Fencibles disbanded when the state troops were called to volunteer in the Confederate army, which would be going to Virginia, and Bratton resigned and joined the Buckhead Guards as a private. He was quickly promoted to second lieutenant of Company C, Sixth South Carolina Regiment, C.S.A.[29]

Word was received that the Federals were advancing into Virginia with plans to take Richmond, and the Confederates received orders to depart for Manassas, Virginia, north of Richmond. When John arrived at Manassas Junction, he had his first good look at war's aftermath of death and destruction.[30] In a letter to his wife on July 23, 1861, he described seeing all of the dead men "strewn thickly over the ground in some places," and was "astonished ... at being so little shocked at the sight. He indicated that his sympathies were "more excited for the dead horses than men."[31] Even with about five thousand dead, the battle was a skirmish compared to some later battles, but both sides realized this would *not* be a ninety-day war.

Lieutenant John Bratton in 1861. Courtesy of South Caroliniana Library, University of South Carolina, Columbia.

Lieutenant Bratton remained in the area for several months, moving from one location to another and basically setting up camp, picketing, fortifying, scouting, and dealing with illness among his men. He was already war-weary and worried that the war would last a long time. When he received word that his second son, John Bratton Jr., had been born, he sent Bettie his congratulations in a letter but expressed his difficulty in trying to relate to life on the plantation or to picture his infant son, stating, "Well, it is a little hard to think that he will be an old stranger before I can see him … ."[32]

≈ ≈ ≈

Lieutenant Bratton's first encounter with the enemy was on December 20, 1861, in Dranesville, Virginia. It was a small battle, but Bratton showed excellent leadership and skill and "attracted the attention and commanded the confidence of the entire regiment," becoming known as the *strict Lieutenant*."[33]

In March of 1862, the Union army's Peninsula Campaign was kicking off. Bratton had re-enlisted and was now part of the First South Carolina Battalion of Re-enlisted Volunteers. He was promoted to the rank of lieutenant colonel, assumed command, and departed for the Peninsula. The battalion set up camp outside Richmond, was brought up to regimental strength, and then elected him to the position of colonel.[34]

Colonel Bratton's first battle during the Peninsula Campaign was May 4–5, 1862, the Battle of Williamsburg. Bratton was part of the rear guard that helped defend Fort MacGruder, an earthen fortification alongside the Williamsburg Road. He noticed Federal troops moving toward an empty redoubt that would make Fort MacGruder vulnerable and acted without orders, leaving the fort to foil the Federal troops. He found himself vulnerable and under heavy fire but he completed his goal and made it back to the fort to continued fighting from there. Both sides claimed victory, and continued towards Richmond.[35]

The Battle of Seven Pines was Colonel Bratton's next encounter with the enemy. He led the Sixth Regiment over obstacles and two enemy camps and took on heavy enemy fire. His regiment had 269 men killed or wounded out of the 521 who entered battle. Colonel Bratton watched as his brother-in-law, Sgt. Maj. Beverly Means, died as he was talking to him.

Colonel Bratton then led another charge and was shot in his left arm and shoulder. He was blinded by the shock but continued to urge his men forward, and then laid down with the dead and dying. He ordered his men to retreat back to Confederate lines, but two wounded soldiers refused to leave him and attempted to move him to safety. Unconscious, he awoke to Union soldiers, who took him to a nearby field hospital. The doctor expected him to die from his wounds.[36]

Special consideration from Union army general Phillip Kearny helped save Colonel Bratton's life. General Kearny did not know Bratton personally but had heard of the gallantry of his regiment. General Kearny contacted the hospital to request that Colonel Bratton receive the best of care, and even wrote him a personal letter letting him know that he had placed a $200 credit for him through his bankers.[37]

Colonel Bratton was transported to Fortress Monroe for further treatment before being held there as a prisoner of war. He was treated with respect and given special privileges during his confinement. He was held until August 31, 1862, when he was exchanged and headed home.[38]

During Bratton's captivity, his brother, Capt. William M. Bratton, was killed on June 30, 1862, during the Seven Days' Battle. Captain William Bratton was with the Alabama Eleventh Regiment and was in the act of capturing a battery of ten guns when he was "pierced through the heart" and killed. He was found with his faithful servant, John, "who refused to leave his body until it was claimed by comrades … ."[39]

≈ ≈ ≈

After Colonel Bratton was released and paroled in August 1862, he spent September and most of October at home recovering from his near-fatal wounds, dealing with plantation matters, and grieving family losses. In addition to the death of his brother, William Bratton, and his brother-in-law, Beverly Means, both of his wife's parents died in 1862, as had many of their friends. His family, now composed of two children with one on the way, needed him, and he needed time to heal.

There was little time for healing, however, as the Confederate army needed to gear up its forces even more. Lincoln's Emancipation Proclamation of September 1862 granted freedom to slaves if the Confederacy did not return to the Union by January 1863, and had taken the idea of support for the Confederacy by France and England

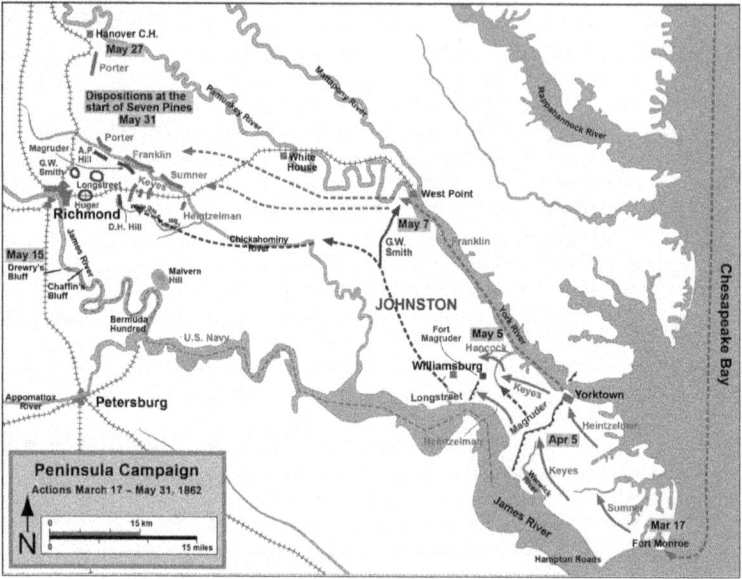

The Peninsula Campaign. Map by Hal Jespersen, www.posix.com/CW.

Battle of Seven Pines, where Bratton was wounded and taken prisoner. Map by Hal Jespersen, www. posix.com/CW.

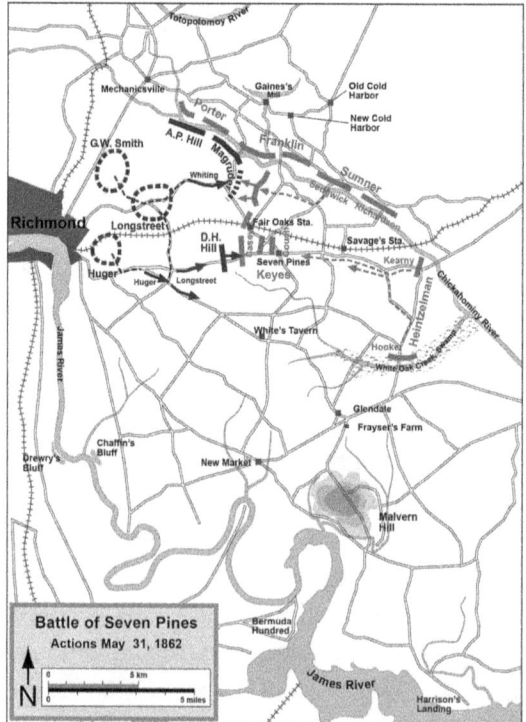

off the table. Southerners were enraged, of course, as were many in the North who were willing to fight for the union of the states but not for emancipation.

Colonel Bratton returned to his regiment in late October of 1862. The regiment had participated in five battles during his absence and had been reorganized, and Bratton became the South Carolina Brigade's senior colonel.[40] The Union army was once again preparing to advance towards Richmond but stopped first at Fredericksburg, a key transportation link for the Confederacy.

Colonel Bratton was with Jenkins's Brigade during the Battle of Fredericksburg on December 11–15, 1862, but participated in very little of the actual fighting; his brigade was basically shifted from one area to another to provide support services.[41] The battle was a huge victory and much-needed morale booster for the Confederacy, though.

The winter of 1862–1863 was even rougher than that of the year before. It was unusually cold, rainy, and muddy, and neither horses nor men had enough to eat. The two greatest armies of the Civil War camped within sight of each other across the Rappahannock River around the city of Fredericksburg, with 60,000 men in the Army of Northern Virginia, and 130,000 belonging to the Army of the Potomac.

Colonel Bratton was demoralized. He had to quarantine one of his companies due to a smallpox scare, his entire arm was hurting from the wound he had received at Seven Pines, and he was worried that he had not received any recent letters from his wife, perhaps because one of their children was ill.[42]

Civil War Service: 1863

In January of 1863, Colonel Bratton was recommended for promotion to brigadier general by his former and current commanding officers. He was passed over, despite glowing recommendations for his courage and management, probably because he had not had an opportunity to participate in more battles or in the summer campaigns.[43]

In mid-February, however, Colonel Bratton was made temporary brigade commander during General Pickens's absence. The brigade was ordered to march south with Longstreet's Corps past Richmond towards an enemy buildup at Suffolk, which laid on two important rail lines and a corridor to Richmond. They participated in skirmishes along the way, but things were fairly calm when they arrived at Suffolk, and Colonel Bratton was allowed to go home on furlough.[44] His third child, Theodore DuBose Bratton, had been born three months earlier, and he was finally able to meet him.

When Colonel Bratton returned, the Confederate army was digging in and laying siege to Suffolk. The main purpose of the expedition towards Suffolk was to forage for food, taking Suffolk if possible. The army was starving, and needed to secure enough food for General Lee to take the war north to Pennsylvania again. Taking Suffolk was not successful, although there were skirmishes and attempts, but the main goal was accomplished.[45]

Bratton's brigade was not present when the majority of Lee's army was at the Battle of Gettysburg in July of 1863 because he was garrisoned near Richmond, but the Confederate's defeat there was a terrible blow for the South. General Lee blamed himself for the defeat, and ordered a retreat to Virginia, his wagon train seventeen miles long and full of wounded soldiers.[46]

By September 24, 1863, Colonel Bratton was in Chickamauga on the Tennessee-Georgia border. The Federal and Confederate forces had battled on September 19, and the Confederacy maintained control of the battlefield. The men were short on rations, and "some of [his] men fasted for forty-eight hours."[47] Bratton's brigade, along with two other brigades, was ordered to cross Lookout Mountain to assault Federal troops camped at Wauhatchie Junction; the attack was well executed but the Confederates met with stiff resistance and were forced to withdraw.[48]

Colonel Bratton was still in charge of the brigade, which had been ordered with other troops around Chattanooga to move into east Tennessee. The Union army had control of Knoxville. When the Confederates reached Loudon, south of Knoxville, Federal troops were waiting on the other side of the river. The Confederates, with the Carolina brigade taking the lead, pursued them, with Bratton's troops sustaining heavy casualties during a battle at Campbell's Station under heavy artillery fire.

Knoxville's fortifications were assaulted, but the Confederates failed to take it, and in December the Carolina brigade—after more pursuits, fighting, and disputes among their senior staff—settled into winter quarters near Morristown, Tennessee.[49]

Civil War Service: 1864–1865

The mood in the South was grim in 1864. Colonel Bratton had participated in few major battles up to that point, limiting his chances for promotion, but this would change in a few months. He was to fight in three more major battles, be promoted to brigadier general after the deaths of his brigade commander and division leader in May, and to participate in the Siege of Petersburg before the year's end.

At the beginning of 1864, he had to deal with the miseries of the winter season again. In letters to his wife in January, Colonel Bratton spoke of his ill health, his concerns about her as she was also ill, and his frustration with his commander, who had been discredited. He also spoke of his efforts to secure shoes and blankets for his men.[50] Food and supplies were scarce, and many of his men were ill.

In April, orders were received to return to Virginia. General Lee was preparing for a commencement of hostilities as spring advanced. Ulysses S. Grant had been placed in charge of all Union armies in March of 1864, and was determined to vanquish the South once and for all. Both armies met and fought for three days in the Battle of the Wilderness, from May 5–7, in Spotsylvania and Orange County, Virginia, an area of dense and tangled forest. Gen. Micah Jenkins was in command of the brigade and was killed the first day, and General Longstreet, Division Commander, was wounded. Fighting was fierce as both sides attempted to maneuver in the jungle-like underbrush, and the morning of May 7 saw Grant's forces withdrawing towards Richmond.

> On the Battle of the Wilderness, where [John Bratton] conducted himself with the greatest valor and brilliancy, he was made brigadier general. General Lee sent a telegram to the war department at Richmond, on the night of the second days fight, requesting the immediate promotion and confirmation of Col. Bratton.[51]

The battle was a tactical victory for the Confederates, but Grant was not dissuaded, and he moved southeast towards Richmond, fortifying

Spotsylvania Courthouse in anticipation that Lee would follow and attack.[52] General Lee guessed his intentions, and some of his army beat them there and began entrenching. Fighting occurred on and off for about two weeks, and in the end, with almost 32,000 casualties on both sides, Grant once again withdrew towards Richmond.[53]

From May 31 to June 12, the Confederates fought the Federals at the Battle of Cold Harbor, about ten miles northeast of Richmond. The Confederates had built a series of fortifications seven miles long, and when Grant attacked on June 3—the turning point of the battle—the Confederates "... were able to hold their positions, cutting down Federal troops until the dead covered more than five acres of ground about as thickly as they could be laid."[54]

The Confederates had fought valiantly but their numbers compared to those of the Union army had been greatly reduced.

> As an acting brigadier since May 6, Bratton had met the mental and physical challenges presented by such arduous service—the effects of which had begun to debilitate thousands of combatants with what a future generation would call shell shock. But was he truly among the dwindling number of general officers capable of maintaining the fitness of their commands? That remained to be seen.[55]

In letters to his wife after the Wilderness Campaign and the Battle of Cold Harbor, General Bratton let her know that he was unhurt, although two bullets had passed through his coat, and that he thought the campaign would probably be a long one. He also mentioned that his body servant, Lewis, who narrowly escaped bullets and shells, was also unhurt. During a brief period of quiet and apparently in response to a letter from Bettie, we get a glimpse of Bratton's frame of mind and philosophy when he says, "You seem to be tormenting yourself into a state of wretchedness about my being killed without professing religion .... We are all made to die as well as live, and there is no sense in making oneself miserable because friends do not die to suit you ... ."[56]

Grant's next strategy was to take Petersburg, which was about twenty miles south of Richmond, to cut off Richmond's supply lines. The attempt resulted in a ten-month siege instead, and the Confederates

Note from General Robert E. Lee recommending Colonel Bratton's promotion to brigadier general. It reads: "Forwarded the promotion of Col. Bratton to be Brig. Gen. for assignment to this command is recommended. I regret that I cannot send in a recommendation at once & request than an these new appointments be made of the same date otherwise the former relative rank of the offers will be interfered with."

Photocopy is from General Services Administration National Archives and Records Service. Courtesy of John Bratton, Sewanee, TN, and Johnny Bratton of Raleigh, SC.

dug into entrenchment. Brigadier General Bratton spent weeks in the trenches, fighting sporadically and repelling assaults by the Federals. Two of his regiments helped save Richmond in August.

General Bratton also fought in the Battle of Darbytown Road on October 13, 1864, and was wounded again, this time by a mini ball that struck his breast and emerged through his back. The Confederates were attempting to retake ground they had lost to Federal forces during battles near Richmond but failed, although Federal casualties were heavy. Bratton went home to Winnsboro to recover, returning to the entrenchments near Petersburg only six weeks later.[57]

While General Bratton and the other Confederate warriors of Winnsboro were still fighting near Petersburg, Union Army General William T. Sherman's forces attacked their home. On November 15, 1864, after taking Atlanta, General Sherman set out on a thousand-mile march through Georgia and Carolina with over 60,000 men in an effort to destroy civilian support for the war by bringing it to their doorstep. His army had been instructed to live off the land, taking food and livestock and destroying stores that could supply the enemy, but not to burn or destroy private homes. The Federals had a particular dislike for South Carolina, though, as it had been first to secede from the Union, and drunken soldiers burned indiscriminately and were often cruel. Much of nearby Columbia, South Carolina, was burned.

General Bratton had written to Bettie in January, advising her what to do if enemy troops should appear. He wrote that she should let their [Negroes] go, take to the swamps, or join with the enemy if they were unwilling to stay. He expressed much concern for them, wishing he could be there to save them from what he considered to be "false promises of freedom." He also advised Bettie to "harness up all the mules and horses and load up the wagons with provisions and drive out of the track of the enemy and camp until he passes and then come back home … ."[58]

On Tuesday, February 21, General Sherman's troops arrived in Winnsboro. The town was expecting them, and the day before, "the citizens met and appointed a committee to meet the army beyond the limits of the town with a white flag in order to surrender the town."[59]

Over thirty buildings were burned in the town, including stores, a hotel, residences, and even the Episcopal church. Corncribs and smoke houses were destroyed, and horses, mules, hogs, and other animals were slain. Some calves were hung with telegraph wire and left to die, other calves' neck and legs were wound together with wire so that their necks would be pierced with the jagged end and they would strangle as they tried to move. Citizens were robbed of jewelry and personal valuables, and some older citizens were threatened and strung up until they nearly died.[60]

Wynne Dee, the large and gracious home of John and Bettie Bratton, was a refuge for several of the Bratton and DuBose women during the Civil War. When Federal troops arrived at the home, they rode their horses through the home's great hall, pulling down the original stairs in the hallway. When they found a rusty old Revolutionary War sword, they accused the women of concealing weapons and further frightened them by saying the house would have to be burned down. A fire was set but it was quickly extinguished, and the troops finally left after looting the house and leaving the pantry bare.[61]

≈ ≈ ≈

As General Sherman's forces were terrorizing their families, General Bratton and his troops continued to fight in Petersburg, sustaining many casualties. The siege finally ended on April 2, 1865, after General Grant's ninth offensive broke the Confederate line southwest of Petersburg at dawn; Lee made plans to evacuate that night.[62]

General Lee's men were exhausted and starving as they withdrew, and the Federals were chasing them without letup or mercy. They fought desperately, but General Lee finally realized that the situation was hopeless and began to discuss surrender with General Grant.[63] The formal surrender took place at Appomattox Courthouse on April 12. General Grant was generous with the terms of surrender; the Confederates would be paroled and allowed to return home.

General Bratton surrendered his 1,549-man brigade on April 9, submitting a written recap on April 10. His brigade contained the remnants of three regiments, including the Sixth Carolina Regiment with 30 officers and 328 men. It was the largest brigade of the surrendered army, containing nearly one-fifth of Lee's men.[64]

The *Cyclopedia of Eminent and Representative Men of the Carolinas of the Nineteenth Century* describes his surrender as follows:

His brigade maintained its organization after the surrender, and volunteered the same respect for his authority that it had under military law, and thus enabled him to conduct them in an orderly march to Danville, where railroad transportation was secured for a part of their weary way home. All other commands disbanded and scattered from Appomattox. This action of his men showed in what great respect he was held by them.[65]

Still officially a paroled prisoner, Bratton submitted his request for amnesty and pardon to President Andrew Johnson on August 10, 1865. President Lincoln had been assassinated on April 14, and Vice President Johnson, who wanted quick reinstatement of the South, had succeeded him. On May 29, 1865, President Johnson required that former Confederate officials, officers above a certain rank, and people owning a certain amount of property apply for individual pardons and take an oath of allegiance. In his request, John Bratton eloquently expressed the reasons he went to war: his belief in "the right of secession as the keystone

"Ravages of the Enemy in South Carolina," *The Daily Dispatch* (Richmond, VA), March 30, 1865. From the Library of Congress, Chronicling America.

RAVAGES OF THE ENEMY IN SOUTH CAROLINA.

The Fairfield (South Carolina) *Courier* gives a long account of the excesses committed by the enemy in the town of Winnsboro', from which we extract the following:

"Our once beautiful town presents now a most pitiful sight. Residences and stores that once lifted their proud heads to Heaven are now numbered among the things that were. Charred ruins now meet the gaze, where once the busy feet of man passed in the daily pursuits of life. And all this is done by people calling themselves men. They have belied their title, not being even fit for an association among the brutes they have slain, whose carcasses meet the eye on our public roads.

to the Citadel of Republicanism,"[66] and then he pledged his oath of allegiance. General Bratton received his pardon on September 2, 1865.

Survival and Loss in Winnsboro

In the summer of 1865, General Bratton returned home to the destruction of Winnsboro and to the arms of Bettie and their children. He was thirty-four years old and had been wounded twice in battle. Bettie was only twenty-seven, and by the end of the year had borne seven children. Half of Charleston had burned, the South was in ruins, and Fairfield County had lost many of its young men. "Out of one hundred and forty-six thousand white males of all ages in the State at the census of 1860, it [had] lost forty thousand by death or disablement … ."[67]

Theodore DuBose Bratton, General Bratton's son, described what life was like in Winnsboro immediately after the Civil War in his book, *An Apostle of Reality*:

> There were no animals and no implements with which to prepare the soil, and no seed if land could be prepared. No one knows how the year 1865 was survived. The problem of the owner was to care for the great number of emancipated servants who were yet a "child race."[68]

Even Southerners like the Brattons, as kind and concerned as they may have been for their "slave family," still considered their servants ignorant, child-like, and not to be trusted with true emancipation. A more immediate problem for the Brattons, however, was survival.

Most Southern slaves had remained on the plantation during the war, but as the war had progressed, there was a shortage of males to manage them. Women, old men, and others less well-equipped to run plantations often resulted in less efficiency, and farm production suffered drastically. Bettie Bratton, who had lived a relatively comfortable, protected life before the war, her education consisting primarily of the social graces, was ill-prepared to deal with managing plantations, although the large DuBose-Bratton presence in the area was surely of support to her.

Winnsboro So. Ca.
Augt 10th 1865

To his Excellency Andrew Johnston
President of the United States
I have
the honor to make, in conformity with the
requirements of your proclamation of the 29th of May
A.D. 1865, this, my application for Amnesty and Pardon
Enclosed is the Oath taken by me and administered
by proper and prescribed authority
To state briefly my case; I did all in my power to
make good the Ordinance of Secession passed by the
Convention of the people of this State in Dec. 1860
and the Obligations afterwards assumed by it to the
Southern Confederacy — I responded to the first call
for Troops made by the State by volunteering as a Private
And remained continuously in the Field until its
surrender on the 9th of April last —
It is scarcely necessary, Sir, to add that I did this
because I thought it my duty —
I was a Brigadier General in the Confederate Army and
am included under no other of the Fourteen Exceptions —
I have never held political office or engaged actively
in politics in any way but pursued quietly my own
private business as physician and planter — My
political creed, however, was strictly Staterights,
running out to the right of a Sovereign State to
secede — The exercise of that right was a different
question, one of policy and to my mind a disputable
one — But when the right of secession was denied, the
Union of the United States was placed in Antagonism to
Republicanism and upon the highway to ruin that was
travelled by Republics of former times — I fought for
the right of secession as the keystone to the citadel

Amnesty and pardon application by General Bratton, page one. From Confederate Applications for Presidential Pardons, 1865–1867.

of Republicanism —

But since we who contended for secession have been overwhelmed, have laid down our arms and submitted to the Forces representing the Union, I conceive it to be the duty of each and all of us, and the part of patriotism, to give faithful and cordial support to the Authorities that be, and thus aid in restoring law and order to the lands —

With this view I subscribed the enclosed Oath and to this end I proffer this my petition for amnesty and pardon —

I have, Sir, the honor to be with highest respect

Your Obedient Servt

Jno Bratton
Brig Gen P. A. C S
& Parolled Prisoner

Amnesty and pardon application by General Bratton, page two. From Confederate Applications for Presidential Pardons, 1865–1867.

When General Bratton returned home, he was land rich but money poor, as were the DuBoses—his wife's relatives—and other leading planters in the area. The DuBoses had three plantations, as did General Bratton, and they decided to advertise their lands for rent to wealthy Northerners. General Bratton had kept in touch with a colonel who had been on his staff throughout the war who had moved to Baltimore, writing him of conditions in the South and his hopes of renting the land to provide an income for his family and emancipated slaves. The colonel, moved by the general's plight, implored his uncle—a Baltimore banker—for assistance. General Bratton soon received a telegraph from the banker who offered him a partnership: The banker would provide the capitol to run the plantations if General Bratton would manage them. With tears of relief, General Bratton ordered the purchase of mules, wagons, and other supplies and "thus the DuBoses and the Brattons, and their great family of Negroes, were enabled to carry on."[69]

Most citizens of Fairfield were not as fortunate as the Brattons, and the local economy did not recover for many years. "The 'Gay Nineties' were dull and lacked luster in Fairfield," and with few exceptions, the economy did not receive a boost until 1898, with the establishment of the Fairfield Cotton Mills."[70] Middle class tradesmen and merchants could no longer earn a decent income and small farmers struggled. According to Winnsboro resident, Robert Gooding, "After the Civil War, our people had no money. We became a one-crop people. Cotton was ready money [but] speculators manipulated all the profit out of cotton by a system of exchanges, grades, and quotations."[71]

General Bratton diversified and survived. He "concentrated on farming and raising livestock on his Farmington Plantation. In 1867 he owned 2,100 acres and imported purebred cattle, sheep and swine [and was] interested in progressive farming methods."[72] General Bratton was not actually the owner of the Farmington Plantation but the manager. When Theodore Samuel DuBose, his wife's father, died in 1862, Bratton had become manager of the Farmington Plantation on Wateree Creek, and the Roseland and Rock Spring Plantations, both on Small Town Road in Winnsboro, until they were all sold by the turn of the century.[73] At the time of the 1860 Federal Census, Theodore DuBose owned 3,000 acres and 204 slaves, which were managed by General Bratton after

DuBose died. General Bratton did own the Wynne Dee Plantation, and perhaps the Canaan Plantation,[74] although I have not been able to confirm the latter's actual ownership other than through verbal comments or assumptions.

By 1870, however, a terrible tragedy had struck the young family. By then, Elizabeth had borne nine of their ten children, all boys. Seven of their little boys had died, according to the *DuBose Genealogy* compiled by Sharon Goff Avery, "during and just after the Civil War, literally from privation and starvation as the result of the Federal invasion and destruction of the family property resulting therefrom."[75] According to a history of St. John's Episcopal Church in Winnsboro, they were all buried at the church's cemetery with their dates of death listed at about 1870.[76] They were as follows:

- John Bratton Jr., born 1861
- Edward Noble Bratton, born 1863
- Frank Gaillard Bratton, born 1864
- Beverly Mans Bratton. born 1865
- McNeely DuBose Bratton, born 1865
- Robert Means Bratton, born 1867
- Richard Nott Bratton, born 1869

The 1870 Federal Census lists John M. and "Betsey" Bratton living in the same home with William D. and Theodore Bratton, their two remaining sons. A person by the name of Marian Porcher—presumably a relative of Bettie's, who had a sister by that name—was also listed as living in the home.

One can only imagine how devastating the loss of seven children was for the Brattons, even though death was a common occurrence during Civil War days and its aftermath when food, medical care, and other necessities of life were scarce.

Reconstruction

The Reconstruction era (1865–1876) was a very complicated effort to resolve the issues involved in reuniting the eleven breakaway states with the Union. Secession had to be repudiated and all forms of slavery had to be eliminated. The Conservative Democrats of the South, who wanted to return ex-slaves to their former status, and Radical Republicans, who had pushed for emancipation and full civil rights for slaves, vied for control. Corruption was rampant throughout southern governments, bitterness and suspicion prevailed everywhere, and voices of high emotion or ulterior motives often overpowered voices of reason.

General Bratton was one of those voices of reason, a man who carefully considered the facts as he saw them before coming to his conclusions. He believed that the Emancipation Proclamation had done almost irreparable harm to the Southern economy, that emancipated freedmen were incapable of living as equals next to whites, and that a restoration of states' rights, including segregation and the denial of blacks to vote, hold office, and more, was necessary for the South's recovery.

The legal end to slavery in the nation came in December 1865, when the Thirteenth Amendment was ratified and abolished slavery and involuntary servitude except as punishment for a crime. Freedmen and slaves had served on both sides during the Civil War, some as body servants, some as soldiers in black Union army regiments, and they rejoiced along with those on the plantations, albeit quietly as they weren't quite sure what to expect.

The South's slaves were finally emancipated, but life did not change much for them at first. There had been rumors during General Sherman's march through the South that freed slaves would be given "forty acres and a mule," on confiscated Southern planters' land. In January 1865, General Sherman issued Special Field Order Number 15, a plan granting each freed family forty acres of land. The Union army also donated some of its mules to the former slaves. Additionally, Abraham Lincoln created the Freedmen's Bureau in 1865 to assist former slaves and poor whites in the South with food, medical aid, and legal assistance, and it also established schools. Abolitionist groups and the Radical Republicans in Congress were as determined as the civil rights activists of the 1960s to achieve equality for all men.

But Southerners were determined to pass laws that basically returned ex-slaves to their former status. President Andrew Johnson, a Southerner and a strong proponent of states' rights, was their ally. He ordered that any lands turned over to former slaves be returned to their former owners, dashing the hopes of many freedmen to become landowners. President Johnson also continually vetoed follow-up Freedmen's Bureau bills; Congress overrode his vetoes, but the bureau suffered from a lack of funds and personnel, as well as controversy, and was shut down in 1872. In fact, President Johnson had so many conflicts with the Radical Republicans that the House of Representatives eventually impeached him, and he narrowly avoided conviction by the Senate.

Most Southerners, including General Bratton, honestly believed that former slaves were incapable of handling freedom and that it would be impossible for them to live side by side with whites as equals. They had always feared slave uprising in the days before and during the Civil War, and some even saw blacks as child-like at best, needing control and instruction. At worse, they also saw them as inherently lazy and lacking in morals and intellectual ability. They wanted to reconstruct the South as closely as possible to its former state; they were fearful that it would totally collapse without a source of free or cheap labor and if blacks were given an education, the ability to vote, and other civil rights. Many Northerners felt the same way or believed that the time was not right for total equality, but the Radical Republicans—members who were committed to equal treatment of former slaves—pushed for reform.

South Carolina's Constitutional Convention of 1865

The South was bristling over Union control and Freedmen's Bureau laws, and during the summer and fall of 1865 most of the old Confederate states held constitutional conventions to discuss how to further take back their rights to self-rule. General Bratton, always a strong proponent of states' rights, was a delegate from Fairfield[77] to South Carolina's Constitutional Convention, which met in Columbia on September 13, 1865.

The South Carolina convention met to repeal the Ordinance of Secession and to remodel the State Constitution. The Ordinance was repealed, but South Carolina also passed laws known as the Black

Codes, which continued to segregate blacks from whites and denied them most of their civil rights. Provisional Governor B. F. Perry set the tone for the convention: "To extend this universal suffrage to the 'freedmen' in their present ignorant and degraded condition, would be little less than folly and madness ... this is a white man's government, and intended for white men only."[78] Gen. Wade Hampton III, a very popular man among conservatives who had been perhaps the wealthiest slave owner in South Carolina, was nominated for governor but declined,[79] and James Lawrence Orr was elected the first postbellum governor of South Carolina and took office in November 1865.

≈ ≈ ≈

Emancipation for freedmen who lived on plantations in 1865 had to have been quite a disappointment for any who expected or hoped for full civil rights. Freedmen could leave the plantations and search for a different or better life or could remain on as sharecroppers with few prospects for advancing economically. A typical sharecropping contract in 1866 was about one page long and would have been similar to the one on page 85, one used by General Bratton's uncle, John S. Bratton, who inherited the Brattonsville plantation in York County from his father, Colonel William Bratton. It required the freedmen to work six days a week, to be "polite and respectful ... to not to entertain idlers or vagrants from other plantations, nor to leave the plantation [without written permission] ... ."[80] In return, John S. Bratton would provide the freedmen with shelter and food grown on the plantation, the use of tools and farm implements, and one-fourth of the remaining crop. Bratton's 1867 contract was longer, and "included restrictions on having dogs, weapons, or liquor ... unannounced searches of their homes, [and denied] them the freedom to sell their crops without permission."[81]

South Carolina's Black Codes, along with those of other Southern states, were declared invalid by the Federals, who accused the South of trying to restore slavery. As a result, the Reconstruction Acts of 1867 and 1868 contained new requirements for Southern states to be readmitted to the Union. The Acts basically required universal male suffrage. All adult males within a political system would be allowed to vote, regardless of income, property, religion, race, or any other qualification. Once voters accepted the new constitution, the state would then need to ratify

Freedmen's Agreement dated December 29, 1865. This was an early agreement, completed shortly after Emancipation, between General Bratton's brother, John S. Bratton, and his freedmen in neighboring York County. Courtesy of Fairfield County Museum, Winnsboro, SC, Bratton Family Collection.

the Fourteenth Amendment to become a part of the Union. The very idea filled most white Southerners with dread, especially those of the planter class and their cohorts. They were terrified that black men, the majority, would then be in control and cause a complete economic and social disaster for the South.

Constitutional Conventions of 1868

South Carolina held its next constitutional convention from January through March 1868, overturning the Black Codes, abolishing race as a limit on male suffrage and property ownership as a qualification for holding office. It also opened public schools to all races.[82] This was a radically different constitution compared to the one in 1865, and South Carolina was admitted to the Union on June 25, 1868.

General Bratton was not present at the constitutional convention; he attended a separate convention for whites only that was held a couple of months earlier in Columbia, South Carolina, in November 1867. The Conservative Convention, as it named itself, was composed of delegates from two thirds of the districts in the state, and General Bratton was listed as being one of seven delegates from Fairfield County.[83] The convention published a lengthy open "Address to the People of South Carolina," which was published in several newspapers. *The Charleston Daily News*, on November 9, 1867, showcased the address on the front page, along with several responses by imminent men.

Following is an excerpt from the address:

> What but disaster could follow in the footsteps of the hasty and inconsiderate policy by which 4,000,000 of slaves, without education, and without the least preparation were turned adrift from the discipline and interested care of the master to provide for themselves? Must it not be self-evident to any thinking man, no matter what his prejudices, that nothing he can now propose will be able to convert an idling, roving, thriftless free Negro population into the steady, healthy, laboring population that we formerly employed in our fields in the South?[84]

The address did have some constructive recommendations for the people of South Carolina, expressing the belief that in time, the state could recover. Their suggestions included that people should grow more cotton, raise more stock for individual use and for sale, and turn more to manufacturing to survive. However, most of the address involved complaints. It stated that the Reconstruction Acts would "place the best interests of society into the hands of an ignorant mob," and claimed that a "gradual system of emancipation" should have been adopted ... and the industry of the country would have received no such shock as now prostrates the South and overwhelms her in despair."

The heart of the address spoke to the authors' fear that freedmen, with the right to vote, would bring further disaster to South Carolina. The authors accepted emancipation as a fact but protested the way it was handled and the belief that the Negro majority, "much more than two to one" in South Carolina and unfit to rule or hold any position of power, in their opinions, would end up in charge. They encouraged whites to register in districts where the election of conservative men was hopeless, and asked them not to vote after they had registered. The new constitution required the support of the majority of registered voters, so if the majority of registered voters failed to vote, the constitution would not be ratified.[85] Their strategy failed, though, and a few months later South Carolina had a new constitution that guaranteed universal male suffrage and much more.

It is important to read the entirety of the address to fully understand its concerns and its tone. Yes, there was obviously racism, paternalism, and hypocrisy involved, but there was also a deep concern for the future of South Carolina. There was also a concern by some who responded to the letter, such as The Honorable James Chestnut in particular, that the letter itself, "filled with adjectives and epithets," would "only increase animosity."[86] Others thought it could do no harm. Wade Hampton, General Bratton's good friend and future political comrade, fully supported the address on moral grounds: "So, if our vessel must go down, let us at least stand true to our principles, and do nothing to deserve reproach. Let us sink, if not with arms in our hands, true to the past and to all of our instincts as Carolinians."[87]

The newspaper article containing the address does not contain any comments by General Bratton, specifically, but as vice president of the convention, it is safe to assume that he shared the same strong beliefs and opinions.

In between General Bratton's participation as a delegate at South Carolina's first Constitutional convention after the Civil War in 1865 and in the "alternative" convention of 1868, in which he was elected to the position of vice president, General Bratton was Fairfield's representative in the state Senate for the Forty-Seventh General Assembly (1865–1866) and served as a member of the judiciary and the military and pensions standing committees for those years.[88] By coincidence, his grandfather, Colonel William Bratton, was involved in military and pensions work when he was a Senator from 1785 to 1790. Both men were concerned about back pay and pensions for their respective comrades in arms.

Charity for Veterans and Their Families

While General Bratton was participating in politics during Reconstruction, he was also participating in local civic activities, especially those involving veterans and their families. In 1866 he was unable to attend a soldiers' meeting at Walhalla, so wrote them a letter on September 17, 1866. He wrote that since the state was "inoperative and ... unable to do her duty to her sons," that he wanted to organize a "Brigade Association for the benefits of the helpless of our Brigade." General Bratton suggested that if the other brigades in the state would do the same, they could establish a "common center from which charity could efficiently and largely be dispensed."[89] An article printed in the *Daily Phoenix (Columbia, SC)* on September 14, 1868, reported that he chaired a meeting of the Fairfield Soldiers' Relief Association that was held "for the purpose of organizing a society for the education of the orphans of the late Confederate soldiers ... and opened the meeting with a few feeling and appropriate remarks."[90]

General Bratton subsequently became president of the Survivors' Association of the Sixth Regiment and was a delegate to the state Survivors' Association Convention in 1869.[91]

The Ku Klux Klan

By 1868 the Ku Klux Klan had come to South Carolina and was particularly active in nine counties in the upcountry, including Fairfield County. In fact, "masked riders rode almost nightly over a period of several months immediately following the election of 1870,"[92] when Republican Governor Robert Scott was re-elected. An interview between 1936 and 1938 with Winnsboro resident Robert C. Gooding provides a hint of local white feeling about the Klan:

> The Ku Klux Klan was a necessary organization and did much to discourage weak white men and ignorant Negroes from lowliness. When the Ku Klux Klan wished to get rid of an undesirable white man or Negro, they would put an empty coffin at the undesirable person's front door. It usually caused the warned one to disappear.[93]

South Carolina's State Constitution of 1868 did not make a dent in most Southerners' attitudes towards racial equality, and as freedmen began to gain in power and to demand wages or tenant farming in lieu of sharecropping, they became more independent, which was threatening to landowners. Union Leagues educated and emboldened freedmen, and many joined the Republican Party, creating even more mistrust between whites and blacks. Blacks were allowed to arm themselves for protection and rode in Federal militias, which didn't exactly sit well with most white Southerners. Whites blamed Federals for inciting blacks, who at times seemed to be more interested in going to meetings such as those held by Union Leagues than in staying on plantations and working. Whites began to stockpile arms, and the Klan resorted to violence and began to act as a secret militia, threatening not only "radicals" (Republicans) but also whites who did not follow their beliefs. The "Klan rode to support traditional local values [and] Southern honor,"[94] and even if whites did not join, the Klan symbolized many of their values and received their implicit support.

It is not safe to assume, however, that General Bratton's beliefs included riding with the Ku Klux Klan or supported them in any way, even though his cousin, Dr. J. Rufus Bratton, was a well-known

Gen. Bratton and the K.K.K

How Fairfield's Republican Officials Escaped Death.

Winnsboro News and Herald.

There are many incidents in the dark days of radicalism and negro rule which will make very interesting reading in a few years to those who were actively connected with the matters pertaining to the country, surrounded as it was at that time by the greatest difficulties which ever beset a Government in the history of government.

There are young men to-day in Fairfield County who have no conception of what our people endured from 1868 to 1876. The Radical government was so bad in the State that an organization known as the Kuklux Klan was perfected for the suppression of crimes and the protection of life and liberty of our people. Much good resulted at first, but like a secret organization of the kind, the tendency was bad and the organization was abused toward the last. Fairfied County never suffered, however, like some of our sister counties for two reasons mainly and for other reasons largely also. In those days it was a common sight to see the streets on Saturday evening filled with armed negroes who came in nearly every Saturday for "a big muster." Crops and business had t o wait. This brings us to our story.

There was trouble with some of the negroes out about the Jack Gladney country and an arrangement was effected whereby they were to return their guns to the State and disband their company. Mr. L. Duval was sheriff and the guns were put in his charge. They were stored in the jail or sheriff's office, and when the Kulux learned that they had not been sent to Columbia they met and determined to put every county official to death, as our narrative will afterwards prove.

Gen. Bratton was not a member of the Kuklux, but on account of his wisdom, prudence and patriotism he exerted an influence by his very course on all matters affecting the public welfare of our depressed country His opinion was sought in a mysterious way.

Article from *The Watchman and Southron* (*Sumter, SC*), October 23, 1895. From the Library of Congress, Chronicling America.

The KKK had decided to kill all Republican county officials because they felt promises had been broken. General Bratton spoke with a member of the Klan and diffused the situation, and no officials were killed.

Klansman. General Bratton's son, Theodore DuBose Bratton, denied that his father was a member of the Klan in a 1935 letter to *The News and Herald*, a Winnsboro paper, as he was reminiscing about his father's life. Bishop Bratton said his father "never was a member of the Ku Klux Klan because of his conviction that disguise could be used by vicious people for vicious ends."

Bishop Bratton recalled how his father was almost arrested for being a Klansman, despite the General's strong feelings against the Klan:

> I recall of that era, though not a member of the Klan, the U. S. post in Chester had listed his name as such. A small detachment of soldiers was sent to Farmington to capture him. We were sitting around the fire in the sitting room sometime after supper, when suddenly there came a knock at the door, somewhat startling in that hour of the night, for our house was not on a highway. Father opened the door. A Yankee officer said, "General, I have the unpleasant duty to arrest you as a member of the Klan. I advise you to make no resistance, for the house is surrounded." My mother, aunts, and we children were stricken dumb when my father replied to the Captain: "You are mistaken; I am not a member of the Klan, but of course you have your order ... but before you attempt to execute it I want you to realize I have you covered with the pistol in my pocket. You will be the first to fall. With my assurance it will be wise to withdraw, and upon investigation you will discover your mistake." The wise course was adopted, and shortly after, my uncle, Col. Robert McCaw of York, died, and father was sent for. The narrow gauge railway from Chester to York had not yet been repaired. After arriving in Chester, my father went to Mr. Nicholson's hotel. He had seen father's name posted for arrest as a member of the Klan. The problem was to get a horse for the ride to York. The Yankee garrison had the only horses fit for duty. Mr. Nicholson at once proposed that he, with other members of the Sixth regiment,

commandeer one of their horses by night. Father, however, determined to storm the garrison in another way. He wrote a note to the Colonel, telling him his dilemma. An immediate reply came with the needed horse, telling him that the mistake had been discovered and offering my father help that might be needed in the effort to reach his sister, Mrs. McCaw, and be with her for the funeral.[95]

In 1871 President Ulysses S. Grant sent federal troops to South Carolina to suppress Klan violence, ordering it to disperse, and placed nine counties, including Fairfield, under martial law. Many Klansmen were arrested but most got off lightly. General Bratton's cousin, Klansman J. Rufus Bratton, fled from arrest to Canada but was later pardoned.

Reconstruction continued; the first black lawmakers were elected to Congress, including one from South Carolina, and integration began in some schools. Southerners continued to despise their Republican governments, not only because blacks had been given civil rights but also because of the money they were now required to spend for education, social services and railway expansion, and because of government corruption.

Carpetbaggers, Scalawags, and Taxes

Carpetbaggers and scalawags were common terms used in the South during Reconstruction. According to most Southerners, the carpetbaggers were evil people from the north who moved south to loot the defeated South, while the scalawags were Southern traitors who sided with the Republican government during Reconstruction. The government was quite corrupt at the time in South Carolina and in other states, both during and after Reconstruction. Many people used their positions for personal gain, and the radicals in the state Congress passed bills that placed Carolina even deeper in debt.

By 1873 the entire country was in a severe economic depression that lasted over five years. Among other things, the largest bank in the US had failed, and there were wage cuts and deflation. The South had yet to recover from the Civil War, so taxpayers in South Carolina were particularly concerned with their government's reckless spending habits and taxation.

General Bratton was a delegate for Fairfield County at the 1871 and 1874 Taxpayers' Conventions of South Carolina,[96] which were held in Columbia. Members at the first convention were extremely concerned about the extent of the public debt, reckless expenditures, and abuses by the government, and discussed numerous examples of these. Committees were appointed to investigate these issues further and to bring them to public attention. At the second convention, General Bratton is listed as a member of the executive committee. He was also assigned to a committee to address the people of the state and to a committee to investigate the Bank of the State of South Carolina. The president's address at the second convention indicated that convention actions had managed to halt the issue of six million dollars' worth of bonds, a major concern. Convention actions and inquiries had also aroused popular attention, and had impressed state authorities. The second convention resolved to continue investigating concerns similar to those of the first convention and to share them further by preparing an address to the people of the United States. The address would publicize the wrongs, fraud, extravagance, and lack of representation (by the property owners, especially, who paid most of the taxes) in the hope that those of other states would more fully understand and sympathize with them. It would also recommend punishment for the offenses, and would advise the people of the state how to counteract the heavy burdens that had been placed on them.[97]

General Bratton was also concerned, as all were, about fraudulent voting, and on December 16, 1874, the *Fairfield Herald* published resolutions he had made at the 1874 convention that were adopted. General Bratton prefaced the resolutions by describing the lack of registration laws in the state as demonstrating "not only a palpable disregard of the constitution, but ... the source of fraud and corruption in past elections." The adopted resolutions were as follows:

> That the executive committee of the Tax Unions be charged with the subject, with instructions to investigate the conduct and character of recent elections, to see if

frauds at the ballot box have not been perpetrated with impunity, and the probable extent of the evil.

That the subordinate Tax Unions of the counties be requested and instructed to canvass the voting of the late elections in their precincts, and ascertain the facts in regard to these frauds, and report the results monthly to the executive committee.

That the executive committee be requested to prepare instructions to the Subordinate Unions as to the best course of procedure in the discharge of their duties in the premises.[98]

Elizabeth Bratton's Passing

In the midst of this period of tremendous conflict, General Bratton and his wife, Elizabeth, had their last child, a daughter, in 1873. Isabel Bratton was born that August, the first little girl in the family. Her older brothers, John and Theodore, were fourteen and eleven years old respectively. Unfortunately, Bettie was not able to enjoy her children for much longer, as she died less than two years later in June 1875. She died in the home of General Bratton's sister and brother-in-law, Mary and Edward Noble

Elizabeth's obituary was printed in several South Carolina papers, including *The Fairfield Herald*:

Mrs. Elizabeth P. Bratton, wife of Gen. John Bratton and daughter of the late Theodore DuBose, Esq., departed this life, at the age of thirty-seven years, on the 23d of June, at the residence of Mr. Edward Noble, in Abbeville. In the deceased, to loveliness of person were added the charms of a true Christian character, and in her daily walk, as maiden, wife and mother, she endeared herself to all who knew her. She had been an invalid for several years, and her death was not un-expected.[99]

1876: Democrats Mobilize and the Tide Turns

Resistance by the Southern democrats continued throughout the Reconstruction period and came to a head in 1876. General Bratton served as chairman of the Fairfield County Democratic Party from 1876 to 1880, and portions of a speech he gave in April 1876 reflect his political feelings. He felt that the issues in South Carolina were "the gravest ... since the war of secession," and felt that the republican administration "had worked [illegible] injury alike to the whites and to the colored people." He felt that whites had been "continuously plundered" and the colored people were "the constant dupes of unprincipled carpetbaggers." He indicated that the object of the current Democratic Party was "good and honest government" and that it was the "aim of the corruptionists to tax the people to death." He indicated that colored people "are becoming tired of republican tyranny ... and need it [good government] far more than do the white people, for in addition to taxation and other like evils, they are slaves to party domination."[100]

At the May 1876 Democratic Convention of South Carolina, Wade Hampton III was nominated for governor. Hampton accepted the nomination, and then left the convention. General Bratton was then nominated by his old friend, Colonel James H. Rion of Fairfield County, who said that the Fairfield County Convention had passed a resolution to nominate him. Bratton withdrew in favor of Hampton. He said the resolution "caused him to feel some embarrassment for some time," but it gave him "great pleasure to withdraw in favor of the distinguished gentleman who had been previously nominated."[101] At this same convention, General Bratton was elected delegate to the national Democratic convention, where Samuel J. Tilden became a candidate for president of the United States.

Wade Hampton was elected governor by 1,134 votes after much ballot fraud and intimidation. Wade Hampton's Red Shirts, a grass-roots paramilitary organization whose goal was to intimidate non-Democratic voters, advocated "bloodless coercion" with displays of power such as demonstrations by rifle clubs, military-like drills, and parades, and they had achieved their aim. Mass rallies had been held in every county and included blacks as well as whites. They were led by the same men who led them during the Civil War,[102] including General Bratton. Louisa

Davis, former slave in Winnsboro, said her husband, Sam, spent "years 'ridin' wid a red shirt long side of General in '76."[103]

The election was disputed by the Republicans, who claimed that black voters had been suppressed. Both parties established separate governments, and Daniel Chamberlain, who was governor in 1876 and had been reelected in 1878 (according to the Republicans), remained at the state capitol guarded by Federal troops.

Meanwhile, the presidential election of 1876 caused yet another major crises between the North and the South. Democrat Samuel Tilden was running against Republican Rutherford B. Hayes, and General Bratton, a strong supporter of Tilden, was there as a delegate. The election became one of the most disputed in US history. Democrats were outraged because they thought the votes had been counted incorrectly. They believed that Tilden should have won, and they refused to accept the results.

The presidential election results for Florida and Louisiana were also disputed. Those states, along with South Carolina, were the only states left in the South with Reconstruction era governments still in power, so the Republicans negotiated with Southern Democrats and agreed to put an end to harsh Reconstruction policies in the South if the Democrats agreed to accept Hayes as president. Hayes was confirmed, agreed to pull Federal troops from South Carolina and three other states, and then Hampton's "Redeemers," as they called themselves, took control. The Conservative Regime was ushered in and the Reconstruction period in the South officially ended.

The Conservative Regime

The Conservative regime lasted from 1877 until 1890 and reversed many of the changes instituted by the Radical Republicans. In 1877 and 1888, the South Carolina General Assembly revised the state's election laws, amended codes, and redrew many voting precincts, and the black vote declined. Funds were cut to state hospitals and public schools, and land taxes for planters were lowered. Planters were favored in all disputes, and laborers could be held on plantations if they were in debt to the plantation owner.[104] In 1890 Jim Crow laws mandated the segregation of public restrooms, schools, restaurants, drinking fountains and much more under the guise of a "separate but equal" status for blacks.

The good news was that Wade Hampton "restored and even increased the reputation" of the governor's office in terms of integrity. Hampton, a brigadier general during the Civil War, had been one of the wealthiest slaveholders in the state. He had organized and equipped his own regiment. After the war, he lost almost everything he had and was forced to declare bankruptcy,[105] so he had a deep understanding of Southern conservative values and pain. People throughout the state loved and respected Hampton, even when they disagreed with his policies.

Political Service: 1877–1890

General Bratton remained politically active to a great extent during the Conservative era, although he was a reluctant politician.

In addition to being the Fairfield County Democratic Party Chairman from 1876 to 1880, he was a member of the state Democratic Executive Committee during those years and its chairman in 1880. As stated earlier, he was a delegate to the national Democratic convention of 1876; he was also a delegate in 1880.[106] In December 1880, General Bratton was elected to the 22nd Comptroller General of South Carolina position to fill an unexpired term and served until 1882. According to *The Newberry Herald and Times*, he "refused to become a Candidate, [but] he was elected by the Legislature."[107]

Wade Hampton was reelected Governor in 1878, again with support from the Red Shirts, but resigned in 1879 to become a US Senator. Two other Democratic governors were elected, and in 1882 General Bratton was once again nominated for governor. Major T. G. Barker, who nominated General Bratton, "spoke eloquently of his high character and manhood, the two qualities which in 1876 the people had sought to combine in the candidate who was to redeem South Carolina." Mr. Dozier, who seconded the nomination, referred to Bratton's "simplicity of character, modesty of demeanor and [to his] natural retiring disposition … [and to] his bravery, his character, manhood and sound judgment."[108]

Lt. Gov. John Kennedy, another follower of Wade Hampton's politics, was also nominated, along with Hugh S. Thompson, the State Superintendent of Education. The two main contenders, Kennedy and

Bratton, were "old school" veterans of the Civil War who were focused on the past glory days of the antebellum South, and some Democrats thought it was time for a change.[109] Thompson won the state nomination, and General Bratton's name was withdrawn.

In 1884 General Bratton was elected to the United States House of Representatives from South Carolina's 4th district due to the death of John H. Evins. He served in the 48th Congress for less than three months, from December 8, 1884 until March 3, 1885,[110] and was not a candidate for renomination.

General Bratton was nominated as a candidate for governor in the 1882 and 1886 gubernatorial elections,[111] but Hugh Smith Thompson carried the democratic ticket in the former race and John Richardson carried the ticket in the latter race.

Bratton, a popular and highly respected conservative, rarely sought political offices on his own initiative but was willing to answer the call of duty if he was convinced there were no better candidates. He was once again nominated for governor in 1890 and was convinced that he was the best chance for conservatives to win against another democratic candidate, Ben Tillman. Before we move on to that highly charged election and to the defeat of the conservative Democrats, it may be useful to review General Bratton's other activities while the conservatives retained power, as they will highlight some of the differences between the General and Ben Tillman.

Offices, Memberships and Farming

As if politics weren't enough, General Bratton was also very active in other civic and business roles.

General Bratton was a prominent member of the Grange and State Agricultural Society. In 1876 he was listed as an officer of Gladdens Grove Grange in Fairfield County,[112] and he was periodically involved in County fairs. In an essay read by General Bratton to the 1877 summer meeting of the state grange, we get a sense of Bratton's love for the land. The essay begins by expressing relief in the change of government since 1876 with hopes that agriculture will be restored. It discusses the need for using different methods for the exhausted soil, and then describes a method using livestock to assist in this effort. Much of the essay was spent crediting agriculture as the keystone of civilization and glorifying the role of the farmer. [113]

In 1879 General Bratton was a Commissioner of Phosphates. Governor William D. Simpson, who had succeeded Governor Hampton, appointed General Bratton and two other men to this position.[114] Phosphate mining had begun in earnest after the Civil War, and the governor appointed the men to "investigate the phosphate question, and report to the next session of the Legislature the condition, extent, cost of mining, shipping, etc." He also directed them to "devise the best system of protecting the rights of the State therein."[115] The state's labor force had remained overwhelmingly agricultural, but technological advancements meant that inexpensive fertilizer was available, and newly freed former slaves as well as poor whites needed employment. Phosphates never became as important as railroads or cotton mills in South Carolina, but between 1877 and 1890 royalties from phosphates were of great benefit to the state financial situation.[116]

General Bratton was also dedicated to education and particularly fond of his alma mater. He was vice president of the South Carolina College Alumni Association in 1881, 1882, and 1889; elective trustee of the South Carolina College from 1886 to 1888; and elective trustee of the University of South Carolina [the new name for South Carolina College] from 1888 to 1890.[117] At one point when he was vice president of the alumni association, whose members were primarily Southern democrats, he called the college "the cornerstone of our system."

General Bratton had already clashed with Ben Tillman when Tillman wanted to turn General Bratton's beloved South Carolina College into an agricultural college, an issue that was shelved during the 1890 election, but they were to clash even harder during the race for the Democratic Party's nomination that year.[118]

The Election of 1890 and Retirement

The Conservatives Are Ousted

The conservatives in the Democratic Party began to struggle more and more after Wade Hampton retired from politics. The South had begun to change socially and economically, and The Farmers' Movement

GEN. BRATTON IN THE FIELD.

Gen. John Bratton, of Fairfield, announces himself through the daily press of the State as a candidate for the gubernatorial nomination. His letter of announcement is as follows:

Be kind enough to allow me the use of your columns to reply to those of my fellow-citizens who have expressed a desire for me to be a candidate for the gubernatorial nomination of the party.

In the expression of their wishes as they reached me, along with the high personal compliment conveyed, there is the ring of a call to duty.

I accept both, and will give my best efforts to deserve the one and to meet the demands of the other. This is perhaps enough; but that there may be no misapprehension, so far as I am concerned permit a word as to the present status as I see it.

I trust and believe that we are all still a unit as to a common sentiment and desire for the best interests of the State and its people, and the great common purpose to guard and promote them. All agree that our Democratic organization is the only agency through which this sentiment can be practically adjusted and this purpose effected by us. Our differences of opinion are confined to the ways and means to be used by our party for their accomplishment. Where such differences exist some of us are certainly in error, and possibly none of us are absolutely right.

In this emergency our Democratic authorities have arranged for the canvass of the State, certainly not to foment a family quarrel or that partisan strife and personal scramble for office which is alleged to prevail in conventions of politicians, but for the fair and square submission of our differences, freely and frankly stated, to the people themselves for final adjudication and adjustment.

If they can be submitted calmly and dispassionately, and the people bring to bear on their public business that practical business discretion which they exercise in their private affairs, the decision reached, while it must necessarily overrule the views of some of us, will be worthy of a free people and command the respect and cordial support of all.

But should it be otherwise, and we become divided in partisan strife and allow passion and prejudice to take possession of our reason and judgment, the decision will be the best that we, as a people, are for a time capable of, and it must be sustained with unanimity. Any clean cut division of us will surely result in graver consequences than unanimity in even error for a season can bring upon us. Hedged about by unprecedented danger and difficulty, we must sink or swim together. We must stick to the ship, for it requires us all to even control her steering gear; and as long as we do that we retain the power, if we exercise it, to rescue her from dangers to which we ourselves may inadvertently or recklessly subject her.

I shall attend as many of the meetings appointed by our committee as practicable, and direct my efforts to the discussion of the situation in its bearings on our common interests in the hope that I may contribute to that rational agitation which will tend to throw the light of truth upon it and enable us to perform intelligently our duty as sovereign citizens.

Yours respectfully,
JOHN BRATTON.

Farmington, May 26.

General Bratton's letter of candidacy for governor. From the *Yorkville Inquirer* (Yorkville, SC), June 4, 1890.

became more popular. The Farmers' Movement originally started with the Grange, a social organization General Bratton belonged to that disseminated information to farmers and provided mutual assistance. It eventually had business interests, such as co-ops, and provided insurance. It then became politically involved, and in 1880 the Farmers' Alliance was formed, comprising the second period of this movement. During this period, it became even more political and sought additional reforms. The farmers "believed they were the victims of a conspiracy generated by the railroad companies, the bankers, the grain elevator operators, and conservative politicians who favored a money system based on the gold standard."[119]

General Bratton was a farmer but he did not support the Farmer's Movement (also known as the Populist Movement) in South Carolina. In 1890 he became the conservative party's candidate against "Pitchfork Ben" Tillman, as General Bratton stood the best chance of uniting the Democrats against him.[120]

Benjamin R. Tillman was a farmer before he became a politician, with limited Civil war experience compared with the conservatives, whose leaders were mostly older men and Confederate War heroes. He was an outspoken, often bitingly crude critic of the conservative party, and in 1890 Tillman condemned General Bratton as an old man whose "gaze was toward the grave."[121] Tillman had been emerging since the 1880s "as a spokesman for poor rural whites in South Carolina in their conflict against both the ruling white aristocracy and the impoverished Negro population." He was also a white supremacist who "considered lynching an acceptable law-enforcement measure."[122]

The political race was heated and full of name-calling by Tillman, but General Bratton, always the gentleman, announced his candidacy with the voice of reason and attempted to maintain his composure throughout the race. A public speaking tour to include every county in the state had been ordered by the Democratic executive committee, and farmers and storekeepers everywhere greeted the candidates with cheers and jeers in a carnival-like atmosphere. Tillman spent his time denouncing the Agriculture Bureau, and denouncing his enemies as aristocrats. His opponents tried to shift the discussion to national issues but ended up spending their time denouncing Tillman's accusations.[123]

When the tour ended, General Bratton hoped that it had served as "an enlightenment of our people as to their public matters," but Tillman had overshadowed him with his "stump speaking" and won the Democratic nomination and the gubernatorial race by a large margin.[124]

General Bratton did not immediately retire from politics after that election, as some sources indicate, although he and almost all of his conservative Democratic friends were no longer in power. General Bratton had been elected to the executive committee of the conservative Democratic convention in 1894, where Ben Tillman's "Tillmanites" dominated the convention, and the new constitution of the party was adopted.[125]

During the last years of his life, General Bratton stayed involved with a few civic or social organizations, and remained on the periphery of the political scene. He was a delegate to the Piedmont Colonization Society of South Carolina convention in 1894, a society that encouraged the introduction of desirable immigrants into ten counties in the area.[126] According to the *News and Herald* (*Winnsboro, SC*), August 10, 1895, he was nominated for the executive committee of the Democratic League in 1895, but declined.

The General remained involved with the educational system, and in 1895 he contributed to the erection of a new Mt. Olivet schoolhouse.

Not surprisingly, he was also a member of the board of managers of the South Carolina Society of the Sons of the American Revolution during his retirement years in 1896.[127]

The Model Farmer

General Bratton loved to farm. It was the occupation he chose instead of medicine, and an occupation that brought him much peace and prosperity. His fascination with farming and the results he produced were also a source of pride for the community. On the next page is an 1888 *News and Herald* article written by a visitor to the General's farm, who describes it as a "model farm." There were cotton fields, corn, chicken coops, sheep, cattle, and a dairy. The visitor described General Bratton's cattle as "the finest herd Ayreshire cattle that can be seen in the state,

"A Model Farm," *News and Herald* (Winnsboro, SC), October 3, 1888. From the Library of Congress, Chronicling America. A description of General Bratton's farm by an acquaintance.

A MODEL FARM.

Mr. Editor: It was announced in your paper that Major Pagan had gone to visit Gen. Bratton, and had let the weather get out of joint. Now the Major is at his post and the weather is about as good as any farmer could desire, and I hope to keep the white flag flying for many months.

I made a visit to Gen. Bratton's and not only enjoyed a very social visit but had the pleasure of seeing a "model farm"—a complete farm from cotton field to dairy and chicken coop.

I have never seen a crop in any respect as good as the General now has. His cotton is a "prize patch" all in one. The most of his cotton is planted on land that has been in grass, and no doubt well fertilized. He has early planted cotton and that which was not planted so early, but all of it seems to be good. Of course it has all been more or less damaged by the rains, but the estimate is that the yield will be at least a 500 pound bale to every acre planted. I saw as fine corn on upland as could be made on rich bottoms, and it was all good.

I saw a large field of kaffir corn that looked like it was as good as could be made, although I'm no judge of that kind of corn.

I saw large barns full of the finest kind of hay made from cultivated grass, and I saw many an acre of it ready for the mower.

Now, this is not all. The General has the finest herd of Ayreshire cattle that can be seen in the State, besides some very fine Guernseys. Any one needing fine cattle can be suited by calling on the General. In addition to all this I saw about two hundred fine sheep of the breed that makes fine mutton. It requires a herder and shepherd dog to care for the cattle and sheep. In the fowl line I saw about one hundred and fifty full blooded game fowls, all in good condition.

besides some very fine Guernseys." The General was often seen at county fairs, sometimes as president of the local county fair association, and won prizes for his heifers, according to the *Fairfield News and Herald* (*Winnsboro, SC*) in an article written on November 21, 1894.

Theodore DuBose Bratton, his youngest son, described his father's love for the land and farming as follows:

> His love of the soil was inborn and intense, and the study of agriculture and animal husbandry a lifelong delight. I never knew anyone who more than he, readily inspired as mutual [an] understanding and trust with animal and even bird life. One of my latest mental pictures of him, on a visit to him at Farmington about 1895, was on a spring day, seated on the front porch, near to a yellow jasmine vine in which was a nest of young mocking birds; with his black pointer dog at his feet, the mother bird eating seeds prepared for her, on the railing of the porch, only few feet away his cat sunning herself on the same railing, all apparently in unafraid fellowship.[128]

In 1889 when he was fifty-seven years old, General Bratton listed two of the plantations he managed, Farmington and Rock Spring, for sale. His advertisement appeared in the *Fairfield Herald* on September 22 and was headed "Fine Plantations for Sale." Farmington, about ten miles from Winnsboro, was advertised as containing "about 2200 acres," a "dwelling house and necessary plantation buildings." Rock Spring, about four miles from Winnsboro, contained "about 600 acres" and "all necessary plantation buildings." The plantations would be sold to the highest bidder at the Fairfield Court House "on sale day in October next." Robert M. DuBose and John Bratton were both listed as executors for the estate of Theodore DuBose, deceased (General Bratton's father-in-law).[129]

Retirement? The General's Final Years

Actually, it is somewhat doubtful that the General ever really retired. In 1896 General Bratton was sixty-five years old. A widower of over twenty years, he had never remarried but he had filled his life with farming and social and civic activities and was a beloved friend and colleague to many. His children were all grown, and he was doubtlessly very proud of them.

William, the oldest and still unmarried, was thirty-six years old and had become a medical doctor. He had attended Mt. Zion School, the University of the South in Sewanee, Tennessee, and South Carolina Medical College at Charleston, where he graduated in 1884. William was commissioned in the Navy as Assistant Surgeon in 1885.[130]

Theodore, his second son, was thirty-four. He had received his education in Sewanee, Tennessee, where he attended elementary school and the University of the South and became an Episcopal priest. Theodore married and at that point already had several children. He was often in the area preaching.

According to the 1880 United States Federal Census, Isabel was living with the family of Mary Noble, her father's sister, in Abbeville, South Carolina, about ninety miles from Winnsboro. Mary and her husband, Edward Noble, had two teenage girls at the time.

Isabel was a charmer by all accounts. She was "a fit representative of the beauty, the chivalry, the past glory and the present aspirations of South Carolina," according to an article written by *The Fairfield News and Herald*. The article, "South Carolina's Sponsor," indicated she had been chosen to represent the South Carolina Division of United Confederate Veterans,[131] so her father wasn't the only one in the family involved in working with veterans of the Civil War.

Friends, including those left from his Sixth Regiment, also surrounded General Bratton. He was dearly loved by them and by the community. He was a long time member of the Episcopal Church, having converted at some point from Presbyterianism after he married his wife. Until 1897, the year before he died, General Bratton's name appeared quite regularly in local newspapers, whether an event was social, political, farm-related, or just the fact that he had arrived in town. One article about a quarry in the county simply mentioned that he was there: His presence at any function or place was considered an honor.

Before his death in 1898, General Bratton was to lose one of his sons to the grim reaper. His oldest son, Dr. William D. Bratton, was fatally wounded by a fall in 1897. He was stationed at Sabine Pass, Texas, at the time, and had volunteered for a post in the yellow fever district. Dr. Bratton died of injuries received when he fell through the hold of a ship while en route to serve yellow fever sufferers. *The Fairfield News and Herald* obituary notice spoke of the esteem in which his commanding officers held him, and described his personality: "Pure, high-minded, gifted at once with talent and modesty—sweet and gentle as a woman, yet in every sense a brave and true man, he has fallen in harness, alas, too soon.[132] William died on October 12, 1897, and was buried at St. John's Episcopal Cemetery. His father was to follow him there only three months later.

A Celebration of Life

The news of General John Bratton's death on January 12, 1898, made the front page of several newspapers all over South Carolina. Tributes and memorial events, some even months after his death, exemplified just how much South Carolina and Winnsboro, in particular, loved and honored this man.

St. John's Episcopal Cemetery, where General Bratton and several other members of the Bratton family are buried. General Bratton was buried next to his beloved wife, Elizabeth. Photo by Pat West, author, June 25, 2015.

"Gen. Bratton Dead: Fairfield's Most Distinguished Citizen Passes Away Suddenly," was a typical headline. The *Fairfield News and Herald* of January 19, 1898, contained numerous columns regarding his public life and career. General Bratton fell ill on a Saturday with what would ultimately be determined to be heart issues, but on the following Wednesday was in "good spirits," telling visitors "war incidents and war jokes." His son, Reverend Theodore DuBose Bratton, was with him when he took a turn for the worse. General Bratton's funeral was attended not only by family but also by friends who had traveled long distances to pay their respects. "Camp Raines, U.C.V., attended in a body, as did Camp Bratton, sons of Confederate Veterans," and pallbearers carried the old Sixth Regiment flag. All of the stores in Winnsboro closed, and the "old town bell and all the church bells" tolled. One phrase in the *Fairfield News and Herald* seems to describe him particularly well:

> Brave as a lion; tender-hearted as a woman. Always giving to the widow and orphan (especially a Confederate widow or orphan). Great believer in Calhoun and the fundamental principals of the Democratic Party. Almost Quixotic in his idea that the "office should seek the man."[133]

I might have added, "Yes, but all he really wanted to be was a farmer," but that would be an oversimplification. General Bratton was a true Southern gentleman, a very intelligent and thoughtful man born to privilege but also born to lead, and with that came a sense of duty and honor. He preferred to be tending to his sheep, cattle, and cotton, but he always answered the call of duty.

A traditional, conservative, and serious soul who could also tell a joke or two, John Bratton basically followed in the footsteps of his father and his grandfather (except for his conversion from Presbyterianism to the Episcopal Church, but I suspect his wife and her family had something to say about that). A doctor by the age of twenty-three, he preferred farming, and began to focus on the lands he had inherited or managed even before the Civil War. During the Civil War, he volunteered as a private and rose to the position of brigadier general, and his reputation for courage, leadership, and fairness were so great that even his enemies honored him. He was wounded in battled twice, and each time returned to the battlefield within a month or two.

Upon his return home in 1865 to a wrecked, devastated plantation, town, and family, General Bratton managed to consolidate family lands and resources and to provide for his large family, including any of his former slaves who had remained on his land. By 1867 he owned 2100 acres and was growing cotton. He began to import cattle, sheep, and swine, and even started a successful dairy. On top of these successes, however, he had lost seven of nine little sons to starvation or privation during or after the Civil War, and his beloved wife, Elizabeth, died at the age of thirty-seven after being ill for several years. General Bratton was left with a two-year old daughter and the couple's two surviving sons. With the help of his family, however, he raised these three children to become successful, respected members of the community. One son, William, became a doctor who died on his way to help yellow fever victims. Another son, Theodore, became a Bishop of Mississippi. His daughter, Isabel, supported the General's favorite cause—that of ex-Confederates, orphans, and widows. She moved to Mississippi after her father's death and married a doctor, Julius Crisler.

Always a somewhat reluctant hero and politician who has been described as deferential to others, John Bratton still responded to the call of his fellow conservatives in politics and was heavily involved with other conservative democrats until 1890, when they began to lose power. The General, as he was always referred to, was a delegate to Democratic conventions, a member of the state Senate, and chairman of the county Democratic Party and of the Democratic state executive committee. Although he declined to run, he was elected Comptroller. With his history of heavy involvement in taxpayer conventions ad concern for the state economy, he doubtlessly did an excellent job.

Bratton was a Commissioner of Phosphates who helped bring much-needed revenue into the state. He was nominated for governor no less than four times between 1876 and 1890, with one serious race in 1890, but he usually managed to bow out graciously. He was happy to see his friends—mostly members of the Confederate War generation—take the lead.

In addition to farming and politics, General Bratton cared deeply for those in need, especially his beloved Confederate soldiers, widows, and orphans, and helped establish a charity for them. He was also committed to education, especially to his alma mater, serving as an officer in alumni associations or as elective trustee.

≈ ≈ ≈

I suspect that the General was not perfect, as honored as he was, but he was also a product of his times. Yes, he was a slaveholder and yes, believed in segregation, but those harsh-sounding terms do not reflect his reality. He truly seemed to care for his family, and he would have included former slaves (or servants, as he would have said) as a part of that family. According to his son, Theodore, who later became a Bishop of Mississippi, General Bratton's "one parting injunction" before he died was: "Son, I want you to look after my old people when I have gone."[134]

Theodore was the executor of his father's estate, and he did his best, I am sure. The Farmington Plantation was rented after the General's death and continued to produce cotton, and hopefully, a home for the General's "old people" until it was sold on October 2, 1912.[135] Theodore, like his father, had strong feelings for the plight of former slaves, as we shall see in the next chapter.

John Bratton (1831-1898)	married	Elizabeth Porcher DuBose (1838-1875)

William	John	Theodore*	Edward	Frank
Beverly	McNeely	Robert	Richard	Isabel

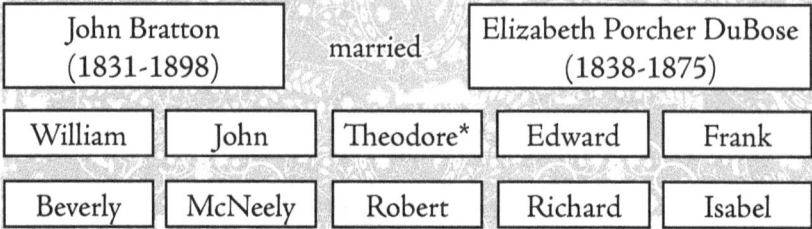

Only William, Theodore, and Isabel survived to adulthood. William, unmarried and childless, was killed when he fell through a ship's hold, and Isabel had no known children, leaving Theodore to carry on his father's branch of the family tree.

*Theodore DuBose Bratton (1862—1944)

Chapter Three

The Rt. Rev. Theodore DuBose Bratton
A Shining Light

———⋆———

THEODORE "ALWAYS FELT A bit timid about preaching because it was a new thing in his family. 'We have always been farmers,' he said, 'or else doctors, and those of us who were doctors were also farmers, but we have not been preachers.'"[1] The Rt. Rev. Theodore DuBose Bratton, third Bishop of Mississippi and Chancellor of The University of the South at Sewanee, Tennessee, had heard the call of God since childhood. He knew he had to follow wherever it led him, even though his path would not always be easy.

Born the year after War Between the States began, he was raised in a conservative South Carolina town that believed in states' rights and fought against the Union army. Theodore was fourteen years old when the Reconstruction era ended and the Conservative era began, and witnessed conservatives in the South passing Jim Crow laws to keep blacks and whites segregated. He had been steeped in the values of the Confederacy and taught to honor and respect white Southern traditions. Like his ancestors, Theodore served during wartime, in his case as a chaplain. Unlike his famous father and other notable relatives, however, his call of duty to God and country would include addressing racial inequalities and the importance of education for women—subjects not always popular in his home state of South Carolina or in his adopted state of Mississippi.

Theodore may have felt timid about preaching but he sang his message loud and clear, and in many ways was ahead of his time and in sharp contrast to those around him. Not only did he preach, Theodore also put his words to action. Schools for women and a several black missions for African Americans were founded. His support for education and enlightenment included his alma mater at Sewanee, a school where his uncle, William Porcher DuBose, created controversy with teaching methods that were ahead of his time. Theodore also lectured tirelessly and authored or contributed to several books.

Throughout his career, Theodore Bratton remained steadfast, pursuing his beliefs while remaining open-minded to changing them. Despite the controversy his words sometimes created, his kind eyes, deep musical voice, and warm handclasp and words never failed to bring joy to his parishioners—whether black or white, male or female—as he continued his family's legacy of courage, honor and devotion to his country.

Early Life

Childhood in Fairfield County

Theodore DuBose Bratton was born on Roseland Plantation near Winnsboro, in Fairfield County, South Carolina, on November 11, 1862. He was the third child out of ten born to General John Bratton and Elizabeth Porcher DuBose Bratton, one of three who would survive to adulthood. Theodore was of Huguenot and Anglo-American ancestry. His father, John Bratton, was a physician and a planter and would become a Confederate war hero and politician. His mother, Elizabeth Porcher DuBose, was a daughter of Theodore Marion and Jane Porcher DuBose, and one of her ancestors was the famed Francis Marion, also known as the "Swamp Fox" of the Revolutionary War. Yet another ancestor explored with the Lewis and Clark Expedition. All of Theodore's family had been prominent and respected members of Fairfield County, York County (home of his great-grandfather, Colonel William Bratton of the Brattonsville plantation), or Charleston. They were primarily planters, doctors, and even politicians, and were leaders in their communities. Theodore had a lot to live up to.

Theodore was born at the end of the Antebellum era in the South about a year after the War Between the States began. His parents had married in 1860, and by the time Theodore was born, he had two older brothers to play with, William and John. In addition to his brothers, he was surrounded by numerous servants (as the Brattons referred to their slave family) and numerous Bratton and DuBose relatives, who were often in and out of his home. His father, John Bratton, was a physician turned farmer, and owned three plantations and at least seventy-six slaves.[2] His early years were spent at Wynne Dee, his parents' home in Winnsboro, although he often visited the Roseland and the Farmington plantations, which were owned by the DuBoses.

When the War Between the States began, Theodore's father was one of the first to volunteer, and Theodore saw very little of him until after the war. In fact, Theodore was born while his father was fighting the Union army, and they did not even meet until Theodore was about three months old. When General Bratton finally returned home for the last time at war's end, he took control of both his and the DuBose family plantations and was fortunate enough to find a northern investor to help them all start over. He moved the family from Wynn Dee in Winnsboro to the Farmington Plantation, about ten miles north of Winnsboro on the Wateree Creek, when Theodore was four years old.

Farmington "was both a patriarchal family and an agricultural and mechanical community and school,"[3] an entire, self-sufficient community before the war. It had been devastated during the war but it did provide Theodore with an excellent educational foundation, preparing him for entry into a college preparatory school at the age of twelve. He was tutored at Farmington until then by his aunt, Marion ("Betsy") Porcher.[4]

Theodore's Aunt Betsy was also a motivating factor in his early exposure to and future love of religion. The DuBose family, including Theodore's mother, came from a long line of Episcopalians. According to Theodore, his Aunt Betsy "was a sort of saint to us all and had a powerful influence over us as children." She was also an influence over the men in the community, and "almost every man in the community, in due time, became a communicant."[5] Theodore's father, who came from Scots-Irish Presbyterians, converted to the Episcopal Church, and the DuBoses, including Theodore's mother, were doubtlessly an influence on his decision.

The Brattons attended St. John's Episcopal Church in Winnsboro. It was built in the early 1840s and "was an educated, cultured community."[6]

The church was burned by Union troops in February 1865—troops from Sherman's March through South Carolina that also ravaged the town and terrorized the inhabitants of Wynne Dee. A second church was built in 1869.

Although Theodore's father managed to revive the family's fortunes after the war ended, the young family suffered terribly during the postwar years. By 1869 John and Elizabeth Bratton had produced nine children, all boys, but seven of them had died by 1870 due to the hardships created by the war. Theodore lost his older playmate—brother John Jr.—and six younger brothers; only he and his older brother William survived.

Education at Sewanee

When Theodore was twelve, he followed his brother William to Sewanee Grammar School, a private college preparatory school that had been founded in 1869 in Sewanee, Tennessee, by the Episcopal Church. Most of its faculty had been officers in the Confederate army, graduates of institutions like West Point, Cambridge, and South Carolina, and they were "men of high ideals and invincible integrity of character … ."[7] It was typical for the sons of planters to attend military academies, as had Theodore's father and his grandfather before him. The school fit the bill, although it was not to officially become the Sewanee Military Academy until 1908. Theodore arrived at the school in 1874, three years after his uncle, William Porcher DuBose, left South Carolina to become Chaplain and Professor of Moral Science at The University of the South in Sewanee.

The grammar school was affiliated with The University of the South, which Theodore would attend after preparatory school. The university's cornerstone had been laid in 1860 and building commenced. There were few Episcopal educational institutions in the South at the time, and the vision of its founders was to create one that would rival Harvard, Princeton, and Yale. The university's buildings were burned during the War Between the States, but construction began again in 1866, and it officially reopened in 1868.

While Theodore was pursuing his studies tucked away in the mountains of Tennessee, South Carolina and other states were embroiled in turmoil and change. The South struggled under Reconstruction politics and economic depression until 1876, when the Conservative era was ushered in. The Democratic Conservatives were back in power in South Carolina, and Jim Crow laws were passed.

Theodore's father, General Bratton, was right in the middle of it all—active in politics, various commissions, and social causes in addition to farming his plantations. Theodore's mother had been ill for some time, and she passed away in 1875. Isabel Bratton, Theodore's baby sister, had been born in 1873, and went to live with relatives, Edward and Mary Noble,[8] in Abbeville, South Carolina, after their mother's death.

Religion in America had been changing as well. Various religious awakenings had been occurring since the mid-eighteenth century, and what some called a Third Great Awakening had begun in the 1850s and would continue even beyond the Civil War into the early 1900s. Religious awakenings in the mid 1800s contained strong elements of social activism.[9]

The Episcopal Church in the South took a middle road, standing with the South and skirting the issue of slavery.

> Unlike other denominations, the Episcopal Church did not formally divide over the issue of slavery. Abhorring schism above all else, and realizing that resolutions on slavery would inevitably bring disputes, the church avoided an official stand on human bondage … . In keeping with their emphasis on personal religion, many evangelical and high church Episcopalians also felt that slavery was a purely political issue … . In addition, those Episcopalians who knew southern planters from college or from summer resorts seem to have been repelled by the characterization of slave owners given in abolitionist publications.[10]

The southern diocese of the Episcopal Church became a part of the Confederacy during the Civil War but quickly reconciled with the national Church after the war; there had never actually been a split of an official nature.[11]

The Church eventually had to find a way to deal with the issue of emancipation, of course, and during most of Theodore's adult life took the path of segregating African American congregations. Theodore also took that path, as we shall see, but did so with much soul searching and advocacy for African Americans—and with more conviction and fortitude than many others in his church.

New religions or religious organizations came onto the scene, such as the Salvation Army in 1865 and Christian Science in 1879. Darwin's theory of evolution, first presented in his 1869 book, *On the Origin of the Species*, caused an upheaval in contemporary religious ideas.

≈ ≈ ≈

The atmosphere at Sewanee, particularly if one's teacher was William Porcher DuBose, fostered discussion and debate on all of these changes. This was considered revolutionary, as "the youth of that day were not encouraged to ask questions," and was so alarming to some of the church fathers that there was an investigation into DuBose's methods.[12] DuBose was cleared, and is now considered to be one of the most profound American theologians of the period. "DuBose was almost a living stereotype of classic Southern upbringing, yet the combination of evangelical fever and Anglo-Catholic modernism which he expounded in several major works was remarkably attuned to the scholarly development and philosophical interests of his age."[13]

Dr. DuBose had been charged with starting the university's school of theology in 1873, and he and his theology students also provided services to the Fairmont School for Young Ladies, which was about six miles from Sewanee. The school "splendidly served a large number of the girls of the Gulf States, at a time when such rare culture as the gifted lady teachers imparted was often sought in vain."[14]

Dr. DuBose was not only Theodore's uncle and had been the rector of Theodore's church in Winnsboro, Saint John's, but he was also Theodore's professor when he attended The University of the South. He had a deep influence on Theodore, who later described him as a prophet: "He was the prophet—this was the ever growing conviction of his students—coming daily from God and speaking both from Him and of Him."[15]

The two were linked by blood, background, and theology. There were differences between them, however: DuBose was about twenty-six years older than his nephew and his parents were wealthy slave owners during antebellum, slave-owning times. Theodore had never really experienced slave ownership, with the exception of his first three years of life during the Civil War when his family still owned slaves. Still, Theodore always had an enormous respect for his uncle and became a leading authority on DuBose when he wrote a book about him, *An Apostle of Reality: The Life and Thought of the Reverend William Porcher DuBose ... .* Theodore wrote the book so that DuBose's philosophy could be "revived and re-studied," and because he believed that it presented "an enduring vehicle of truth, of universal application to the expression of the Truth and its molding power in thought and life."[16]

Theodore's strong beliefs about the importance of Christian education likely had their deepest roots in his uncle's influence. He expressed not only his uncle's feelings but also his own when he wrote in *An Apostle of Reality,* "The Church must ever be a teaching Church if her members are to be really living daily and growing daily."[17]

≈ ≈ ≈

Theodore studied civil engineering at the University of the South as well as divinity under the watchful eye of his Uncle William,[18] but his studies were periodically interrupted. "After beginning study in the university proper, he had to return home for two years to manage his father's plantation while General Bratton directed the Democratic campaigns for South Carolina offices in 1880."[19]

Theodore returned to the university and continued his studies, but he developed a serious eye affliction two months before graduation and had to withdraw from his classes. "He was appointed a proctor. A year later he became a teacher in the preparatory school and while thus engaged pursued his divinity studies at Saint Luke's Theological Hall, the theological school of the university."[20] On a biographical form he later completed for the Mississippi Archives and History Department, Bratton wrote that he was "Assistant Master, Sewanee, Elementary School, 1883–1886," and was a member of the "Alpha Tau Omega" fraternity.[21] According to his grandson, John Gass Bratton, he was the fraternity chaplain and signed the contract to build the ATO fraternity house, which was the oldest frat house in the South before it burned and was rebuilt.[22]

Bratton received his BA in 1887 and his BD in 1889 from The University of the South.[23] He later received two honorary doctoral

Saint Luke's Hall at The University of the South, Sewanee, TN. Courtesy of University Archives and Special Collections, The University of the South.

degrees, a Doctor of Divinity from The University of the South in 1901 and a Doctor of Laws from The University of Mississippi in 1911.[24] Information regarding the circumstances of his honorary doctorates will be provided later in this chapter.

Priesthood in Carolina

W. B. W. Howe, Bishop of the Episcopal Diocese of South Carolina, ordained Theodore DuBose Bratton deacon at Trinity Church, Columbia, South Carolina, on September 25, 1887.[25]

Bratton's love and admiration for his Uncle William DuBose and his early exposure to religion by his parents and by his charming, lovable, and pious Aunt Betsy were surely among his reasons for entering the priesthood. His kind and generous spirit, fostered by a family who provided him with an abundance of love, support, and a sense of responsibility for his fellow man, were also factors in the equation.

As one of Bratton's friends, the Rev. Holly Wilberforce Wells, observed:

> He seemed to know and understand all living things
> … . It always hurt him to see life starved or deprived;
> his instinct was altogether for the care and culture of
> life, its healing and fulfillment. In the field or at the
> bedside his fathers had been farmers and physicians;
> he himself was a farmer and physician in things of
> the spirit … . He knew that human beings are never
> artificially reconstructed; if they are to become better
> they must grow better, and it is only as they grow into
> the likeness of Christ that they fulfill their normal life.[26]

Mr. Bratton's first charge in the church was to serve as an Episcopal missionary for two years in Lancaster and Chester counties—which bordered Fairfield County—and in York County, where his ancestors had immigrated to South Carolina in the eighteenth century.

Spartanburg: Church of the Advent and Converse College

The Church of the Advent in Spartanburg, South Carolina, heavily in debt and in much need of repairs, had been seeking a minister but no one seemed interested. "On July 30, 1888, the vestry called Mr. Bratton, who was the deacon in charge of the Church of the Good Shepherd in York, South Carolina. Bratton was on the verge of being elevated to the priesthood and seemed to possess the energy needed."[27] A couple of months later, on September 23, 1888, Mr. Bratton was ordained priest at Christ Church, Greenville, South Carolina, and in the same year became Rector of the Church of the Advent. The church, located about ninety miles northwest of Winnsboro, was "home of the first Episcopal congregation organized in Spartanburg County, and was an excellent example of a Gothic Revival sanctuary and church complex designed before the Civil War."[28]

Before the Jim Crow laws in South Carolina in the 1880s, African Americans had attended the Church of the Advent, but when Mr. Bratton arrived, segregation had taken hold and African Americans and whites had separate churches. Bishop Howe, who was in charge

Church of the Advent, Spartanburg, SC (*above*). Photo by Bill Fitzpatrick, February 18, 2012.

Converse College (*right*), original campus. Courtesy of Converse College.

of the Diocese of South Carolina and who had ordained Bratton as a deacon, had ruled that African Americans should be seated in the church's annual convention, "but the Vestry of the Advent, along with many others, was furious that Howe would even entertain such an idea and passed heated resolutions of objection."[29] In 1893, however, Bratton founded the Epiphany Mission, a mission that located a place for African Americans to worship that also included a school for them, The Colored Industrial School. He also organized the first mixed choir at the Church of the Advent. Following is an excerpt from a newspaper article that included some of his history with the Church of the Advent:

> During his pastorate of eleven years, he founded the Epiphany mission for the colored, in the neighboring city of Greenwood, and [he] organized the first mixed choir at the Church of the Advent. By this time, the church built in 1884 was in great need of repair. Dr. Bratton and his vestry, looking to the future, enlarged the church by the addition of transepts and choir. The first building, its roof raised, forms the nave of the church as it is today.[30]

Mr. Bratton was very popular at the Church of the Advent, and an article in the *Charleston News and Courier* of July 28, 1890, described him as "one of the most eloquent preachers in the diocese of South Carolina. He is an able student, and in every way acceptable to the congregation and the people of Spartanburg." The congregation grew, the church's debt was eliminated, and the building was repaired, and Bratton was given a raise in 1893 and an assistant. A school for community children and one run by ladies of the Advent was started, as were more plans for community outreach. In addition, Mr. Bratton also formed the women's Altar Guild.

The church had outgrown its buildings by 1894, and Silas McBee, who had designed the chapel at Bratton's beloved alma mater, was retained as a consultant. Construction began in 1897, and a special service was planned for October 10, 1897, to consecrate the church. However, the service became "a service of farewell, for Theodore DuBose Bratton had resigned on June 19, 1899, to take charge of Saint Mary's School in Raleigh."[31]

From 1890 until 1899, in addition to his position as Rector of the Church of the Advent, Mr. Bratton taught at Converse College in Spartanburg as a professor of history.[32] The college had been started by "citizens concerned with the lack of educational opportunities for young women ... [when] the importance of education for women was being supported in the South,"[33] and it opened its doors in 1890. Mr. Bratton was very popular at the college, and his students faithfully attended the Church of the Advent. While the church was being rebuilt due to its growing membership, services were held in the chapel room of Converse College.

Marriage and Family

In the same year that he was ordained as a priest, in 1888, Theodore DuBose Bratton married Lucy Beverly Randolph on July 17 in Tallahassee, Florida. Lucy's parents were Dr. James F. Randolph and Elizabeth Beard Randolph, descendants of the Randolph family of Virginia. Mr. Randolph was the grand nephew of Thomas Jefferson and was raised in Jefferson's home. Lucy's family was well-known in Florida, active in the Episcopal Church and in education:

> Dr. Randolph was a surgeon in the provisional army of the Confederacy, and was mayor of Tallahassee in 1876. In 1881, Dr. Randolph was appointed superintendent and physician in charge of the Florida State Hospital in Chattahoochee. With his father, he co-founded Saint John's Episcopal Church. The Randolph daughters conducted the first girls' school in Tallahassee.[34]

Mr. Bratton's marriage to Lucy Randolph was quite fortunate on a number of levels. Lucy was a beauty, inside and out, and became not only the mother of their nine children but also a very important part of Bratton's ministry. Among other things, Mrs. Bratton would have participated in the church's women's auxiliary, which had been organized after the church's 1871 General Convention.[35] The auxiliary became an important part of the Episcopal Church, collecting funds for missionary work and other purposes. The fact that the Randolphs were involved in education for women would have been an added advantage, especially when Theodore would later become rector of a women's college in Raleigh, North Carolina.

By April 13, 1899, Mrs. Bratton had borne three little boys and four little girls. Sadly, three of these children had died: Elizabeth (1891–1892), Lucy (1894–1895), and Harriet (1896–1898). The children were all buried in the Church of the Advent Cemetery, which surrounds the sanctuary.

Another sad occurrence during that period of time was the death of Mr. Bratton's brother, William DuBose Bratton, on October 2, 1897. William was a surgeon connected to the US Marines and was in Sabine, Texas, when he died. He had volunteered to assist victims of the yellow fever epidemic, even though he was still recovering from an illness. He was checking on the disinfecting of a ship when he fell through a ventilating hold, striking his head. He died a few hours later. William was only thirty-seven years old, and "his literary and scientific attainments were of a high order." His supervising surgeon general described him as "of modest and reserved manner, yet frank and manly in his demeanor, and actuated by a high sense of honor in all relations."[36]

Raleigh: Saint Mary's College

Saint Mary's College in Raleigh, North Carolina, wanted to lure Mr. Bratton away from his native South Carolina and was concerned it might be difficult. They came up with a plan to elect him trustee, and after so doing, they surprised him at his first meeting as a trustee by electing him rector of Saint Mary's! Mr. Bratton was thirty-seven years old and his wife Lucy was thirty-six when he was elected the third rector of Saint Mary's in 1899. Bratton accepted, and the *News and Herald*, his hometown paper in Winnsboro, wrote all about it:

> For years, Mr. Bratton has had charge of the Episcopal Church in Spartanburg and in that time he has won the love and admiration, not only of his parishioners, but also of every one in the town with whom he has come in contact. Although his election to the rectorship was highly complimentary, yet his friends are deeply grieved at the thought of his leaving the state, and especially his friends here in his native town.[37]

Mr. Bratton moved his wife, four young children, his widowed mother-in-law, Elizabeth Randolph, and his sister, Isabel—who would teach at the school—to Raleigh in the summer of 1899. The two-story frame house meant for them was in need of so many repairs that he offered to donate $500 of his first year's salary to fix it. The trustees declined his offer, but it made them more certain than ever that they had the right man.

Lucy was appointed the "school mother," and supervised daily living for the students.[38] Saint Mary's had been founded in 1842 as a church school for young ladies, "designed to furnish a thorough and excellent education equal to the best that [could] be obtained in the city of New York, or in any Northern school," and was successful from the first, even remaining open during the Civil War. In 1897 the Episcopal Diocese of North Carolina took charge of the school and the Board of Trustees was created, and by the time that Mr. Bratton was elected rector, it had become a college.[39]

Although Mr. Bratton was only rector at Saint Mary's for four years, he made quite an impression. Bratton reorganized the curriculum and divided the school into preparatory and college departments to put Saint Mary's on an equal track with other colleges for women. "The University of the South conferred the honorary degree of Doctor of Divinity upon Mr. Bratton in 1901 in recognition of his contributions to Christian education."[40] Mr. Bratton was also involved with the buildings and grounds. He did some landscaping and added music practice rooms, the north dormitory, and an infirmary, and he enlarged or remodeling other buildings. He also kept cows, pigs, and a five-acre vegetable garden.

All of the girls at the college "worshipped" him, and thought, "he was the handsomest and sweetest man [they] ever knew." They privately called him "T. D."[41] Saint Mary's had a very loving atmosphere; there was discipline, although some considered it lax—girls were even allowed to stand on their heads in the snow. Formal dances, sorority banquets, and team sports were encouraged. And of course, Mr. Bratton made sure that the chapel was at the center of it all, and instituted Founders' Day as part of the All Saints' observance.[42]

The Muse was Saint Mary's yearbook, and in 1901 it was dedicated to the college's beloved rector. In addition to being the rector, Mr. Bratton

Family portrait, 1901, taken in Raleigh, NC. Theodore DuBose Bratton is in the center. *First row, from left to right:* his son, William DuBose Bratton; his wife, Lucy Randolph Bratton; his son, John Bratton; a goat named Snow; and his sister, Isabel Bratton.* *Top row, from left to right:* Mary Bratton (held by a maid); his son, Randolph Bratton, on the knees of his mother-in-law, Elizabeth Beard Randolph; Marion Bratton (held by a maid); and a cousin, John Bratton DuBose. Image from State Archives of Florida, *Florida Memory.* Information courtesy of John Gass Bratton, Sewanee, TN.

was also on the college's board of trustees, on the athletic association advisory committee, and a member of the tennis club. In the 1903 yearbook, he and Mrs. Bratton were honorary members of the Epsilon Alpha Pi Literary Society;[43] Mr. Bratton had assisted his students with its creation in 1901.[44] The Muse also dedicated their 1904 yearbook to Mr. Bratton after he was elected Bishop of Mississippi in 1903:

> His magnetic personality, his unswerving determination not to be ruled by prejudice, his never-failing tact, made him a head to be respected and loved; his kindliness, tenderness and wisdom, a friend from whom to seek advice and sympathy; the purity, charity and unselfishness of his character, a priest whose life is an incentive and inspiration to all who know him. To him we dedicate this book in loving gratitude for all he has done for us and for our Alma Mater.[45]

About two weeks before Mr. Bratton was elected Bishop of Mississippi, his wife was busy having their last child, Isabel Bratton, who was born on April 5, 1903. Isabel may have been named after Bratton's sister, Isabel, who was living with them at the time and had come with them to Mississippi. Isabel would have been twenty-nine years old in April 1903 and was surely a help to the growing family. In late 1903 the Brattons had six children under the age of fourteen: William (14), John (11), Randolph (8), Marion (4), Mary (2) and Isabel (infant).

The times were changing rapidly, and the Bratton children would grow up in a society that was quite different than that of their parents. The industrial revolution of 1865 to 1900 meant the coming of steam engines, trains, the light bulb, and the telegraph. The Wright brothers took their first flight in 1903. Technology, science, and inventions were proceeding rapidly. Coca-Cola was here to stay, as were radio and radar, cars and bicycles.

Dr. Bratton's challenge was to move into the twentieth century and to deal with a multitude of social and economic changes while advocating for changes he considered critical for the church and for society as a whole. As you will see while reading of his years as a bishop, he worked tirelessly and accomplished much. He would not be able to completely escape his roots as a conservative white Southerner, but as a Bishop of

Mississippi, he would prove to be quite outspoken—especially given the time and place.

Election to Bishop and the First Years

Theodore DuBose Bratton was elected the third Bishop of Mississippi on April 29, 1903. He was consecrated in Saint Andrew's Church, Jackson, Mississippi, on the Feast of Saint Michael and All Angel's day, on September 29, 1903.

Bishop Bratton had entered a diocese that tended to be evangelical, or "low church," a church that was concerned with reaching out to everyone, whether they were black or white. The Episcopal Diocese of Mississippi had been created in 1826 and had jurisdiction over the entire state of Mississippi—a state whose population was half black. Provisional bishops were in charge until 1849, when the Rev. William Mercer Green was elected as the first Bishop of Mississippi. Bishop Green encouraged the church's ministry with blacks, both before and after the Civil War. After the Civil War, the church was open on several occasions for freedmen who worshipped

The Rt. Rev. Theodore DuBose Bratton. Courtesy of John Bratton, Sewanee, TN.

with white congregations. The first ordination of a black person in his diocese took place in 1874 and was "one of the first such ordinations in the South."[46] A council Green organized convened at Sewanee in 1883 to "draw up a program for ministry to black people," and sent resolutions to the General Convention calling for "the inauguration of active work and the building up of a black priesthood and laity."[47] When the Rev. Hugh Miller Thompson became Mississippi's second bishop in 1887, he continued Bishop Green's work in this direction, and several black congregations were organized under his leadership.

Bishop Bratton was to serve for a total of thirty-five years, during which there were many economic and social changes in the state. Industrialism increased, many blacks left Mississippi for the North, and there was a world war and the Great Depression. Despite financial constraints, however, the number of communicants under Bishop Bratton doubled.[48] Bratton also maintained close ties with his alma mater, and "in 1914, the diocese voted to take part in the work of the Fourth (Sewanee) Province consisting of most of the southern dioceses."[49]

As Bishop, Bratton traveled throughout the diocese during the year. He visited each congregation periodically; examined candidates for ordination; reported to the national church; conferred the Rite of Confirmation; consented to marriages of those who had been previously married; mediated disputes between a rector and vestry; handled financial issues; and much more. *The Journals of the Diocese of Mississippi* details Bishop Bratton's hectic, almost non-stop schedule, which was primarily by railroad until after World War I, as there were more railroads than roads at that time.[50]

Priorities of Bishop Bratton's Episcopate

Bishop Bratton made his priorities clear in his first address to the council in 1904. His address fit right in with the diocese's history of evangelism, including its reaching out to blacks, and placed more of an emphasis on sharing resources within and without the parish and on the importance of education. Since his consecration, he had "visited every parish and mission in the Diocese, and several towns besides in which [the church had] ... no organized work." His first address was quite lengthy and set the tone for his episcopate. He saw the diocese as "one big parish" with the smaller and weaker divisions deserving help from the larger and more prosperous divisions.

In his address, Bishop Bratton spoke of changing the church policy against allowing non-Episcopal churches to use their buildings and property. He expressed concerned at the lack of attendance among men in the parish, decried the lack of suitable parsonages for the rectors, and reminded the rectors that pledges were their duty. He emphasized the importance of education for the young, referring to The University of the South at Sewanee and how it represented to his mind the best

Christian education available. He said, "we must not be satisfied until we have provided the means of training our boys and girls for life here and hereafter."[51]

The principles inherent in Bishop Bratton's episcopate were "an emphasis on missionary activity and education, for whites and blacks, and a willingness to cooperate with those outside the church, while maintaining a faithful adherence to the church's canons and traditions."[52]

Lucy Randolph Bratton's Passing

Just two years after Bishop Bratton's arrival in Mississippi, his cherished wife, Lucy, was stricken with nephritis and died four days later on January 5, 1905.[53] She was interred at Cedarlawn Cemetery in Jackson.

The Muse, the yearbook of Saint Mary's in Raleigh, dedicated its 1905 yearbook to Mrs. Bratton, describing her as having "the precious gift of sympathy—not alone in joys and sorrows—but in trifles, those so-called little things, the petty pleasures and worries that return each day, and are strong to make or mar life's happiness." The St. Etheldreda's chapter of the junior auxiliary at Saint Mary's changed its name to the Lucy Randolph Bratton chapter to honor her memory.[54]

Her obituary in the *Laurel Ledger* (Laurel, MS) on January 7, 1905, was written by someone who had known her "almost from her girlhood," and described her as "one of such unusual graces of mind and heart and with such a useful sphere to fill as mother of a large young family and spiritual mother of the diocese ... ."[55]

Mrs. Bratton was only forty-one years old when she died. She left behind six children ranging from two to sixteen years old, her stricken husband, and the deep sadness of all who knew and loved her.

MRS. THEODORE DuBOSE BRATTON

"Mrs. T. D. Bratton." Courtesy of *The Muse*, 1905 (Saint Mary's Yearbook).

John Gass. Courtesy of John Gass Bratton.

Ivy Wardlaw Perrin Gass. Courtesy of John Gass Bratton.

Second Marriage

On August 15, 1906, Bishop Bratton married Ivy Wardlaw Perrin Gass in Sewanee, Tennessee. It was "a quiet affair," according to the announcement in the *Clarion Ledger*, which described Mrs. Gass as a "lady of rare culture and charm, well known in Jackson."[56]

Mrs. Gass was the daughter of James Monroe Perrin and Kitty Calhoun Tillman Perrin. The Perrins were prominent citizens of Abbeville, South Carolina, and Mr. Perrin practiced law and was in the South Carolina House of Representatives. He was a colonel with the South Carolina Volunteers, and died in Chancellorsville during the War Between the States.[57]

Ivy Wardlaw Perrin Gass was the widow of the Rev. John Gass. The Gass and Bratton families were well acquainted and were good friends. Gass graduated from The University of the South in 1887, the same year that Bratton received his BA there, so they were schoolmates; and they were both ordained by Bishop Howe on September 23, 1887, at Trinity Church in Columbia, South Carolina.[58] Mr. Gass was the rector at Saint John's Episcopal Church in Winnsboro, Bishop Bratton's home church, and was also the rector of churches in Augusta, Georgia; Charleston, South Carolina; and St. Luke's Episcopal Church in Atlanta. He died from appendicitis in 1898, shortly before his fortieth birthday.[59] After Mr. Gass died, Ivy moved her family to Sewanee, where she served as a matron.[60]

Mr. and Mrs. Gass had two sons and three daughters, but the oldest daughter died when she was a few months old, so Mrs. Gass had four remaining children when she married Bishop Bratton: Ivy Wardlaw Gass, Henry Markley Gass, John Gass Jr., and Katherine Perrin Gass. Bishop Bratton was forty-three years old and his new wife was forty-seven, and together they had a house full of ten children ranging in age from about two to twenty years old. Isabel Bratton, Bishop Bratton's sister, did not marry until October 23, 1906, so she probably remained with her brother and new sister-in-law until that time.

The marriage of Bishop Bratton to Ivy Gass was the beginning of a history of unusual coincidences, connections, and intermarriages between the Brattons and the Gasses, beginning with their immigration to America. John Gass Bratton, grandson of Bishop Bratton, wrote an amusing story about this titled "A Tale of Two Families" and presented it to the Rotary Club of Monteagle on September 20, 2000. For those interested in more details of the Bratton/Gass connections and history, it may be found in appendix E.

All Saints' Junior College

Bishop Bratton's passion for Christian education began to manifest even more as he spearheaded the development of what would become All Saints' Junior College. In 1905 the diocesan council resolved that a diocesan school for girls be established. The bishops and trustees of Saint Katherine's School in Bolivar, Tennessee, telegraphed Bishop Bratton with a request to make their school an inter-diocesan girls' school for Mississippi and Tennessee. Bishop Bratton recommended this to his diocese, and also came up with a detailed proposal for a boys' military preparatory school that would be located in Mississippi. The Mississippi diocese declined both recommendations and decided to establish a girls' school in Mississippi. In 1906 a committee was appointed to raise $100,000 for All Saints' Junior College with Bishop Bratton as its chairman. Vicksburg, Mississippi, was chosen as the location. By 1908 property and sufficient funding were acquired and Bishop Bratton officially founded the school. All Saints' Junior College,

All Saints' College, Vicksburg, MS. From freepages.history. rootsweb.ancestry.com.

originally a junior college and high school for women, opened in the fall of 1909. Bishop Bratton was president of the trustees when it opened, and then became president of the school from 1912 to 1937. The Rev. William M. Green II was the school's first dean.

Bishop Bratton's words in a 1911 speech describe how he felt about All Saints':[61]

> In my own mind and heart All Saints' College and The University of the South stand upon equal terms in consideration and affectionate interest, representing as they do, the Church's will to fulfill her Divine Head's exhortation to teach .... My desire, my purpose, is that no member of our diocesan family will be satisfied to permit a year to pass without investing something in the Christian education of our young people.[62]

"The school was Bishop Bratton's own Saint Mary's and for many years he served as the president and board chairman of All Saints' in addition to his other duties."[63]

Bishop Bratton's Mission to Black Episcopalians

Bishop Bratton spent much of his time addressing the needs of the African American community throughout his episcopate, and was interested in the subject long before he entered the priesthood. In 1905 he said,

> For twenty-five years, I have been devoting as large a share as possible of my ministry to the Negro race, beginning my labors before being admitted to Holy orders. My interest in the work has grown with the years .... That we should preach the Gospel to them and teach them is not, I suppose, an open question to any healthy Christian mind.[64]

Why did Bishop Bratton spend so much of his time on this issue? Why did he give numerous talks on the subject; write a book on the subject; work actively on starting or supporting black educational and church ministries; and basically do everything he could to encourage the advancement of African Americans at a time when many of them were migrating to the North to escape lynching and Jim Crow laws? Remember, his was a conservative church in Mississippi, the state where some of the bloodiest racial conflicts after the Civil War took place.

We know that Bratton's predecessors, Bishops Thompson and Green, believed in outreach to the black community, but there may have been other motivations as well.

One theory involves the possibility that he had a half-brother named Ruffus Bratton, a mulatto whose father was General John Bratton, Bishop Bratton's father. Elliott Bratton, a black descendant of the Brattons, has done extensive research on the subject and has come to that conclusion. According to Elliott, Ruffus and Theodore Bratton were best friends, and Ruffus was also close to Isabel, Bishop Bratton's sister. The reader may draw his or her own conclusions after reviewing Elliott's research in appendix D, but if this is true, it could explain at least some of Bratton's motivation for being so deeply involved in this issue.

In addition to the support from his predecessors in the church and to his close relationship with Ruffus, there were several other factors that could easily have come into play. Bishop Bratton was raised in a home that saw its black servants as an extension of their family and—from all known accounts—treated them with kindness. Bratton was mentored first by a beloved aunt who was deeply religious, and then by an uncle whose teaching methods, both in terms of academics and religion, encouraged Bishop Bratton to think for himself and to love all men equally. His personal attributes, highly respected Southern roots, and early success as a priest in education and in race relations lent credence to his words, and success encourages success. Finally, he had inherited a duty of caretaking from his family: As you saw at the end of the preceding chapter, one of his father's last charges to him was to take care of his father's "old people," former slaves who had remained with General Bratton on his plantation after the Civil War.

When Mr. Bratton was called to be rector in 1888 at the Church of the Advent, the man who ordained him into the priesthood, Bishop Howe of the Diocese of South Carolina, had ruled that African Americans should be seated in the church's annual convention, and this ruling caused quite an uproar. Episcopal congregations and most of their leaders were all part of the Southern culture, which saw African Americans as inherently inferior to whites or child-like, at best. Fortunately, when Mr. Bratton was consecrated as third Bishop of Mississippi, he also inherited a diocese in which his predecessors had reached out to black people and had been one of the first dioceses in the South to ordain a black person. He quickly followed suit, and his first ordination of a priest after he became a bishop was a black man, the Rev. Richard Temple Middleton.[65] It seems obvious that Bishop Bratton would not have ordained as a priest a man he considered inferior or child-like.

We can theorize at length as to his motives, but the fact stands that Bishop Bratton was driven to spend much of his time reaching out to African Americans.

Christian Principles and the Race Issue

Bishop Bratton did believe in segregation of the races, as did the vast majority of Southern white conservatives; he had known nothing else during his lifetime. He never maintained that whites were inherently superior to blacks, however, and urged blacks and whites to resolve what was commonly referred to then as "the race issue." His thoughts on the matter also seemed to evolve as time went on.

In a chapter of the book, *The Development of Segregationist Thought*,[66] the book's editor has reprinted part of an address Bratton gave on April 23, 1908, to the Conference for Education in the South, in Memphis, Tennessee. The title of Bratton's address is "The Christian South and Negro Education." The editor uses Bratton as an example of moderates who consider themselves "friends of the Negro;" who "consider Christianity the best guide to racial policy and interracial conduct;" and who "hoped to eliminate the harsher aspects of white supremacy and neutralize its most brutal consequences."[67]

In the first two pages of Bishop Bratton's 1908 address, Bratton prefaced his comments about the Christian South with an explanation of how the relationship between slaves and their masters, who became freedmen working for their former masters after the Civil War, changed with the Reconstruction era. Bratton felt that the races got along better before Reconstruction, and described the Reconstruction era as a "period of anarchy and destruction." He said, "The races emerged with the conviction that they could not dwell together upon the footing of equality, social or other equality, which had been the fond dream of the Negro race, and that there must be clear and distinct separation."[68]

While Bratton's 1908 address reflected an obviously paternalistic attitude towards Negroes, he also stated that "the Negro is capable of development to a point whose limit I have not yet discovered," and that "no solution of difficulties growing out of the relations of two races is going to be permanent and satisfactory unless both races have made contributions to it."[69] Bishop Bratton did believe, based on his experiences, that "the vast majority of Negroes [were] still children intellectually and little short of savage morally,"[70] and that it was the Christian responsibility of whites to "raise" them through education, cooperation, and an ongoing, thoughtful re-examination of their needs. Distressed at interracial violence, especially with lynching in the South, Bratton wanted to resolve race issues with dialogue and cooperation.

In 1909 he addressed the Missionary Council of Sewanee at Montgomery, Alabama, on the "Best Method of Work for the Colored People." In this address, Bishop Bratton expressed his conviction that education through a "teaching church" was the answer, and discussed his opposition to the adoption of the plan of black Suffragan Bishoprics then before the church. The suffragan plan involved a way "to address the issue of African American autonomy while maintaining the unity of the denomination ... [but] they would not be allowed to vote in the House of Bishops and would always remain under the authority of white bishops."[71]

In 1914 the Southern Sociological Congress published his article, "Race Co-Operation in Church Work." Bishop Bratton began by summarizing the damage that the Reconstruction era had caused, during which "politically the Negro had been practically annihilated, and religiously he had emancipated himself from his best guide [white churches]." He then moved on into an acceptance of the "modern period" of segregation, which he felt was "very generally accepted as the best condition of racial development." He expressed the belief that it was God's hand that placed the Negro in America, and that it was within "the power of cooperative religion to solve this problem of race relationship, as indeed all other moral problems." He expressed concern that young black people were often not joining the churches around them because, while the young people had advanced educationally and culturally, the churches had not. Bishop Bratton condemned those who spoke flippantly of the black race, saying such words were "ignorant and vicious by the white man who would deny him a school and herd his family in a one-room hut!" In conclusion, he called white Christians to reach out to their black brethren, "with divine compassion toward their need."[72]

≈ ≈ ≈

The race issue was one of the most complicated issues of Bishop Bratton's time, and his emotions seemed to go back and forth during his episcopacy. He seemed to struggle with the issue, often reminiscing with nostalgia during his addresses about black and white relationships in the South before the Civil War. While it is true that on at least one occasion he described the vast majority of blacks as little better than savages, Bishop Bratton also condemned white people who spoke of the black race as one that was ignorant and vicious. In any event, he continued to tackle the issue in an effort to improve race relationships and to encourage Negro education, believing that education was the key to the Negro race's advancement.

In 1918 the Southern Sociological Congress published his article, "An Open Door to Industry on the Basis of Efficiency," in which Bratton discussed the race problem and the attitude that white men should take toward encouraging Negroes to realize "racial achievement and success." He chastised men who wanted to limit Negro education and stated, "He is not confined in the South to menial tasks. Law, medicine, the pulpit, the school, the mercantile lines are all open to him. His real problem is the gaining of a measure of efficiency that will reward his industry with success." Bishop Bratton praised Negro leaders, and went on to state that "the Negro, as a race, has not yet measured his own capability, and the white man is equally ignorant of it."[73]

Bishop Bratton also took his plea for justice regarding racial issues to a national level, even becoming involved in politics.

In 1916 an article in the *Chicago Defender* on May 6 noted that Bishop Bratton "took a prominent part in the defeat of the Stevens' bill, which sought to keep white people from teaching in race schools ... ."[74] The *Chicago Defender* had written an article about the bill on February 26, 1916, indicating that its passage would "make it unlawful for any person to serve as a teacher in any school attended in the state by any pupils of a different race ... [and that it] would apply both to public and private schools."[75]

In 1919 Bishop Bratton attended an annual Conference of Governors held in Denver. He was president of the Southern Sociological Congress, and part of a committee that brought race relations before the body due to mob violence. When World War I was over, returning white soldiers had been welcomed home as heroes, but "black soldiers who had fought shoulder-to-shoulder with their white comrades were now expected to resume their "proper place" as second-class citizens. Resentment grew and violent race riots resulted in several Southern cities."[76] The position of Bratton's committee was that race problems were a "national rather than a sectional concern; and it was felt that if a policy could be for-mulated which could be endorsed by the governors of all the states, a starting point would be secured from which the whole problem might be worked out along common lines."[77]

Bishop Bratton "went on to found biracial committees to work for better race relations, and as limited as his sympathies were, his help was the best black leaders got from Mississippi whites during the depths of segregation."[78] These bi-racial committees or groups were very unusual for those times, and one of these organizations, the Council for Interracial Cooperation, sponsored Councils in Human Relations in all of the Southern states.[79]

≈ ≈ ≈

Bishop Bratton believed in separation of the races and in something he referred to as "racial integrity." He believed that God had created many different races—why, he did not know. He said, "Race integrity is obedience to God's own creation and appointment." Bratton's thoughts on the subject of race would continue to evolve, and when he wrote a book in 1922, *Wanted–Leaders! A Study of Negro Development*, he described his experiences with Negroes in his city's administration, in board meetings, and in council meetings in the Episcopal Church. These experiences, along with his discussions with African American leaders and with his parishioners, led him to believe that segregation was a mutual choice. One of the African American leaders who influenced him was Booker T. Washington and, in his book, *Wanted!—Leaders*, Bishop Bratton quoted some of Dr. Washington's words:

> We are a unit like a man's hand; in our inner social life, in all that contributes to racial integrity and the separate trusts that God imposes, we are separate as the fingers of that hand; but hand and fingers unite in striving to perfect the human family, to strengthen and build up, to guard and to purify, the great living Temple of God.[80]

Booker T. Washington, an educator who had founded the Tuskegee Institute, reassured conservative whites in his Atlanta Compromise speech of 1895 that most black people were not interested in being accepted as their social equals but simply wanted a chance to develop skills needed to make a living.[81]

Despite Bishop Bratton's beliefs in racial integrity and in segregation as the correct path for society to take at that time, his conclusion in *Wanted–Leaders!* seems quite unusual for his time and place: it demands equal rights for African Americans. His book is a study of the Negro culture and development in Africa, Liberia, Haiti, and America, slavery and freemen in America, and the Civil War and Reconstruction periods in the South. It also covers the education and the Christian development of the Negro in America and the emergence of black leadership. His conclusion is open-ended regarding the eventual relationship between whites and blacks, and it ends with an excellent and powerful summary of his position on racial equality in terms of justice and equal rights:

> The Negro knows even better than his white critics how faulty a living building is in which the majority of the living stones are still rough, unpolished, unsquared. He asks, and he has the right to ask, that, as a free man, he be treated as a man; that, as justice is the right of life, he be accorded it; that, as a citizen, he be granted the rights of citizenship—the equal right of life, liberty and the pursuit of happiness; that laws governing citizenship be applied with equal justice to Negroes and to Whites.

If the Church of God (that is, her members) can bring
herself to stand for less than that, it is difficult to find
ground for forgiveness at the hands of the Son of Man
who died upon the Cross for the salvation of all.[82]

Black Missions and Education

Bishop Bratton felt it was his Christian duty to minister to every man
or woman of any race, and particularly emphasized the importance of
black leaders in this regard. The emphasis for the education of African
Americans in Mississippi at that time was "placed on vocational training
in the industrial, domestic, and agricultural arts ... thereby securing first
for them economic welfare."[83]

Bishop Bratton and many in the Episcopal Church "wished to
assist African Americans without disturbing traditional patterns of
race relations," and Bratton often referred to the affectionate relationship blacks and whites had before Reconstruction, calling upon "white
Christians to work closely with African Americans once again—estab-
lishing schools where they could learn practical and useful skills."[84] The
American Church Institute for Negroes, begun in 1906, was founded
by the Board of Missions of the Protestant Episcopal Church. It was "a
response to the alarming disparity between educational opportunities
for African Americans and privileged whites within the church."[85] Its
ultimate purpose was to assist all the schools in the Southern dioceses,
and several schools eventually came under its supervision.

There were only two black missions in the diocese when Bishop
Bratton started his episcopate: Saint Mary's, Vicksburg, with its school,
and a mission in Jackson that would become St. Mark's Church. By
1912, St. Mark's Church in Jackson was known as St. Mark's Mission
(Colored). Several more black missions were established under Bishop
Bratton's leadership or encouragement. Some of the black missions established during the early years of Bishop Bratton's episcopate were Trinity
Chapel, in Natchez, consecrated in 1903 by Bishop Bratton; Mound
Bayou, opened in 1913; the Redeemer, Greenville, also opened in 1913;
and St. Luke's in Gulfport, opened in 1914. A Colored Convocation of
the diocese was established in 1912, with the Rev. R. T. Middleton as
archdeacon of colored work.[86]

The Okolona school is another example of how Bishop Bratton put his words into action. The Okolona Normal and Industrial School was founded in 1902 in Okolona, Mississippi, and in 1921 it became affiliated with the Episcopal Diocese of Mississippi and a member of the American Church Institute for Negroes.[87] Bratton often visited and spoke at various black industrial or agricultural schools, and "due to his interest in the education of the colored people, Okolona Industrial School was given to the diocese and [Bratton] labored long and well for that institution."[88] He was present for many events there, and the T. D. Bratton Memorial Dormitory was named after him.

In 1920, during a visit to the school when a gift to the school of $5,000 from the Church Institute Board of New York City was being announced, Bishop Bratton was introduced by the school's president and founder, Wallace A. Battle, with these words:

> If solving hard problems of humanity, as they exist in the southland, in the wisdom and spirit of Jesus spells greatness, then, fellow teachers, students and friends, here is to speak with you one of the greatest men and Bishops of the world.[89]

Social Justice

Bishop Bratton's interest in social justice extended to all genders, races and social groups, and his ongoing efforts in this area regarding African Americans have already been established. While always adhering strictly to church principles and teachings and the Book of Common Prayer, he felt that "the human race is God's family."[90]

Bratton felt that women were the foundation of civilization. Both of his wives worked with him during his ministries, and his commitment to education for women was demonstrated as a builder and organizer of women's colleges. In a newspaper article, "Bishop Bratton Says Womanhood Is Foundation of Civilization," by Dolly Dalrymple, Bratton said,

> If I had to choose between the education of men and women, which, thank God, is not necessary, I would always chose to see that the womanhood of a nation

was educated; for it is the woman who makes the home, lays the foundation and promotes the spiritual education at the fireside, where children and husband abide.[91]

Bratton's words seem to reflect his personal experiences, considering how well educated and devout his mother and other female relatives were. His was certainly not a modern point of view, but for a male Southerner to espouse that education for women was even more important than education for men was certainly radical for his day. Bratton was also talking about an academic education—not a privileged Southern woman's charm school type of education. His first wife, Lucy, was given the position of school mother at Saint Mary's in Raleigh, a position to replace that of lady principal, which had been abolished after their female principal left the college. It is unclear as to whether or not it was a paid position but it definitely involved the daily supervision of students. Bratton's sister, Isabel, taught at the same college. His second wife, Ivy, worked with him constantly in his ministry and for causes involving social justice. At a meeting of the Commission of Inter-Racial Co-Operation, of which Bishop Bratton was a member, Ivy was listed as a member of the Women's Committee in the Commission's publication of its meeting on October 6–7, 1920.[92]

Bishop Bratton's passion for social justice also extended to the political arena, not only in terms of racial issues but also regarding war and its prevention. During and after World War I, Bratton was also quick to give his opinion about his country's shortcomings. Regarding the war itself, he said,

> If we are struggling only to beat a physical foe ... that our self-indulgence and mammon-worship and material supremacy may be perpetrated, then I frankly confess that I see no reason for anxiety as to the termination of the war or as to the victim. What difference does it make who wins if Mammon is to receive the fruits of conquest? But if in the struggle we are consecrating ourselves to God ... (so) that God's Kingdom be exalted and His Truth and Righteousness

abound, then there is nothing that may be withheld from the offering to Him.[93]

In speaking of his country's lack of participation in the League of Nations, an organization dedicated to preventing another world war, Bratton said,

> I consider that our country not only committed a positive blunder, but a positive sin in not taking part in its functions ... . America was the logical umpire, the only nation strong enough to be respected, and disinterested enough to be impartial. It is a positive sin for America to sit quietly by, and not fulfill the office of friend without invitation when called to this service, but to refuse the nations when they have gone down on their knees to us, figuratively speaking, to intervene, is absolutely sinful.[94]

World War I, the YMCA, and France

Bratton had been chaplain of the Spartanburg, South Carolina, company in 1898 during the Spanish American War but had not been called to serve.[95] When World War I began, the religious forces of the nations were unprepared, and it wasn't until 1917 that the Federal Council of Churches met to organize the General War-Time Commission of the Churches. This commission was "a coordinating agency consisting of official delegates of thirty different religious organizations ... [including] a representative group of Protestant Churches except for the YMCA, which had interdenominational support."[96]

Bishop Bratton decided to become a missionary chaplain for the YMCA and left for France in October 1918 to serve at Brest and in the Le Mans and Chaumont area. Because he would be absent for at least a year and because the diocese was growing, a Special Council met at his request in Jackson, Mississippi, and elected the Rev. William Mercer Green II as bishop coadjutor and rector of St. Andrew's in Jackson.[97]

> In the World War Bishop Bratton rendered effective service as a lecturer in behalf of the war work of the Young Men's Christian Association, doing duty

both in American camps and with the American Expeditionary Forces overseas. He was a veritable angel of mercy to thousands of American soldiers at the port of debarkation at Brest, especially during those dark and tragic days when that French harbor was so sadly infested with Spanish influenza.[98]

Why did Bishop Bratton, a man who was almost fifty-six years old, choose to leave his home, his wife, and his busy, growing episcopate to become a missionary chaplain? David Stetson Langdon, who wrote his master's thesis on Bishop Bratton's episcopate, thoroughly explored the possibilities. Langdon concluded that Bratton did it not only to honor his country but also with thoughts of his son, William DuBose Bratton, a young soldier who had also gone to France as a chaplain, and thoughts of his mentor, William Porcher DuBose, who had died earlier in 1918. Additionally, service to country was important to the Bratton family, his church had a history of evangelical/missionary work, and Bratton had full confidence in the abilities of Mr. Green as coadjutor.[99]

Langdon, who reviewed the bishop's journals, noticed that in 1918 Bishop Bratton made repeated visits to his oldest son, William DuBose Bratton, who was a chaplain in the US Army. William Bratton was with the First Mississippi Regiment; he was based in Indianola, Mississippi[100] and went overseas with the regiment during the war.

William Porcher DuBose, who died two months before Bishop Bratton left for France, had also served as a chaplain in the Civil War. Bratton wrote about attending his funeral and DuBose's service in the Civil War, along with the fact that DuBose was wounded three times.

Service to country, especially during wartime, was a strong tradition in Bishop Bratton's family history, and "applying for and obtaining canonical leave to serve in France during the First World War, Bishop Bratton upheld the SPG and English tradition of the importance of military and other hardship chaplaincies."[101]

By October 18, 1918, Bishop Bratton was shipboard on the HMS Euripides, an English vessel, and "no one in Jackson was surprised."[102]

≈ ≈ ≈

Mr. Green originally declined the appointment to coadjutor due to a technicality with the election, but when the regular diocesan council met

in 1919 and reaffirmed him, he accepted.[103] Bishop Bratton wanted Green
to take over "the biggest parish, St. Andrews, Jackson, … [and Green]
maintained a satisfied diocesan constituency through it all … [Bratton's
choice of Green] was a hallmark of the genius of Bishop Bratton's
leadership."[104] Green was the son of the first bishop of Mississippi and
the first dean of All Saints' Junior College in Vicksburg when Bishop
Bratton founded it in 1909. Green and Bratton were an excellent match.

Bishop Green excelled at moving forward with Bishop Bratton's
ideas for his episcopate, and remained on as his coadjutor after Bratton's
return. He "relieved Bishop Bratton of much of the burden of episcopal
supervision, and moreover, made definite contributions toward system-
atizing diocesan work and strengthening church life."[105]

The Episcopate After World War I

Upon his return from France, Bishop Bratton was ready to begin what
he saw as the church's responsibility to establish a "new social equilib-
rium." He said, "The church and only the church has the power to still
the social unrest of today." He called for a "great spiritual awakening,"
and "asserted that the Episcopal Church will take the lead in assuming
its share of the responsibility … ."[106]

Bishop Bratton worked with Bishop Green to increase organizations,
committees, and activities. They established a "Colored Archdeaconry"
in 1912 and an Executive Committee in 1921 that was "composed of
representatives from chief diocesan departments and committees."[107]

In 1923 a new revision of the constitution and canons was approved,
and "four years later, full-time field workers for the advance of Church
School and Young People's work." The Episcopal Laymen of Mississippi
was organized in 1927 to promote the programs of the church; to interest more laymen in evangelicalism; to help place *The Church News*
in every Episcopal home; and to recruit new members for the layman's
organization. It secured pledges of over $100,000 for All Saints' Junior
College in Vicksburg, among many other accomplishments.[108]

With Bishop Green as coadjutor, Bratton was also able to continue
to spread his beliefs within and without the church. As previously noted,
the diocese accepted oversight of the Okolona Industrial School, and
Bishop Bratton continued his outspoken mission to African Americans

through speeches, publications, social and political activities, and church activities.

His mission to African Americans also included some quiet, small attempts to desegregate the church. According to Bishop Duncan M. Gray Jr. seventh bishop of Mississippi:

> Some measure of desegregation also took place at the diocesan level. For example, blacks and whites met together for Diocesan Council from way back for Diocesan business sessions; but when mealtime came, they went their separate ways … . Bishop Bratton moved to change this by having an official Council Dinner at which everyone would eat together. Of course, this had to be done in the parish house of the host parish, since certainly no restaurant or public facility would allow any such. When this was announced, the story was that the ladies of the parish that was [sic] to host the next Council weren't real excited to say the least about having to serve their African American brothers and sisters at the dinner table … . Bishop Bratton responded in his gentle, but firm way that he would do the serving. Needless to say, the ladies changed their minds, and another small step was taken on the long road to real racial reconciliation.[109]

By 1930 the diocese had grown considerably. Parish membership and receipts had increased parish receipts, along with parishes and rectories, and schools—including educational endowments. These endowments benefited All Saints', Sewanee, Okolona, and St. Mary's School in Vicksburg.

Then came the Great Depression and Bishop Bratton's blunt warning about it: "We must recognize that we have brought this on ourselves. We must become completely awake to the danger that is threatening and testing both Christian civilization and the Christian character in each of us."[110] Bratton, ever critical of mammon, used strong words to blame both a country and even Christian churches who placed money and power over morality. Not surprisingly, he was a Democrat, highly supportive of Franklin D. Roosevelt and his social and economic reforms.

By 1932 Bishop Bratton began to turn over more diocesan work to Bishop Green, and in 1936, when he was seventy-four years old, he wrote *Apostle of Reality: The Life and Thought of William Porcher DuBose*. He also served as chancellor of his beloved University of the South from 1936 until 1938.

The Ninth Chancellor of Sewanee

Bishop Bratton spoke often of Sewanee, holding The University of the South close to his heart. His 1912 journal for the dates June 12 and 13 contains but one of many entries recording a visit to Sewanee. He wrote that he went to St. Luke's Chapel on June 12, and on June 13 to Commencement Day exercises and "to Fairmont, nearby, to visit my uncle, Dr. DuBose, now growing old, and his family."[111]

Sewanee, as local residents often refer to the university, "follows in the same tradition of many English universities in having a distinguished person named as chancellor, while the president is named vice-chancellor," according to John Gass Bratton, grandson of Bishop Bratton, and former alumni director. "Sewanee's version of this is to have the board of trustees, over which he [the chancellor] will preside, electing a bishop as chancellor from among the owning Episcopal dioceses of the university."[112] The board of trustees also elects a vice chancellor and a president who serves as CEO. As Sewanee's ninth chancellor, Bishop Bratton continued to reside in Jackson, Mississippi, but he traveled to Sewanee several times a year. In addition to presiding over the board of trustees, which met annually, he also attended quarterly meetings with the board of regents.

Elizabeth N. Chitty wrote an article in the March 30, 2000, issue of the *Sewanee Mountain Messenger* (page 148) describing the circumstances of Bratton's arrival as chancellor. Bishop Bratton was the first "son of Sewanee" to be chancellor. His relationship with Sewanee had spanned sixty-two years: it began with his entrance to the Sewanee Grammar School in 1874, and his graduation from the university and the college of theology, to his role as trustee and regent for forty-five years.

Thursday, March 30, 2000 THE SEWANEE MOUNTAIN MESSENGER (3

Sewanee Now & Then

by Elizabeth N. Chitty

Chancellors 9 & 10

Bishop Theodore DuBose Bratton

The 9th Chancellorship came in June, 1936, to Bishop Theodore DuBose Bratton of Mississippi at the first meeting of the Board of Trustees following the death of Bishop Thomas Frank Gailor in October, 1935. Bishop Bratton was the first "son of Sewanee" to be Chancellor after his 60 years of relationship as a student in the Sewanee Grammar School, the College, and the School of Theology, and a total of 45 years as trustee and regent.

Bratton came to the Chancellorship at a crucial time. Vice-Chancellor Benjamin Ficklin Finney had announced that he would retire in 1937, after 15 years as VC at a time when changes in the administrative structure of the University's Constitution would put more authority in the hands of a smaller body (the Regents) than in the 108 men who made up the Board of Trustees. The total number of trustees entitled to seat and voice now reaches in the neighborhood of 150.

Alexander Guerry, elected Vice-Chancellor in December, 1937, to succeed Dr. Finney, declined that election. It fell to Bishop Bratton to persuade Dr. Guerry to reconsider; and Dr. Finney stayed on as VC one more year. The University's smaller enrollment and budget deficits made understandable the necessity for Finney's successor to be chosen. Bishop Bratton's plea was to Dr. Guerry to "save Sewanee," and Bratton himself devoted the second year to raising church support from Episcopal parishes.

The Reverend Theodore DuBose Bratton about 1902. He was rector (president) of St. Mary's Junior College in Raleigh, N.C., before his election as Bishop, and then 9th Chancellor of the University. Pictured with him are his wife, Lucy Randolph and relatives including Manions, Jeffersons, DuBose, Means. After the death of Lucy Randolph Bratton, the Bishop married the widow of the Reverend John Gass, '75, and a Sewanee dynasty was created, continuing into recent Brattons and Gasses in the College.

From left to right: The Rev. McNeely DuBose (St. Mary's School, Raleigh, NC); Haskel DuBose (Sewanee, TN); the Rev. William Porcher DuBose (Sewanee, TN); and Bishop Theodore DuBose Bratton, Bishop of Mississippi, circa 1903–1910. The portrait was probably taken immediately before or after a service of Holy Communion due to the Eucharistic vestments, with Dr. DuBose as celebrant and the others assisting. Courtesy of John Gass Bratton, Sewanee, TN.

Chitty also noted that Bratton became chancellor at a critical time for the university. Bishop Thomas Gailor, who had been chancellor since 1908, died in 1935, and Benjamin Finney, who was vice chancellor at the time, was due to retire in 1937. Alexander Guerry, President of The University of Chattanooga, had been offered the job of chancellor but turned it down. There had been changes in the administrative structure of the university's constitution, a smaller enrollment, and budget deficits.[113] Bishop Bratton did not take well to the news that Guerry turned the job down and pleaded with him to accept the position. John Gass Bratton remembers the situation quite well, and wrote:

> Not long after we moved to Sewanee in 1938, Dr. Guerry offered me a job assisting his secretary, Mrs. Walter Byers ... helping her in the office, which I recall was mostly filing. On several occasions, when I would meet Dr. Guerry—usually walking along the sidewalk in front of his home, Fulford Hall—Dr. Guerry told me of the circumstances leading to his acceptance of the board of trustee's election of him as vice chancellor.
>
> My brother, Theodore DuBose Bratton ("Ted"), often said that Dr. Guerry was somewhat offended by the rather perfunctory invitation of the board of trustees in informing Dr. Guerry of the honor they were bestowing on him by his election as vice chancellor. I don't know if this is true, but I do know that the university at that time was in destitute financial condition and Dr. Guerry turned the election down.
>
> On his second election, Dr. Guerry told me that Grandfather (Bishop Bratton), as chancellor, had taken the news of his election to him personally with this challenge: "Alex, I want you to save Sewanee." Dr. Guerry then said to me that this was a challenge he could not refuse. I am convinced that had Dr. Guerry not so responded to Bishop Bratton's challenge, Sewanee would not have survived as we know it today.[114]

Dr. Finney remained on as vice chancellor for another year, "Bishop Bratton himself devoted the second year to raising church support from Episcopal parishes,"[115] and together they began to save Sewanee. After he accepted Bishop Bratton's challenge, Dr. Guerry resolved long-standing issues of university governance, employed a strategic vision for the university, raised money alongside of Bishop Bratton, made several physical improvements to the university, and returned enrollment to its peak of the late 1920s.[116]

Bishop Bratton "invariably voted with Dr. Guerry on vital and sometimes controversial issues."[117] One controversial issue involved Sewanee's football team, a favorite form of entertainment with the school and community—even though Sewanee's team, the Tigers, rarely won a game. Sewanee had joined the Southern Conference in 1922 and the Southeastern Conference in 1932. In 1935 the Southeastern conference decided to publicly award athletic scholarships. There was much debate at the university about the professionalizing of football, and some believed it was not a proper function of a college. Others, including most of the students, thought scholarships would draw better athletes and more income. When Dr. Guerry was involved in negotiations to become vice chancellor, he demanded an end to scholarships and a withdrawal from the conference, and made this one of the conditions of his acceptance. In a meeting with the student body in 1938, he expressed his conviction "that a small liberal arts college would 'destroy its sense of values' if it decided to play big-time football," and Bishop Bratton agreed.[118]

Other Activities and Publications

In addition to the activities already delineated in this chapter, Bishop Bratton "served several years as a member of the national board of missions, and a three-year term as president of the Synod of Sewanee." He was also a member of the Rotary Club; Grand Chaplain of the Free and Accepted Masons in Mississippi; a grand chaplain of his college fraternity, Alpha Tau Omega; and in 1930 he was Chaplain General of the United Confederate Veterans. He was also a member of the Board of Trustees of the Mississippi Department of Archives and History from December 11, 1913, until the day of his death.[119]

In addition to writing his two well-known books, *Wanted–Leaders!* and *An Apostle of Reality* ..., and other publications already noted, the Mississippi Department of Archives and History lists four other books that he authored or co-authored. They are: *The Diocesan School* (1906); *History of the Afro-American Group of the Episcopal Church* (co-authored with George Freeman Bragg, 1922); *The Jefferson Davis Memorial in the Vicksburg National Military Park* (authored along with other members of the Mississippi Jefferson Davis Memorial Commission, 1927); and *Craig (Robert E. Lee) Scrapbook* (authored with four other people, 1837–1904).

Randolph Bratton's Passing

On August 7, 1937, Bishop Bratton's son, Randolph, died by a self-inflicted pistol wound and was buried in Saint John's Episcopal Cemetery in Winnsboro, South Carolina.

James Lyles, who was ninety-six years old at the time he was interviewed in Winnsboro, remembers Randolph and his family:

> When I was a child, my family lived next to Randolph's family on High Street. Randolph Bratton's wife was Eula Boulware. She was raised out on the Newberry Highway. I can remember what she looked like and I remember what their children looked like. They had three children: Randolph Jr., Isabel, and Lucy.
>
> Every morning, Randolph would start out walking to town with his head down, looking at the ground—I think to Mr. Jim Macon's barbershop. He was despondent. He would spend the day out there, and that morning we heard that he had shot himself in the barbershop. I can very vividly remember hearing that he had killed himself. His grave is at Saint John's Episcopal Cemetery. Randolph was highly decorated in WWI. He was 42 years old when he killed himself. Randolph served in WWI, the First division— probably the best division in WWI. The commanding

General was General Summerall, who later became the Chief of Staff for the whole army.[120]

Randolph may have been a victim of what we now call Post Traumatic Stress Disorder (PTSD). In a letter to Randolph's wife, Eula, dated August 17, 1937, the Rev. John Gass, who lived in New York, wrote to express his condolences and said, "He was a victim and a tragedy of the war for worse, as you know better than the most of us, than those who were killed on the battle-fields." A newspaper article, in speaking of the tragedy, said, "He had a brilliant war record ... and was several times cited for outstanding bravery." The article also noted that he had been both gassed and wounded, and that he had been hospitalized two months prior to his suicide "undergoing treatment for his nerves."[121]

Bishop Bratton wrote several letters to Eula, expressing his condolences and his love, and doing his best to make sure she and the children were taken care of financially. He inquired into the possibility of having his son awarded the Distinguished Service Cross, and received a response from General John Pershing dated January 13, 1922. General Pershing indicated that, while he believed the Distinguished Service

Image of Ivy Gass Bratton, widow of William DuBose Bratton. Courtesy of John Gass Bratton.

Cross should be awarded to Randolph, it was not possible at the time due to a "defect" in the law.[122]

William DuBose Bratton's Passing

Only five months later, Bishop Bratton's oldest son, William, also died. William DuBose Bratton was rector of Grace Episcopal Church in Memphis, and had been elected Dean of the West Tennessee Convocation on January 7, 1938. Like his brother, Randolph, he was also a victim of suicide. On January 10, 1938, William jumped off a bridge into the Mississippi River in Memphis after driving his youngest son to school. According to his wife, he had been "very depressed"[126] recently. Dr. Charles F. Blaindell, rector of Calvary Episcopal Church, attributed Mr. Bratton's action to "strain and overwork .... He had been under a strain for several years. He was a very hard worker and took very little rest. The strain brought on a depression he could not break."[123]

The *Lexington Advertiser* (Lexington, MS, January 13, 1938) published an article titled "Tragic Deaths" in sympathy with Bishop Bratton, and quoted Mayor Frederick Sullens who said, "Tears in the eyes for you, beloved Bishop Bratton. The tragic deaths of your precious sons, occurring within a few brief weeks, must truly seem to be a cross too heavy to bear, a cup of sorrow too bitter to drink."

William Bratton's body was never recovered, and he left behind his wife Ivy, and three sons and a daughter: Theodore DuBose Bratton, age twenty-one; William DuBose Bratton Jr., age seventeen; John Gass Bratton, age nine; and Lucy Randolph Bratton, age nineteen.

After her husband's death, Mrs. Bratton moved her family to Sewanee, where she had family support and was the School of Theology's first librarian. Mrs. Bratton and the children resided on North Carolina Avenue while a house was built for them through the generosity of Mrs. Bratton's brothers, Henry Markley Gass and John Gass. Henry was a popular classics professor and eventually an acting vice chancellor at the university, and John was then a rector in New York.[124]

Retirement

On January 18, 1938, Bishop Bratton wrote a letter to the diocesan council announcing, for what was apparently the second time, his intention to retire in the fall of 1938. In the letter he also said, "If God spares me, I will hope to be of whatever assistance my successor thinks I can render."[125]

He was seventy-five years old and it was time. He had worked tirelessly for many years but needed to spend his last years enjoying his remaining children and grandchildren. Two of his sons had died within a few months of each other, his son William about a week before Bratton wrote his second letter of retirement. Although he had no idea at the time of that letter, his second wife, Ivy, would also die later in 1938.

Bishop Bratton would live almost seven more years, longer than Bishop Mercer Green II who succeeded him, and he would continue to do good works and to enjoy his remaining family until the day he died in 1944. True to his word, he continued to give himself unsparingly to the service of his church.

Bishop Bratton and his family had always lived at 1903 Battle Hill, Jackson, the home of the bishops of Mississippi, and was provided with a home in retirement in West Jackson "through the benefaction of my beloved and lamented friend, Mr. Richard H. Green." He also had a summer home on the Gulf Coast at Gautier, Mississippi, where his children and grandchildren would come to visit, and where he enjoyed spending part of each day working in the yard.[126] He was looking forward to retirement.

Ivy Perrin Bratton's Passing

Bishop Bratton was only able to enjoy retirement for a few months before his wife, Ivy, died unexpectedly on December 10, 1938, at the age of seventy-nine. According to a Greenville, Mississippi, newspaper, she was visiting her daughter, Ivy Gass Bratton, in Memphis, when she was "stricken" and "died suddenly" in her daughter's home. "Funeral services for the beloved Jackson woman, known throughout the state for her devoted church activities, [were] held in Memphis ... with the Bishop William Mercer Green of Mississippi and Bishop James M. Maxon of Tennessee officiating."[127]

Mrs. Bratton was buried at Christ Episcopal Church Cemetery in Greenville, South Carolina, where her first husband, the Rev. John Gass, was also buried.

Beloved, Faithful Episcopal Church Leader Is Laid To Rest In Cedarlawn Cemetery

Simple but impressive rites at the St. Andrew's Episcopal church here yesterday morning at 10:30 o'clock marked the triumphal entry of the Right Reverend Theodore duBose Bratton, 81-year-old retired Bishop of all Episcopal churches in the southeast, into his Maker's house.

Bishop Bratton, beloved and faithful leader of Episcopal congregations in the southeast for many years, passed away at a local hospital Monday following a heart attck.

As the procesesional entered the flower-filled church, the congregation stood in final respect to his memory. The Rev. Louis O'V. Thomas, assistant-rector of St. Andrew's, served as crucifer and led the processional of bishops and clergy. During the processional, the Right Reverend Duncan M. Gray, D. D., Bishop of Mississippi, read the opening sentences of the service.

Following the singing of triumphal songs by the vested choir, the Reverend John Gass, D. D., of Troy, N. Y., stepson of Bishop Bratton, read the lesson from Roman s8:14-39 and St. John 14:1-8.

The Reverend Walter B. Capers, D. D., rector of St. Andrew's, who's father served as Bishop Bratton's bishop in South Carolina many years ago, led in the recital of the apostles creed.

The Right Reverend John L. Jackson, Bishop of Louisiana, led in the prayers at the church after which the remains were taken to Cedarlawn cemetery for interment. The Right Reverend R. Bland Mitchell, D. D., Bishop of Arkansas, led the prayers in the graveside service and Bishop Gray said the benediction.

A purple velvet pall centered with a large red cross covered the bier. It was the same pall used at the final services for Bishop Hugh Miller Thompson and Bishop William Mercer Green.

A small section of the church was reserved for negroes for whom Bishop Bratton had done so much during his lifetime.

Clergy of the Diocese of Mississippi, serving as active pallbearers, were the Reverend Warwick Aiken of Pass Christian, the Reverend George R. Stephenson of Gulfport, the Reverend Joseph Juehnle of Natchez, the Reverend Cecil B. Jones of Columbus, the Reverend Jones S. Hamilton of Greenwood, the Reverend E. Lucien Malone of Clarksdale, the Reverend Edward J. Jones of Yazoo City and the Reverend W. G. Christian of Vicksburg.

Lay officials of the Diocese, serving as honorary pallbearers, were Garner W. Green of Jackson, E. H. Simpson of Jackson, Nash K. Burger of Jackson, Lester W. Dawley of Jackson, Zed D. Hawkins of Meridian, Charles H. Russell of Jackson, Lloyd G. Spivey of Canton, Captain T. H. Shields of Jackson, Dr. S. B. Caruthers of Grenada, P. T. LaGrone of Greenville, Robert E. Lake of Jackson, James D. Thames of Vicksburg, D. S. Wheatley of Greenwood and J. Webb Wilson of Meridian.

Bishop Bratton, who served as Bishop of Mississippi for 25 years before his retirement in 1938, had resided in Jackson for 41 years. He received his Bachelor of Divinity degree from the University of the South in 1887 and his Doctor of Divinity degree from the same institution in 1902. The University of Mississippi awarded him an honorary LL. D in 1911.

During World War I, Bishop Bratton served with the Y.M.C.A and for a time was acting chaplain at the Port of Brest in France. He served as rector of the Church of Advent, Spartanburg, S C. and at St. Mary's School for Young Women, was professor of history at Converse College and was chancellor of the University of the South.

He was ordained as deacon in 1887, made a priest in 1888 and consecrated Bishop of Mississivpi in 1903. He was chosen chaplain general in the United Confederate Veterans in 1930.

Survivors are a son, John Bratton, Raleigh, N. C.; three daughters, Mrs. Robert E. Conner of Houston, Texas, Mrs. James Harris Brister and Mrs. Isabel Edmondson, both of Jackson; and four stepchildren, the Reverend John Gass of Troy, N. Y., Major Henry Gass and Mrs. William Bratton of Sewanee, Tenn. and Mrs. James R. McDowell of Memphis, Tenn.

Article courtesy of John Gass Bratton, Sewanee, TN, personal collection (name of newspaper and date unknown).

Bishop Bratton's Legacy

Bishop Bratton lived for about five and a half years after the death of his wife, Ivy. He died at a local hospital in Jackson on June 26, 1944, when he was eight-one years old. "Death came quickly and mercifully to end a long period of physical infirmity and much suffering. A brief heart attack was the immediate cause."[128] Bishop Bratton's funeral was held at St. Andrew's Episcopal Church in Jackson, and he was buried at Cedarlawn Cemetery.

Long articles containing accolades and biographical information appeared almost immediately in numerous newspapers. Among many messages sent was one to the Rt. Rev. Duncan Gray, who officiated at the funeral, from Alex Guerry, chancellor at Sewanee, who said, "Distressed to hear the sad news about Bishop Bratton. I hasten to send this expression of the love and sorrow of all Sewanee."[129]

Bishop Bratton was survived by one son, three daughters and four stepchildren, and approximately seventeen biological or step-grandchildren. Among the grandchildren were at least three named Theodore.

His remaining children were John Bratton, Raleigh, NC; Mrs. Robert E. Connor [Mary], Houston, TX; Mrs. Isabel Edmondson [Isabel], Jackson, MS; and Mrs. Harris Brister [Marion], Jackson, MS.

His stepchildren were the Rev. John Gass, Troy, NY; Major Henry Gass, Sewanee, TN; Mrs. William Bratton [Ivy], Sewanee, TN; and Mrs. James R. McDowell [Katherine], McDowell, Memphis, TN.[130]

Memorials and Tributes

After Bishop Bratton's death on June 26, 1944, memorials and tributes began to pour in and continue almost to this date. Some of these provide additional insight on his personality and priorities.

On July 4, 1944, a sermon on the life and character of Bishop Bratton was delivered by Dr. W. B. Capers, the rector of St. Andrews Episcopal Church in Jackson. He commented on Bishop Bratton's devotion to his family, saying, "However, his work came first." Interestingly enough, considering Bratton's popularity, Dr. Capers added, "As a young man, Bishop Bratton was not an eloquent preacher. Without any way being didactic or pedantic, his sermons and addresses were characteristically instructive." Dr. Capers further described Bratton by quoting the humorous words of a Biloxi man (name unknown): "Bishop Bratton has more personal religion than any man I ever knew, and annoys you less with it." Capers also spoke of how tolerant and sympathetic Bratton was with the doctrine of other Christian churches, what a good sense of humor he had, and that he "was both physically and morally one of the most courageous men I ever knew ... There was no fear or surrender in his brave soul."[131]

On July 13, 1944, an article written by the Rev. James W. Emerson, Priest-in-Charge of All Saints' Episcopal Church in Tupelo, Mississippi, also described Bishop Bratton in glowing terms and helps us understand how Bratton survived all of the tragedies in his personal life:

> There were many heartaches and heartbreaks in the life of Bishop Bratton, periods when he was plunged into veritable seas of sorrows and depths of despair, but they never broke his rare courage or soured his sunny nature. He was sweet-souled, even when bearing the heaviest cross. Always he looked upward and above his cross and beheld the shining throne of God. His faith could not be broken; his indomitable spirit could not be quelled. Fate decreed that he should outlive most of his children, also loved ones who were so near and dear to him, but even when bereavements and disappointments came thick and fast he bravely tried to turn a bright and smiling face to the world and to prove that when serving God one can find consolation for all sorrows.[132]

By July 27, 1944, donations were coming in to the Baptist Hospital in Jackson, "to be used specifically for the treatment of Negro children," and the article about this memorial fund considered it a "beautiful example of the immortality of good and righteous deeds," and commented on his genuine and generous interest in Negroes and his concern for their educational advancement.[133]

On November 26, 1946, yet another memorial, this one a proposal for the All Saints' Chapel for the All Saints' Episcopal College in Vicksburg, Mississippi, got off the ground with tributes and comments in booklet form written by Colonel Alexander Fitz-Hugh of Vicksburg;

Plaque (*left*) dedicated to Bishop Bratton at St. John's Episcopal Church, Winnsboro, SC. Photo by author.

Interior of Chapel of St. John's (*below*). Photo by author.

the Rev. Holly W. Wells, who later wrote a book about his recollections of Bishop Bratton; the Rt. Rev. Duncan Montgomery Gray, Bishop of Mississippi; the Rt. Rev. James M. Mason, Bishop of Tennessee, George A. Wilson, Chairman of the Bratton Memorial Fund; and W. G. Christian, rector of All Saints' College.[134] With all of these heavy-weights involved, it will not surprise you to know that the college now has its chapel.

Bishop Bratton's portrait hangs in the Mississippi Hall of Fame in Jackson, Mississippi. In Sewanee, one can visit the Theodore DuBose Bratton Memorial Bridge [and the Ivy Gass Bratton Memorial Bench], Lake Bratton, and Bishop Bratton Hall at Saint Andrew's Sewanee School.

Another portrait of Bishop Bratton has also been presented to The University of the South by John Gass Bratton, and currently hangs in the Jessie Ball duPont Library at the university. There is also a tablet dedicated to the memory of Bishop Bratton at All Saints' Chapel at the university.

Finally, there are two tablets and stained glass windows dedicated to the memory of Bishop Bratton and to Dr. William Porcher DuBose, his uncle (one tablet and window each), that hang in the chapel of Saint John's Episcopal Church in Winnsboro, South Carolina, Bishop Bratton's very first church in the town of his birth.[135]

One final view of Bishop Bratton's character was one seen by many, is a sweet ending to this chapter, and is especially poignant because it comes from his grandson, John Gass Bratton:

> Bishop Bratton chose neither to live in the past nor to shut the door on it. He honored the past that deserved to be honored, but he chose to seek justice and bring about change.
>
> Gentleness describes not just his demeanor but also his character. His gentleness was apparent to me once in the yard of his summer place at Gautier, Mississippi, which he called Fair Haven. He was commenting on a pear tree, which he called "this little fellow." He gave personality to living things. I don't know if all men were sons, but women always seemed to be "daughters."

He wrote and spoke his view of the role of women in society, and it was forward-looking. He was led by the Spirit of God. He fought the good fight. That was Bishop Bratton.[136]

Bishop Bratton's legacy lives on with his church, his country, and his descendants. We will see this reflected in our final chapter through the life of one of his grandsons, John Bratton Jr., who was a well-known businessman, churchman, and philanthropist in Raleigh, North Carolina.

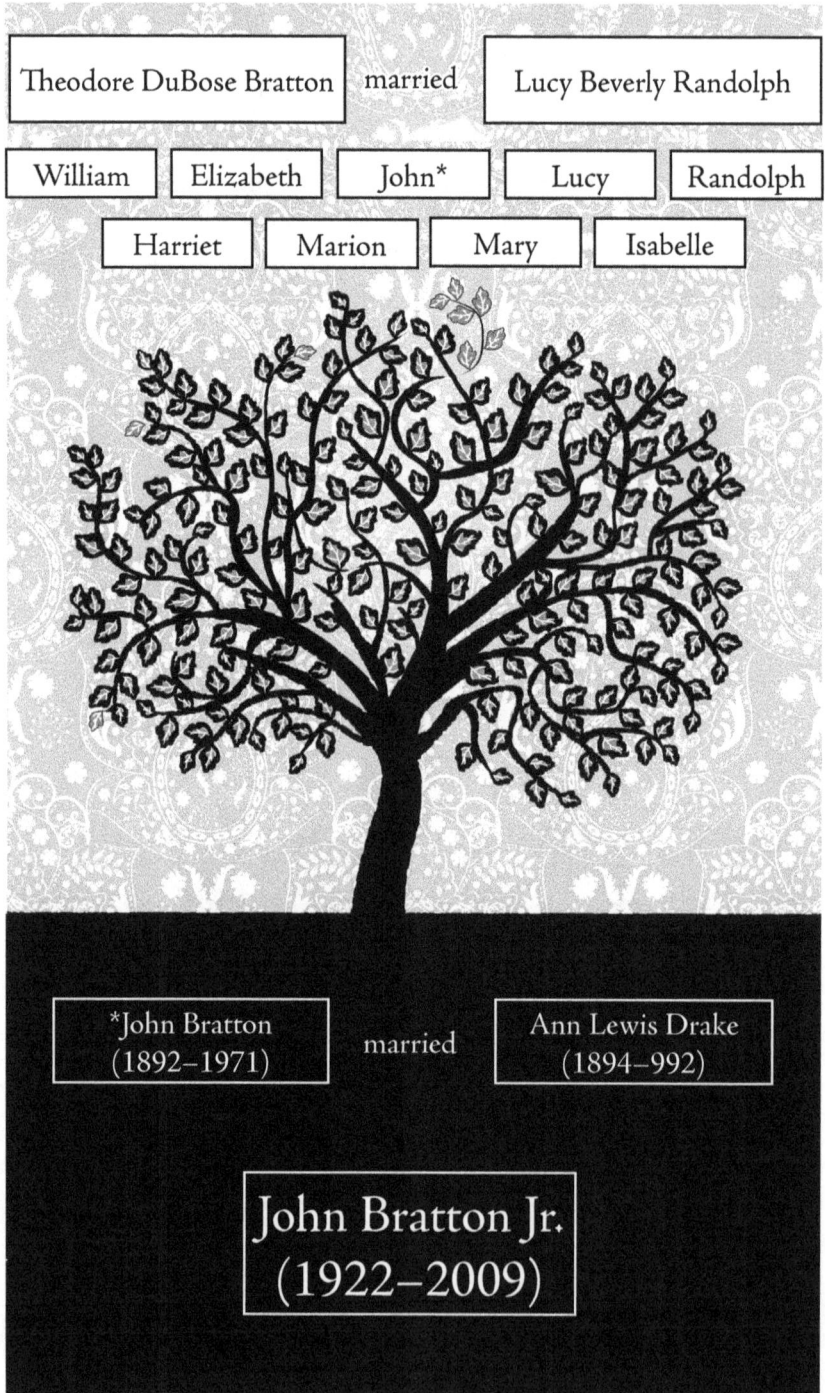

| Theodore DuBose Bratton | married | Lucy Beverly Randolph |

| William | Elizabeth | John* | Lucy | Randolph |

| Harriet | Marion | Mary | Isabelle |

| *John Bratton (1892–1971) | married | Ann Lewis Drake (1894–992) |

John Bratton Jr. (1922–2009)

CHAPTER FOUR

John Bratton Jr.

Crushed Stone and Community

—————★—————

A PERFECT SYMBOL OF that Greatest Generation, John Jr. believed in hard work, God, country, and family, and that a man is as good as his word. Although he was born into a noble, well-educated and prosperous family, they literally lost the farm during the Great Depression. John had to move with his family from the plantations he loved to a city, but he never forgot his roots. When he went to work as a civil engineer and started his own business, John was a staunch conservationist. He treated the quarries he owned as though they were the farms he had left behind, and made sure that streams, ponds, and wildlife were protected. John also made sure that his neighbors were pleased with the view. His love for his family extended to his community, and John gave generously of his time and money, both as an individual and as an employer. He loved his life, and his only regret may have been that he could not have stayed around a bit longer to enjoy it even more.

Early Life

John Bratton Jr. was born during the Roaring Twenties, a time of great social and political change. It was also a time of increasing prosperity for the nation. Home refrigeration and air conditioning, radio broadcasts, and television brought comforts that we take for granted today. Medical advances like penicillin and insulin saved many lives. Women won the right to vote, and families began to buy ready-made clothes. Going to the movies became a routine for many, and people were able to drive there in affordable cars. Jazz was in full bloom and many young people danced the Charleston. Prohibition was in effect, but this just drove the consumption of alcohol underground.[1]

John's father was John Bratton and his mother was Annie Lewis Drake Bratton. Neither John nor his father had middle names, so for the sake of clarity, we will sometimes refer to John's father as John Bratton Sr. or John Sr.

John's parents originally lived in Winnsboro, South Carolina, possibly on Canaan Plantation, which was owned by his grandfather, General John Bratton. His older sister, Anne, was born on Canaan Plantation in 1920.[2] By 1922 the family had moved to Clarendon County, South Carolina, where John was born on August 6, 1922.

Parents and Family

John Bratton Sr. was born in Spartanburg, South Carolina, on September 25, 1892.[3] His parents were Theodore DuBose Bratton, Bishop of Mississippi, and Lucy Randolph Bratton. Both were from prominent families. Bishop Bratton, originally born and raised in Winnsboro, South Carolina, moved to Jackson, Mississippi, after he was elected Bishop of Mississippi in 1903. John Sr. and his siblings were raised with comfort, kindness, and a good education, reflecting the character and values of their parents.

John Sr. attended Mississippi State University where, according to his 1911 school yearbook, *Reveille*, his nickname was "Hungry" Bratton. John Sr. was active in several clubs or organizations including The Midnight Crew (Serenaders) and the Wall Street Club whose motto was "Lovers of good-looking women."[4] Judging by his yearbook picture, Hungry Bratton was quite good-looking himself.

Mississippi State, originally named the Agricultural and Mechanical College of the State of Mississippi, prepared John Sr. for life

John "Hungry" Bratton, 1911. Image from his college yearbook, the *Reveille*, p. 257, taken from a group picture titled "The Wall Streeters."

as a farmer, and 1916 found him engaged in farming in the Winnsboro area, where his family was quite well-known. His draft registration in Winnsboro indicated that he had served in the Mississippi National Guard for three years and that he was single. His occupation was listed as "farmer, general farming, [and] employer."[5]

John Sr. married Annie Lewis Drake on December 3, 1919, in Bennettsville, South Carolina, where she had been born. "Lewis," as she was called (and as she will be subsequently be referred to), was born on May 28, 1894, to James Alexander Drake and Gabrielle (Palmer) Drake. Mr. Drake was a Clerk of the Court in Bennettsville, South Carolina, and had also been a warehouse inspector.[6]

John Sr.'s older brother, Randolph Bratton, was living with John and Lewis in 1920. Randolph had returned to Winnsboro after his service in World War I.[7] Randolph married in 1921 and remained in Winnsboro with his wife after John and Lewis moved to Clarendon County.

≈ ≈ ≈

Even though John Sr. had good connections to farming in terms of land, family, and social connections, he would have experienced the same struggle as many other farmers in the South, which was primarily rural and agricultural. The Roaring Twenties, while bringing about change in many other ways, did not bring as much prosperity to Southern states as it did elsewhere, and when the Great Depression hit, times were tough. Masses of homeless and unemployed men were roaming the country, looking for work. The stock market crashed, unemployment nationwide was about 25%, and farm income, which had already been on the decline, completely crushed the dreams of many farmers.[8]

John Bratton Sr. was one of many farmers who lost the farm, as the old saying goes. One of his grandsons, John Randolph Bratton, remembers what his father and grandfather told him about hard times during the Great Depression:

> Dad's father had Roseland Plantation and Canaan Plantation in Winnsboro. It was the depression, and he had given one of them to his brother [Randolph Bratton] to help him, but they lost them both. My grandfather went to work for Palmetto Brick Company when my father was about four years old, so the family

moved to Raleigh. They lived in a nice neighborhood with some people who also grew up in Raleigh, and remained Dad's friends all his life. A lot of them went to school together, went to war, got married, and came back here and raised families. He and Mother lived in a really nice community with a lot of nice friends.[9]

John and Lewis Bratton had their third and last child, Lewis Palmer Bratton, in Raleigh on December 2, 1926. John Sr. worked as a salesman for the brick and tile company, and Lewis worked as a clerk with the title of "Executor: Mail and Files."[10] By 1930 the family lived at 1510 Scales Street and owned their own home, which was valued at $9,000.[11] Their home was located in an upper middle class neighborhood northwest of downtown Raleigh and was in a suburb created in "an estate-like setting."[12]

Raleigh was not unfamiliar territory to John Sr. He had lived there for four years as a child when his father was rector of Saint Mary's from 1899 to 1903, and he probably had some contacts through that relationship and the Episcopal church there. Considering the environment for farmers in the 1920s and the Great Depression, he was fortunate to have found a job during a time when so many were unemployed and going hungry.

≈≈≈

Lucy Bratton Doak, one of John Sr.'s granddaughters, has warm memories of her paternal grandparents.

I knew Dad's father, John Bratton, whom we all called "Pop." He was nice—really sweet. Pop was a big, tall, man—or at least, he seemed that way to me—with a big, kind heart. He went through a difficult time when he lost their plantation and had to start all over. He was such a warm figure and loved having us all around. Pop always loved planting—he was kind of a farmer—and he planted the fruit trees and grape orchards at Wake Stone.

Dad was very good to his parents. He took care of them, particularly my grandmother. She was an artist and made things: One Christmas, she and my father built a dollhouse. They made the furniture together and she made many of the furnishings, even the rugs and curtains. She also painted, made charcoal drawings of all her grandchildren, and made beautiful doll clothes for them. Dad and his mother were very close.[13]

Growing Up in Raleigh

John Bratton Jr. and his siblings, Anne and Lewis, grew up in Raleigh, the capital of North Carolina. A beautiful city known for its oak trees, it was a city that valued education, culture, and history.

John was an adventurous little boy. His daughter, Lucy, related a family story in which John and some friends decided to canoe down the Neuse, a fast-flowing river that flows through the Raleigh-Durham area. John's parents gave their permission for the trip, which was supposed to take a couple of days. The plan was for John to contact his parents when he stopped to spend the night with friends, but he did not get off at the right place and never called. He nearly "scared his mother to death!"[14]

John attended Hayes Barton Elementary School and Needham Broughton High School. He played on the football team at the high school, graduated in 1940, and received a football scholarship to attend North Carolina State University. At the university, he majored in civil engineering and was a member of the Kappa Sigma fraternity.[15] According to his school yearbook of 1943, the *Agromeck*, John participated in the Intra-fraternity Council, Engineers' Council, Inter-honorary Council, freshman football, wrestling, and varsity football.[16]

John's family had moved to 1530 Carr Street by 1941, only a few blocks away from their first home in Raleigh. All three Bratton children were still at home and were very active in school. Anne, John's older sister by two years, had graduated from Saint Mary's (then a two-year high school and junior college for women and now called Saint Mary's School). She then transferred to the Women's College, University of North Carolina. Lewis, John's younger brother, was following in his brother's footsteps—playing football at Needham Broughton High School.[17]

The United States was still recovering from the Great Depression while John Jr. and his siblings were going to school. The New Deal, a

John Bratton Jr. as a football player. Courtesy of
Lucy Bratton Doak.

John Bratton Jr., 1942. Image
from his college yearbook of
1942, *Agromeck*.

series of new domestic programs and executive orders signed by President Franklin D. Roosevelt, was a response to the depression that included the beginnings of the Social Security system. President Roosevelt was enormously popular, and John's family surely listened to his famous "fireside chats," the first time an American President communicated directly with millions of citizens. Also very popular on the radio was the big band music of Benny Goodman and Glenn Miller. Big-screen actors Clark Gable, Bette Davis, Fred Astaire and Ginger Rogers were household names.

World War II and the United States Marines

While the Bratton family was busy with work and school, and perhaps dancing to swing music, the winds of war were blowing towards the United States. The rise of Hitler in Germany, genocide against the Chinese by Japan, thousands of deportations to Siberia by the communists in Russia, and fascism in Spain had been setting the scene for World War II since before 1938. When the Japanese bombed the American naval base at Pearl Harbor on December 7, 1941, Americans were horrified and finally entered the war. World War II involved the world's greatest powers and more than 100 million people from over thirty countries, and it was the most widespread and the deadliest war in world history. The United States and other countries involved threw all their resources into staunching the spread of dictatorships. Entire families participated, whether that meant enlisting in the military or supporting the troops from home, and the Bratton family was no exception.

At the age of twenty, while still a student at North Carolina State, John Bratton registered for the draft.[18] On July 21, 1942, he entered the US Marines. His sister, Anne, had married a month earlier, and became a Red Cross nurse's aid while her husband served in the US Army.[19] John's younger brother, Lewis, joined the Army Air Corp in 1945, right after his graduation from high school.

John continued his education while in the Marines and graduated from Duke University with a BS in Civil Engineering. He subsequently became a second lieutenant and served in Okinawa and in Manchuria, China, in 1945. While in China, he built roads and airports.[20]

Following are selections from comments made about John's college days, the Marines, and World War II. The selections are taken from interviews with John's oldest son, Johnny; his youngest son, Sam; and Tom Oxholm, who came to Wake Stone as a consultant in 1981 and became an employee and a good friend. Their reminiscences were filled with respect, affection, and humor.

John Bratton Jr., US Marine. Courtesy of Lucy Bratton Doak.

JOHNNY: The war was about over when he got to it. He joined the V–12 Marine program that allowed those young men to continue their education and graduate. And then the Marine Corps sent them to officer training school and then to the Pacific where they were stockpiling, getting ready to invade Japan. He was in the Pacific after the bombs were dropped [on Nagasaki and Hiroshima] and the war was over. He went to North China from there for the rest of his commitment. So he really was more [a part of] a cleanup detail than in the action.

SAM: Every time he went to a Chinese restaurant, he asked every waiter if they knew where Chiang-Wan tau was. I still don't know where Chiang-Wan tau was. He had a great time in China. It was a great adventure for him.

TOM: One of his favorite stories was when he was in [the corps] two and a half years or something. It was time to go to war and they had this Going Off to War Day and went down to the train station. He said, "Everyone came down and waved goodbye, and we left Raleigh."

Sam: They didn't have enough rooms in Durham, and he actually came back that evening!

Johnny: That was after he had gone in the Marine Corps and had been to OCS. He was back home and [he] was living at his parents' house. His mother, his new wife, and his sister were all there, and the Marines were shipping out. His family took him down to the train station in Raleigh down to Seaboard. Pop [Johnny's paternal grandfather] told me all the women were crying, and he was crying and sending his son off to war. They got on the train, and when they got to Durham there was nowhere to put them so they sent them back home. Later that afternoon, Daddy came walking back in the house. His father said, "We're not doing this again tomorrow!"

Sam: The Marine Corps wouldn't tell you anything except where to be. You never knew—you just showed up.

He was a very loyal Marine. He went back in the 50th anniversary of the group that went to China. In '94 they took a trip—the China Marine program. He would have been in his mid-70s when he went back over there.

Tom: He got the magazine *China Marine* every month forever and would put it on his desk.

Tom: He finished his engineering degree at Duke, then was shipped overseas. Although he appreciated his time at Duke, his heart was always at North Carolina State.

Sam: And he played football at North Carolina State— very proud of playing, going to North Carolina State or State College as he called it, playing football there and being in the Marine Corps. If anybody was a Marine, he was top notch with him.

TOM: He was 5′ 9″, at 170 pounds when he played football as an offensive lineman. Woody Jones, an old friend who was a real big guy, played right next to him.[21]

Marriage and Family

When John Bratton Jr. was twenty-two years old, he married Mary Constance Michelle Telfair on October 14, 1944, in Wake County, North Carolina.[22] "Michelle," as she has always been called, was nineteen years old, a wartime bride whose husband spent the next year or so in the Pacific and China.

Michelle Telfair Bratton

Michelle was born on September 16, 1925, in Ticonderoga, New York, but her father and his family were originally from the Raleigh area. Michelle's parents were from prominent families, and she is also "a great-great-granddaughter of George Edmund Badger, Secretary of the Navy under Presidents William Henry Harrison and [John] Tyler."[23] Michelle returned to Raleigh, where her father grew up, to attend Saint Mary's Junior College.

Michelle Telfair, 1943. Image from a group picture titled "Juniors" in Saint Mary's College 1943 yearbook.

Michelle's father, Samuel Fowle Telfair Jr., graduated from the University of North Carolina in 1917 and received his Master of Arts degree from Fordham College in New York in 1923. He served as a second lieutenant in the Army in World War I, receiving the Distinguished Service Cross in France in 1918. He was an assistant professor of history at Fordham College, where he was a member of the faculty for thirty-two years. He and his wife had four daughters, including Michelle, and a son.[24]

Michelle's mother was Constance M. Warren Telfair, who was born in New York and whose father was a well-known expert and beloved figure in the pulp and paper business in Ticonderoga.[25]

The Bratton Bunch in Raleigh

After his service during World War II and his discharge from the US Marines, Lieutenant Bratton returned to Raleigh—and to Michelle and their first child, who had been born during his absence—and he went to work as an engineer for Superior Stone Company.

John and Michelle eventually had a total of seven children. The first of their seven children, Michelle Telfair Bratton, was born in July 1945, and was followed by Johnny; Connie; Lucy; Ted; Jane; and Sam. The children were born from 1945 to 1964.

The Bratton children grew up in a time of great prosperity for both the United States and for Raleigh. Prior to the war and in 1945, "nearly a third of Americans lived in poverty. A third of the country's homes had no running water, two-fifths lacked flushing toilets, and three-fifths lacked central heating. More than half of the nation's farm dwellings had no electricity."[26] That was to change rapidly during the '50s and '60s, when John and Michelle were raising their children.

The city of Raleigh was prosperous during those decades, and it was also quite progressive. Raleigh elected the first African American mayor of a Southern city. Its North Carolina Fund, established to end poverty in North Carolina, became a model for programs across the nation in the 1960s. Raleigh is the home of North Carolina State University and the Research Triangle Park, which is home to numerous high-tech companies. It was also consistently voted one of the best places to live and work.[27]

The decade of the 1950s was called the Atomic Age or the Fabulous Fifties, and the Unites States' economy was robust—the biggest in the world. The largest generation in the nation's history, the Baby Boomers, arrived in great numbers. The size of the middle class increased dramatically, housing was affordable, and motherhood became glorified. The Cold War—a period of up to three decades after World War II—also saw "postwar Soviet expansionism in Eastern Europe [that] fueled many Americans' fears of a Russian plan to control the world."[28] However, the postwar economy also bred the belief that anyone who worked hard could succeed.

The Sixties, as the next decade was called, began on a bright note with the election of John F. Kennedy. However, his assassination in 1963, the beginning of the Vietnam War in 1964, the fight for civil rights, and the rise of the counterculture "hippies" radicalized many young Americans and pitted many Baby Boomers against their parents.[29]

The changing times often resulted in conflicts between children who were born after World War II and their parents, but the Brattons pulled together as a family. They weren't really into protesting or into the counterculture, and Mr. Bratton loved Big Band music. All the children were interested in the family business, had a long family history to be proud of, and were raised by parents whose values included the importance of hard work, love of country, and Christian values.

Mr. Bratton was an Episcopalian but his wife was Catholic, and the children were raised as Catholics. He attended church with his parents, while his wife took the children to a Catholic church, and then they all met for Sunday dinner at his mother's house. Michelle Bratton had begun life as an Episcopalian but converted to Catholicism because of her father. One of her sons, Sam, provided an interesting anecdote related to her conversion:

> It was a very interesting route she took to Catholicism. Her father—I'm named after him—grew up in Raleigh, and he was a cradle Episcopalian. During or right after World War I, he converted to Catholicism because he was moved by the faith of the Catholics that he experienced during the war. So mom was raised a Catholic. [When] she moved back to Raleigh, the town her father grew up in, Dad was going to the church that her father grew up going to. She finally converted back—made the full circle. All of us were raised in the Catholic Church. We've all switched to the Episcopal Church except for Lucy, I think. Dad was a member of Christ Church in Raleigh from the time he moved to Raleigh when he was four years old.[30]

Three of the Bratton children described their experiences of growing up with their parents and children, beginning with Johnny Bratton and Sam Bratton.

JOHNNY: I really grew up more with my grandfather than with my father, who was working most of the time. My grandfather was retired and I spent a lot of time with him, but my father and I worked together for a long, long time. Hard work. My father was tough to work for.

I admired his honesty. My dad was a true Southern gentleman. He'd look you in the eye and shake your hand, and that's all he needed. I've had a number of people over the years tell me that they noticed and admired that about him.

I can't say that I specifically know why Dad became an engineer. He liked to build things; he was very good at math; and he couldn't spell, so he was a pretty typical engineer. I don't know that he entered college knowing he was going to engineering school, but he soon decided to major in engineering. Dad was a classic engineer; everything had to be level and square. He was an engineer's engineer. He would measure a wall before he would put a picture up for Mother.

SAM: There's eighteen years difference between Johnny and myself. Johnny was pretty much out of the house by the time I was coming along, so I really don't know how to compare my experiences to his—but I can tell you about mine. Dad was really busy, but there were things that he was starting to be able to have time to enjoy doing.

Dad was in a different phase of his life when I was coming through. I think he had mellowed some. I was the youngest of seven, and they had all broken him in pretty well by the time I came along! I can't attest to it, but I hear, quite often, that the youngest had it easier. I get told a lot, "Well, you don't know what it's like being this old," so I've got to wait to figure it out.

By the time I was getting to be fifteen or sixteen, maybe earlier than that, I would go hunting with Dad. He loved to quail hunt. I spent a lot of time enjoying that with him. We' would also go fishing.

I would get up a lot of Saturdays with him and then he would come into work. I would come out here [to the quarry at Knightdale], ride horses, and spend my Saturdays here—not necessarily with him because he would work most of the time.

We enjoyed a lot of the same things. I felt like we became close friends as he got older, and I tried to take him out and do things with him—and to appreciate my time with him as much as possible. He was a lot of fun—certainly miss him—but we shared a lot of good times together, mostly in the outdoors.

Dad loved having his birthday party. Lots of times we would have it out at the quarry—his birthday was during the summertime and everybody was around. We always got together for Thanksgiving and for Christmas—a big social gathering. He enjoyed being around his family more than anything. There was certainly a lot of activity, but it was always positive and fun.

Dad was relentless if he was focused on something at work; he would grab hold of a concern and really not let go of it until he was satisfied with it. But if he was able to let go, he liked to go to different social functions with Mom, like parties.

Our family would always have dinner together at night. Dad would come in and he'd like to have me fetch his slippers and maybe a jacket during the winter, and we would have a fire going. He would read the *Raleigh Times* in his chair until we had his plate set— something that doesn't happen at my house. Then he would get up, say the blessing, and eat. When dinner was over, he would get up, finish reading his paper, and we would all clean up. You knew he had worked hard that day, so everybody had a role to play. Those were good times.

All of the brothers and sisters get along just fine. All in all, everybody got along and still does.

Mom had her hands full with seven children in and out at home, and with Dad starting a new business. I think that he could channel all the pressure into his productivity at work, but I don't think she had the ability to channel it anywhere else. So I think it was a real stressful time for her—I know it was. There was a lot going on, but we all made it through it. Mom liked to swim for exercise in the summertime and to play some tennis, but there was no time for any of that while Johnny was growing up. Mom made sure we had meals, clothes, got to school and anywhere else we needed to go, and he took care of everything on the other end, the work side. It was a very traditional marriage.

Parenting back then is not the same as parenting today; it's a lot different, but she and Dad always had a deep love for each other. As they got older, I think that love grew stronger. When they were younger, there was so much going on, I don't think they had time to think about it much.

Mom has some dementia now. I was with her about an hour and a half or two hours yesterday. She's very pleasant, so she's not uncomfortable, but she doesn't have much to do during the day—so she's just kind of existing. She has fine care and a very comfortable place to live, but she's not self sufficient at all. And that's tough; that level of independence is gone. She's going be ninety in September.

JOHNNY: I think you ought to know something that I was very impressed with. Dad was very dedicated to his mother. His mother—my grandmother, who I was close to and crazy about—was a wonderful person. I have wonderful memories of all us going to my grandparents' for Sunday dinner. My father always took his mother to church on Sunday after his father died. She moved to a retirement center in New Bern where her only daughter lived. She was in her eighties and lived to be ninety-nine, but he went down there about once a week to see her, which was pretty remarkable.

Lucy Doak, the fourth of the Bratton children, echoed many of the same comments and sentiments expressed by her brothers, and added a few of her favorite memories, beginning with her father:

He loved people and was always interested in everybody around him—everybody who worked for him and all of our friends growing up. I don't think of him as an extrovert, but I do think he just really enjoyed people: knowing their background and knowing them.

I just think he was raised in such a way that he always did the best for everybody that he could. It was natural for him to do things that way. It wasn't like, 'Oh, he's trying to be such a gentleman …' He really *was* such a gentleman—to the core. When people needed him, he would be there. When [someone] died, he was always the first to go.

Sundays out in the car were fun. He would take all of us for a ride. Many Saturdays and Sundays were spent at the quarry with his children and grandchildren. He was so happy out there. He kind of made it a farm; there were orchards and fruit trees. He loved riding, so he always was putting a child on a horse. He bought tiny ponies so that little children could ride them. Those are pretty good memories.

Overall, I think [among the best memories are] his generosity, his desire be with his children and his grandchildren, and that he made sure there was time to do that.

He was kind to everybody in his world.

Lucy described her mother with these words:

> Mother was very admiring of Dad and his family. He was trying to do research, to put together a family tree, and she was very interested his ancestry. She and Dad always tried to make things special for each other. She was very adoring of my father—and all of us, really. I think you can say she really appreciated the Bratton family and how wonderful they were, and felt very lucky to be a part of it.
>
> Mother loved to cook, and always made our birthday cakes. She loved babies. She also gardened a little bit—loved flowers. She loved to read and always took us to the library. She also belonged to historical societies.[31]

While John Bratton Jr. was busy with his career, Michelle Bratton was not only busy with managing the household of her ever-growing family; she also found time to contribute to her school, Saint Mary's, as a member of the alumnae association. One article she wrote for the Saint Mary's School bulletin was titled, "Presentation of the Smedes Memorial Tablet," and described a ceremony and speeches involved in presenting a tablet to the founder of her school and his son.[32]

As you will see later in this chapter, she was also active, individually or with her husband, in various social causes and philanthropies as her children grew older and occupied less of her time.

A Career in Crushed Stone

John Bratton Jr. spent his entire career as an engineer working with aggregate companies. He eventually founded his own aggregate business, but his first twenty-four years were as an employee with Superior Stone Company, which grew and became a part of the Martin Marietta Corporation.

Superior Stone/Martin Marietta

Mr. Bratton's degree in civil engineering and his employment with Superior Stone Company after the war was an excellent career choice for the times. Stone is the basic building material for highways, used in concrete and asphalt, and the car culture had been developing even before World War II. Americans were spreading out to the suburbs, and the need for roads and building materials was growing. Superior Stone, an aggregate company, had been founded in Raleigh in 1939. The company grew rapidly, went through various mergers, and by 1961 it became Martin Marietta Corporation, "a leader in cement, aerospace, aggregates, electronics, and chemicals."[33] Mr. Bratton worked for them for about twenty-four years. He rose to the position of Vice President of Operations,[34] but he gradually became dissatisfied with the job. His oldest son, Johnny Bratton, tells the story:

> When he was discharged from the Marine Corps, Dad went to work for Superior Stone Company. His next-door-neighbor was one of the owners of Superior Stone Company and hired him. Dad was the first engineer that they hired to build rock-crushing plants to make construction aggregate. The company grew rapidly because of the interstate system that Eisenhower was implementing. They would put in quarries to furnish the stone requirements for road projects in North and South Carolina, Virginia, and even Georgia. Dad moved around a lot building crushing plants for Superior Stone.
>
> I think Dad had wanted his own business for a long time. Superior Stone Company had merged with American Marietta in the late '50s. American Marietta was a large company that had some cement interests, built grain storage silos, and had a paint company— Marietta Paint. A few years later, American Marietta merged with Glenn L. Martin Company to form Martin Marietta. My father was running the operations for the quarries for the southeast, and really wanted

to be on his own. It was different working for those great big companies than when he worked for Superior Stone. So in 1970, we found a farm here in Knightdale that had a granite deposit on it, and he left Martin Marietta and we started this business. We bought the farm—it was 170 acres initially—and the equipment, and opened a quarry. I like to say "we;" I started with him, but actually he started the company. He had to borrow some money, but he had his profit sharing from Superior Stone, and equipment companies helped finance the purchase of equipment. We've been very fortunate. We've worked hard and grown the business to five operations now.[35]

Johnny Bratton is being a bit modest in his description of how this family-owned quarry company got started. It may have been his father's idea, but according to Tom Oxholm, the company's longtime CPA, financial advisor, and employee, "Mr. Bratton and Johnny started in '70 with two employees. Mr. Bratton pulled Johnny out of college to come to work here. When it got started, he needed as much free labor as he could get. So Johnny was almost an indentured servant the first five to ten years."[36]

Wake Stone Corporation

John Bratton had worked hard during his years with Superior Stone, and he was to work even harder after he decided to form his own company in 1970. Superior Stone had changed into a huge company, and he wanted his own business with a family-like atmosphere that reflected his values and could become his children's legacy.

The granite reserves under the 170 acres of farmland near Knightdale that Mr. Bratton purchased in 1970 resulted in the company's first quarry about five months later. Since then the company has grown from one quarry to five. "Wake Stone is the fourth largest stone quarrying company in the Carolinas and is among the top forty in the United States."[37]

John Bratton Jr. died in 2009, but two of his sons, Johnny and Sam Bratton, and his longtime CPA at Wake Stone and friend, Tom Oxholm, graciously agreed to meet with me at Wake Stone's headquarters in

Knightdale to discuss Mr. Bratton's work and his life. (Their comments used previously in this chapter took place at Wake Stone headquarters.)

When I arrived at the main building, it reminded me of a lovely Southern plantation home: a white frame house with porches and dormers with beautiful landscaping. The interior furnishings and house were spotless. From Johnny's office facing the back of the property, I could see outbuildings, orchards and horses behind a fence. I could see no signs or sounds of equipment or a quarry, although I'm sure it was back there somewhere!

The Beginnings of Wake Stone

John Randolph Bratton—Johnny—is currently Chairman of the Board of Wake Stone. He joked that he thinks his father gave him a middle name because not having one caused some problems for his father when he was in the military.

Samuel Telfair Bratton—Sam—is President of Wake Stone. The third Bratton brother, Theodore DuBose Bratton—Ted—is Chief Executive Officer, and Tom Oxholm is Chief Financial Officer. Ted Bratton was the only corporate officer missing, but he was out of town.

Johnny Bratton had arranged the meeting, and he, along with Sam and Tom, managed to carve out almost 2½ hours of a busy workday to speak with me. All three were extremely kind, courteous, and fun to be with—and after a few minutes I had almost forgotten that they were the leaders of a multi-million dollar corporation! Much of the conversation seemed to center around the Wake Stone business rather than on John Bratton Jr.'s personal life, but after a while I realized that Wake Stone is a clear reflection of John Jr.'s personality and values: the man and the company are intertwined.

Johnny Bratton appeared to be a somewhat quiet, thoughtful man, who gave questions careful consideration and listened closely to what others had to say. Sam seemed a bit more carefree, a typical youngest child who enjoys teasing and being teased. He jokingly described himself and the other two men as "the good, the bad, and the ugly." Tom Oxholm spoke as much, if not more, than the other two, and obviously has an enormous admiration and affection for the family and for Wake Stone.

I spoke with Johnny alone for a few minutes, and then Sam and Tom joined us for a group interview. Tom Oxholm is like a member of the family but has a slightly different perspective. His first involvement with Wake Stone was as a consultant in 1981, then as an employee in 1986.

> JOHNNY: Wake Stone is family owned. I'd like to tell you we planned that, but in the early '70s, I was so naïve I didn't know enough to be afraid. We were trying to survive—trying to meet payroll. My father had seven children; he left [Superior Stone] and started a business ... and still had five of them to educate, so it was a pretty gutsy move.
>
> I would be the Chairman, for what it's worth. Titles come pretty cheap around here. We all pitch in and just do whatever it takes. And we support our employees and their families. The reason we've done well is because of our employees. It's not that we made it happen; they made it happen.
>
> Tom Oxholm is our accountant. A friend of my father's was our accountant originally. He retired and picked Tom to help us, and we eventually hired Tom to come in. He's our Chief Financial Officer, but is much more than that. He's an advisor for the family, the brains behind all of this. Tom worked with Dad from when Dad was actively working until he really was incapacitated. Tom worked with him as a close friend for a long time, even though he was much younger than Dad.
>
> TOM: Mr. Bratton had two original investors, himself and a friend in a related field. The friend then felt that he needed to get out—that he was too intertwined in Mr. Bratton's business—so he sold to another friend and neighbor, an attorney. The attorney instituted a ten-year buyout program so that Mr. Bratton could buy him out.

Mr. Bratton came into a territory to set up one quarry, a territory that was dominated by the company he had worked for. He went out on his own with a relatively small amount of money and tried to make a go of it in a very capital-intensive business, knowing that his former employer would not take kindly to it. He started preparing the quarry. Well, right next door was a former Martin-Marietta quarry that had been shut down for a while, and Martin-Marietta got it open again before Mr. Bratton was able to get his [quarry] open.

What Mr. Bratton had was a business plan very dependent on two key customers who said they would stick with him even if the dominant player in the market, Martin-Marietta, dropped their prices—which they did. Those two customers held true to their word and kept buying product from Wake Stone, at that time [named] Perfect Land Corporation.

JOHNNY: These were handshake deals; these weren't written contracts.

TOM: Right. After a few years, Mr. Bratton had gotten his feet on the ground. Johnny could tell you typical entrepreneur stories of how making payroll every week was a challenge. One of his first employees, Duncan McCormick, had to get customers to pay just to make payroll.

It was a real challenging sort of a business for a fellow who was forty-seven years old with seven children. Not too many people take that kind of risk. We remind the third generation how big a risk it was to get started in the business. That's always been the most impressive thing: starting like that and having it become so successful.

Three or four years after the company started, Shearon Harris Nuclear Plant was going to be built, and the power company, Carolina Power & Light, sent out for proposals from quarry companies to provide the stone for that nuclear plant. Mr. Bratton's company put a proposal in that won. So a second quarry [Moncure Quarry, Lee County, North Carolina] was started that ran for about nine years while the nuclear power plant was constructed (then it went dormant for about six years and then started again).

The company had a very detailed buy-sell agreement about how Mr. Bratton could buy out his partner. That is what led to my involvement. I was the staff tax accountant working for an appraiser on a fair valuation for the company; the company would be appraised and then Mr. Bratton would pay his partner half of the appraised value. That turned into a very contentious lawsuit; I think Mr. Bratton and Johnny had a lot of scars from that. It was not the right thing for that investor to do. He made a twenty-to-one return in ten years, a 2,000% return. He didn't feel that was enough, so he sued his neighbor, friend and partner. They settled for about 20% more. That left the company with new sets of debts and other new things, so I started working with Mr. Bratton and Johnny in the early '80s as an outside accountant.

The next big thing that happened, right about the eleventh year and while this lawsuit was going on, was that the third quarry [Triangle Quarry, Cary, North Carolina] got started—right next to a state park on an interstate, a very sensitive area. Once I was in, the company really had its foothold in the community, and once a quarry company gets that kind of foothold, it has a lot more stability.

That first ten to eleven years were critical. There were seventy hours weeks every week. Mr. Bratton was a hard worker, a taskmaster, and I don't think Johnny got many days off. The idea was great customer service and a can-do attitude.

JOHNNY: We started about first light, depending on the time of year, and stopped when we got to a good stopping point after a long day.

TOM: I'm not sure I saw the same side of Mr. Bratton as Johnny did in the early years. By the time I came to work, he was sixty-three or sixty-four, so I'm sure he had mellowed quite a bit from when he was forty-seven during the high stress [days]. My perception was that Mr. Bratton was a very hard worker with high standards: he expected people to do it right. He had started twenty quarries for Martin Marietta. He knew how to start a quarry, but he actually hadn't done the work himself. With Johnny they were erecting the plant, putting up the headwall for all the equipment ....

JOHNNY: We hired an experienced foreman, a young man who had worked for him previously at a quarry, who knew how to run daily operations. [Dad] also hired Duncan McCormick, a very dedicated employee who took over the office—accounting, the daily ticketing, customer billing payables, and things like that—so we had two men who were capable and doing a good job.

TOM: In '83 Mr. Bratton wanted to start a profit sharing plan for the employees. Everybody would be on the same plan with the same benefit package—no difference between the salaried and the hourly employees. He very much wanted to do that. Since the early '80s, we have had what is called an old school profit sharing plan where the employees don't have to defer any pay to get matches, and it's there for their retirement. They can't borrow from it, they can't take anything out, and they can't do anything with it until retirement. Although it was a bit paternalistic, Mr. Bratton said, "We're going to take care of the employees. I want to pay them as well as they would get paid anywhere else, and they're going to have better benefits."

While we were working on the profit sharing plan, Mr. Bratton asked me to look at payroll and tell him whether or not I thought he could have a raise. At that time the company had expanded to three quarries, gone through the lawsuit, and started a profit sharing plan, but he wasn't sure he could afford to pay himself any more! I said, "Well, sure," and he said, "How much?" It was a significant increase. It was like the best news he had ever had. I felt like a hero for telling someone he could pay himself more. Then about a year later, he asked, "Do you think it's possible for us to build a beach house?" Seven children had been raised, grandchildren were here now, and he had never had a beach house. I said, "Yeah, no problem." That was the second easiest question of all time. It was funny that he would not do that without somebody giving him an approval. He never thought first of himself. He was in his early sixties before he really started ramping up his pay, had a beach house, and that kind of thing.

SAM: If he made up his mind he was going to do something, he was going to get it done. Dad told me he felt the key to his success was his determination—his unwillingness to comprise. He would make sure that he would accomplish what he wanted to accomplish. Failure wasn't an option for him. I didn't see too much self-doubt in him. Even when he was older, the man thought he was going to live forever. Thinking of his mortality and things like that was kind of like accepting defeat, and he just wouldn't do that. He would talk to you about planning to do something and I would think, "Dad, you're in your mid-eighties, and I don't know if that's really possible," but I didn't want to tell him that.

TOM: Mr. Bratton treated the quarry as a farm, but part of it was to buffer the town and the area from the quarry. It looked like a farm from the road. When [Mr. Bratton] started the company in 1970, his father [John Sr.] must have been in his seventies, and he planted a garden behind the company building with pecan trees, pear trees, and apple trees. When we moved up here in '87, Mr. Bratton said, "I'm going to have the same thing," and he built this little orchard of trees.

Most people would think a quarry is a nuisance. Nobody wants it. Wherever we have one, we try to be an asset to the community or area where the quarry is located. Triangle Quarry is really not in a community, it's next to a state park, so we're very careful about being friends to the park, lending equipment, materials and such to the park. Here we're right in the town at Knightdale. If you called the mayor of Knightdale and said, "Who's your best corporate citizen any time in the last thirty years, they would say that it's Wake Stone. We've donated trucks, fire trucks, and even the land for a town hall. We're going to benefit the community where we live so that they don't think, "Oh there's that awful quarry."

Talking about the farm-like atmosphere of the Wake Stone quarries reminded Tom of a funny story involving Mr. Bratton and his expense reports. Following is the story as recounted by Tom Oxholm:

In 1988 Mr. Bratton was in the habit of turning in his expense reports to Duncan McCormick, and one time Duncan showed me the reports. There was this expense for "Jim," $2500 or so. Duncan said, "I'm not sure what that is, you better go ask Mr. Bratton." So I did, and he said, "Well, that was my hunting dog, Jim, that I bought." I said, "Mr. Bratton, a bird dog? Don't think it would look too good as a business expense if the IRS came. You really ought not to have cows and horses and dogs on the books." He laughed and said "okay."

Tom Oxholm continued with reflections on Mr. Bratton's love of tradition and on the family business:

> Mr. Bratton loved the tradition of things; he had great memories of his father and mother, and did the same kind of things. When he would see a fox running out there [behind the office], he would pull out a gun and shoot him right from the office. [On the property] there were dogs, horses, cows, and even some chickens for a while. The Brattons always had all the children and grandchildren come out to ride horses. There are six or seven horses around back now.

> We've gone through the transition from the first to the second generation, and are spending a good time now trying to get [the third generation] trained in what it takes to run a family business. All the Brattons who work in the company have the same work ethic. You can count on that. Al Parker—Johnny and Sam's nephew—is superintendent of the [Knightdale] quarry. Johnny's son, Hunter Bratton, is twenty-eight and is now at Triangle Quarry. John Doak, Lucy's son, is here now. They see how hard everybody still works, and they're not going to be outworked by employees as that would set the wrong standard.

> I don't think the family members get treated any more special than the employees. I think the average employee has been with us fifteen years. There's a lot of company loyalty, especially through this last recession. All employees got forty-hour paychecks, even when we didn't have forty hours of work.

John Bratton Jr. and his sons. *From left to right*: Ted, Mr. Bratton, Sam, and Johnny outside main office, 1979.

Wake Stone Corporation, a family-owned business, was a rising star in the quarry business in 1979 and soon drew nationwide attention.

During his presidential campaign, Vice President George Bush tours the Triangle Quarry with Mr. Bratton and Johnny Bratton, 1988.

Wake Stone corporate officers in 2011. *From left to right*: Theodore D. Bratton, Chief Executive Officer; John R. Bratton, Chairman of the Board; and Samuel T. Bratton, President.

The three Bratton brothers, Ted, Johnny, and Sam, now lead the corporation. Wake Stone continues to give back to the communities located near its five quarries in North and South Carolina and to preserve or restore existing wetlands. All four images on this and the preceding page are courtesy of the Wake Stone Corporation and were taken from its 40th Anniversary publication in 2011.

The construction crew with the help of men from several quarries restored wetlands and a stream at the Nash County Quarry (before and after pictures), 2008.

When I asked the men how Mr. Bratton handled retirement, they agreed with Tom Oxholm when he said,

> Frustration for an entrepreneur is letting go of being in charge from day-to-day. I remember being in meetings with him when he wasn't keeping up to speed; he would hear something that just didn't sound right to him. He had very good business instincts, but he really didn't have much information about why we did this or why we did that, so that was very hard for him. When Mr. Bratton was about seventy, we had a retirement party for him. He said, "Okay, I'm just going to step back—I'm just going come to one meeting a month." I think it wasn't until after that day that I saw him being really relaxed.

Johnny Bratton added,

> He retired much more than we ever thought he would, but he still maintained an office. He would come in, straighten us out, check his mail, and he was still on some boards.[38]

The Wake Stone Legacy

Wake Stone was founded by a member of the Greatest Generation, a term made popular by Tom Brokaw, who wrote a book about the Greatest Generation in 1998. Mr. Brokaw described them as "the greatest generation any society has ever produced."[39] That generation lived through the Great Depression and World War II, and the vast majority shared common values: a sense of personal responsibility; duty and honor; faith in God; unwavering patriotism; and a belief in commitment. They also believed in community involvement, and were involved in Boy Scouts, Rotary Clubs, community associations, and more.

The Greatest Generation, including Mr. Bratton, learned skills and self-discipline in the military and fought for their country but were humble about their roles in the war—they remembered those who did not survive it. They wanted to put the war behind them, come home, and take care of their families and communities.

John Bratton Jr. appears to have been an excellent example of this generation, an example that is reflected in the way he started his business and ran it. Mr. Bratton became a leader in the aggregate industry, and his company won many awards. He was president of the North Carolina Aggregates Association from 1978 to 1979 and served on the board of the National Stone Association.[40] Mr. Bratton also participated in noise abatement research at the Knightdale and Moncure quarries, and "with the bureau of mines in a program aimed at protecting crusher operators from harmful noise."[41]

Mr. Bratton had a can-do"attitude that is still reflected in the work ethic at Wake Stone, which also has a high employee retention rate.[42] Mr. Bratton always took care of his employees, and his son, Johnny, felt that Wake Stone's employees were the main reason for the company's success.

Mr. Bratton also took care of his children, and happily enough, all of them worked or are still working for Wake Stone in one capacity or another. His three sons lead the company now, and all four daughters have worked there. Jane has worked in the offices, Connie oversaw computer operations, Michelle has handled landscape design, and Lucy remembered weighing trucks at some point.[43]

In 1984 Mr. Bratton began to make plans to hand over the reins of his corporation to his children.

> In 1984 in the prime of health, John Bratton gave his stock in Wake Stone equally to his seven children, but with strings attached. Johnny Bratton and his two brothers, who run the company, got shares with voting rights. Their sisters got nonvoting shares, with provisions that let them borrow against their stock and sell back shares at fair value. By granting the stock to his children before his death, Bratton sidestepped a common threat to family businesses: inheritance taxes, which can force sell-offs.[44]

Mr. Bratton, according to his son, Johnny Bratton, retired in 1984,[45] although he often appeared in the office. Wake Stone, under the leadership of his sons, continues to operate with the same high standards and values set by Mr. Bratton. One of those values is being a good neighbor.[46] Mr. Bratton believed in being an active part of one's community, and

Wake Stone continues to follow his lead. An avid outdoorsman, he was also committed to protecting the environment.

Every effort is made to create a pleasing view for quarry neighbors. Quarries are screened with vegetative earthen berms, and attractive landscaping is placed around offices. The quarry lands contains trees, farmland, orchards, and even animals. At the same time, the company also makes every effort to be environmentally responsible. According to an article in *Stone Review*, they have even used a wildlife biologist as a consultant on some of their projects.[47] They have hired environmental staff to make sure that all permits are in order, meeting all governments regulations, and each Wake Stone site has an environmental management incentive program.[48] The goal is to not only comply with industry standards but to exceed them. "Water wagons spray the roads and stone to control the dust," noise levels are monitored, crushing structures are enclosed, and advanced explosives are used.[49] Quarry planning and operation includes an eventual restoration of the land, including changing quarry pits to lakes that could eventually be surrounded by a housing development or a golf course. It also includes protecting and expanding ponds already on the property.

In 1988 Wake Stone received the Environmental Eagle Awards for each of their quarry operations. In 1999 and 1998 its Triangle Quarry received a Gold Environmental Eagle Award for environmental achievement. In 1998 the National Stone Association in conjunction with the EPA gave them an award for excellence in environmental achievement. In 2000 the North Carolina Landscape Association awarded them with the Environmental Improvement Grand Award. They have received awards from the North Carolina Wildlife federation and for beautifying the area around their quarries. The list goes on and on. Wake Stone's corporate website lists almost four pages of awards for their company.[50] In Mr. Bratton's own words,

> People think you are destroying the land when quarrying, but you can't be in this business without taking care of the land. We appreciate it and leave it in proper condition for future generations. I am and intend to continue as a good steward of the land.[51]

Wake Stone is also an active part of the communities in which their quarries are located, donating time and money. Wake Stone has donated equipment to the Knightdale Fire and Rescue Squad, and many of their employees, including corporate staff, donate their time to community projects.

Philanthropy

In addition to giving to the community through Wake Stone, Mr. Bratton was very active on a personal level, donating his time and money to a wide variety of causes. By the time of his death, he and his wife had donated generously to various nonprofit and educational organizations.

Mr. Bratton was a cradle Episcopalian, always very active in his church, Christ Church of Raleigh. He was a big financial contributor and served on the church vestry for twelve years and as a junior and senior warden. Mr. Bratton was also involved with several other organizations. According to his friend and employee, Tom Oxholm, "He was a donor to a lot of organizations. He liked giving money away. The older he got, the more he loved doing that. He had half a dozen charities that he was real dedicated to."[52]

Serving the Homeless

One of these charities, The Ark, was related to Mr. Bratton's work at Christ Church and was originally a homeless shelter for men in Raleigh. Johnny and Sam Bratton spoke of his work at the Ark; they said that when he was on the church vestry (for twelve years), he had a commitment to spending one night a month at the Ark. According to Sam, "He went to work there. Spending the night means staying up all night, keeping the peace, serving meals and cleaning up."[53]

Oakwood Cemetery

Mr. Bratton was also very involved with Oakwood Cemetery in Raleigh, where he was buried in 2009. Johnny Bratton spoke of his father's involvement with Oakwood:

> Oakwood Cemetery is an old, historic cemetery that
> was given to the state or the city by the Mordecai family,

and it's an independent nonprofit historic cemetery that has lots of old Raleigh families. The friends that my parents grew up with in high school and all my parents' ancestors are there. Dad served on that board for years. Once you're on it, you don't get off, but he enjoyed it and worked hard for its preservation. My father's parents were originally buried in a small family cemetery in Marlborough County, South Carolina, and my father moved them to where [my father] and his family would be buried.[54]

Historic Preservation

Mr. Bratton was interested in preserving the history of his country, both locally and nationally, and he and Mrs. Bratton donated to several organizations for this purpose. One that was very close to his heart was Historic Brattonsville.

Historic Brattonsville

Historic Brattonsville is a living history and Revolutionary War site located in York County, South Carolina, and was originally a plantation founded by Colonel William Bratton (1742–1815), John Bratton's paternal descendant in South Carolina. Sam Bratton spoke of his father's involvement with Brattonsville:

Dad did like the idea of a family home place that was being restored. He was always very proud of Brattonsville—the history behind it—and enjoyed visiting it. One time he went back and was told they needed a pair of mules, so he bought them a pair of mules. He thought that was a neat thing—a working colonial farm with oxen, mules, and other animals.[55]

In 1999 John and Michelle Bratton donated $150,000 to the Culture & Heritage Foundation to create the Historic Brattonsville Fund, a fund that would be used to improve the living history site museum. In announcing their contribution, John said, "Michelle an I are pleased to make these funds available to further the excellent work being done to preserve the culture and customs of the Revolutionary War and ante-bellum periods in the South Carolina Piedmont."[56]

Other Donations or Memberships Involving Historic Preservation

Some of the other historic preservation societies the Brattons donated to were: the Classical American Homes Preservation Trust; the Joel Lane Museum House; and North Carolina's WWII Experience, the latter honoring North Carolina's Greatest Generation with a two-hour documentary presentation. All of these

Campus scene, Saint Mary's School, Raleigh, NC, circa 1930–1945. Postcard by Tichnor Bros. Inc., Boston, MA, Boston Public Library.

donations were over $1,000, some significantly more.[57]

In addition to monetary donations, Mr. Bratton also enjoyed a membership in the Society of the Cincinnati, the oldest patriotic organization in the country. Now an international organization, the society's members have Revolutionary War ancestors.

> The Society of the Cincinnati was founded in 1783 by officers of the Continental Army and their French counterparts who served together in the American Revolution. Its mission is to promote knowledge and appreciation of the achievement of American independence and to foster fellowship among its members."[58]

The society is organized both as a fraternal and as a non-profit corporation, and as a non-profit it has a library, a museum, and educational programs.[59] Mr. Bratton's son, Johnny, said, "He did very much enjoy it later in life—the meetings and the camaraderie. He made some nice friends there."

Education

Mr. Bratton understood the value of a good education and supported it wholeheartedly. His daughter, Lucy Doak, said, "Dad always gave to the schools our children went to, [even when] Daddy could barely pay his children's tuition."[60] One of Mr. Bratton's favorite schools was doubtlessly Saint Mary's School in Raleigh, where he had a rich history of family connections and to which he made very generous donations.

Saint Mary's School and Bratton Hall: Raleigh

Mr. Bratton's grandfather, Theodore DuBose Bratton, had been the third rector at Saint Mary's from 1899 to 1903, and many of the women in the Bratton family attended Saint Mary's. In other words, the Bratton family in Raleigh has been involved with Saint Mary's School for over 100 years.

Saint Mary's School was founded in 1842 with the support of the Episcopal Diocese of North Carolina. It was originally a school for young ladies, and "during the Civil War [it] was a safe haven for relatives of both Union and Confederate generals."[61] It is now a college preparatory school for girls in grades nine through twelve. Saint Mary's website, annual report, and other publications contain numerous references to the Bratton family's involvement, and in 1996 the Bratton family donated one million dollars to the school. John Bratton Jr. said,

> For many years, I have wanted to make a substantial gift to Saint Mary's to honor the school and my grandfather. Saint Mary's, with its history, outstanding faculty and devoted alumnae, has meant a great deal to me and to the women in my family.[62]

In recognition of this gift, the fine arts building on the school's campus was dedicated in October 1996 as Bratton Hall in memory of Theodore DuBose Bratton. In addition to donating money to Saint Mary's, Mr. Bratton also served on Saint Mary's Board of Trustees.

Bishop Bratton Hall: Sewanee

Three or four years after his donation to Saint Mary's, Mr. Bratton and his family made yet another major donation, this time to St.

Andrew's-Sewanee School (SAS) in Sewanee, Tennessee, where his grandfather and other family members had attended school. His gift helped make a spacious new academic building possible: the 7,100 square-foot building was dedicated on September 30, 2000, and was named Bishop Bratton Hall in honor of Theodore DuBose Bratton.[63] Johnny Bratton, who had attended Sewanee Military Academy, was present at the dedication and spoke of how the donation came about:

> The university wanted the Sewanee Military Academy campus for the School of Theology, so in the late '80s, Sewanee Military Academy (SMA) [by then known as Sewanee Academy] and St. Andrews School were consolidated. Dad wanted to do something to honor Bishop Bratton in Sewanee and thought there was a need there that he could help with, so he put up a million dollars.[64]

All Saint's School, Vicksburg, Mississippi

Mr. Bratton was also a generous supporter of All Saints' School, an Episcopal school founded by Bishop Theodore DuBose Bratton in 1908.[65] It was originally known as All Saints' College for Girls, and became co-ed in 1970 and a college preparatory school. It struggled financially—despite the support of Mr. Bratton and others—and closed, unfortunately, in 2006.

Other Donations

John Bratton made numerous other donations to organizations, such as Hospice of Wake County; the WakeMed Foundation; the Boys and Girls Clubs of Wake County; and to his Duke University alumni fund campaigns.[66] As one of his daughters, Lucy Doak, said, "He was a softy for many causes. He really liked supporting things that he felt were important.[67]

John Bratton Jr.'s Legacy

Mr. Bratton died on December 12, 2009, at his home in Raleigh, with his family by his side. The family received friends on December 14 in the Smedes Parlor at Saint Mary's School, the school he and his family had such fond memories of.[68] He was eighty-seven years old.

Mr. Bratton was the sixth generation of Brattons descended from Colonel William and Martha Bratton, who settled in South Carolina in the 1700s. His father, also named John Bratton, had died in 1971, and his mother, Lewis, died in 1992. His sister, Anne Bratton Allen, also preceded him in death as had his brother, Lewis Palmer Bratton. His parents and siblings had all settled in New Bern, North Carolina, a couple of hours away and near the eastern coast.

When he died, Mr. Bratton left behind his wife Michelle, who still resides in Raleigh, seven children, and numerous grandchildren and great-grandchildren.

John Bratton Jr. with various family members. *From top to bottom rows, left to right:* Johnny Bratton; Jane (Bratton) Fleming; Sam Bratton; Michelle (Bratton) Parker; Connie (Bratton) Grine; Ted Bratton; Michelle and John Bratton Jr; and Lucy (Bratton) Doak. Courtesy of Lucy Bratton Doak.

Current information (provided by his daughter, Lucy Doak) on Mr. Bratton's children, their spouses, and the number of their children is as follows:

1. Michelle Telfair (Bratton) Parker, her husband, Alton Parker of Wrightsville Beach, and their two sons

2. John "Johnny" Randolph Bratton, his wife, Katherine Hunter Bratton, and their son

3. Mary "Connie" Constance" Bratton Grine (who died in 2012), her husband, William "Pete" Bark Grine of Wilmington, and their two sons

4. Lucy Beverly (Bratton) Doak, her husband Hoyt "Trey" Buchanan Doak III, and their two sons

5. Theodore DuBose Bratton, his wife, Margaret Foerster Bratton, and their son and two daughters

6. Jane Telfair (Bratton) Fleming, her husband, Lawrence "Pat" Patrick Fleming Jr., and their three sons

John Bratton Jr. and Michelle Telfaire Bratton. Photo taken in the mid–1990s. Courtesy of Lucy Bratton Doak.

7. Samuel Telfair Bratton Jr., his wife, Cooper Parham
Bratton, and their daughter and two sons

Mr. Bratton's memory and his values remain with Wake Stone in the way they do business, treat employees, and maintain close ties with the community, and I'm certain the Bratton children echo many of the same behaviors. I asked his sons, Johnny and Sam, and his daughter, Lucy, if they could identify any common themes that seem to run in their family history.

Several common themes were identified, but the most important for Mr. Bratton were a love of family, love of the land and being a good steward of the land, and being a good neighbor. The importance of religion, education, patriotism and service to country were also obvious themes or values throughout the Bratton generations. Political involvement was just about the only theme common to his ancestors but not to John Bratton Jr., and politics was definitely something he didn't care much for! Before his generation, however, politics was considered an honor and an obligation; much has changed since then.

Mr. Bratton's love for his family and for the land were emphasized repeatedly by his children and his friend, Tom Oxholm. All of the Bratton children have remained in North Carolina, and Mr. Bratton was able to enjoy his retirement years with them. His love for the land is reflected in the conservationist approach he always used when building quarries and by his purchase of property that he named New Canaan, which has been used primarily for hunting by the family. New Canaan was likely named for the Canaan plantation owned by his grandfather, General John Bratton. As Sam Bratton, his youngest, said,

> He was really a conservationist. Coming from an agricultural background, even though that was at a very young time in his life, he felt very connected to agriculture and farming—caring for the land, working the land, and using it as a resource. And that kind of all worked with his concept of being in the quarry industry. [69]

I asked Mr. Bratton's daughter, Lucy, if she knew of any unfulfilled dreams or regrets her father might have had. She said,

> I don't know of any regrets. He wanted to live longer— he didn't want to go! Dad loved living long enough and being well enough to be with his grandchildren and to watch them grow up. He was so happy to be there for them. He made sure he had time with everybody, knowing he wouldn't be there forever.[70]

I wish I could have met John Bratton Jr., a most excellent example of the Greatest Generation, but I can imagine him through his family and through his company, Wake Stone. His heritage, along with that of his ancestors, is a one of courage, honor, country—and much, much more.

John Bratton Jr. portrait. Courtesy of Lucy Bratton Doak.

Appendix A: William Bratton's Military and Civil Service

Compiled by Michael C. Scoggins, Culture & Heritage Museums, December 2008

I. Military Service and Battles, 1775-1782

Captain, New Acquisition Militia Regiment (senior officers: Colonel Thomas Neel Sr., Lieutenant Colonel Samuel Watson, Major Francis "Frank" Ross)

December 1775	Snow Campaign, Greenville County, SC (including Battle of Great Cane Brake, Greenville County, SC, December 22, 1775)
July-October 1776	Cherokee Campaign, western SC/NC (including Battle Hole, Macon County, NC, September 19, 1776)
March 3, 1779	Briar Creek, Screven County, GA
March 29, 1779	Rocky Comfort Creek, Richmond County, GA

Major, New Acquisition Regiment (promoted after Maj. Francis Ross was killed in action at Rocky Comfort Creek, Georgia)

June 20, 1779	Stono Ferry, Charleston County, SC

Lieutenant Colonel, New Acquisition Regiment (promoted after Col. Thomas Neel Sr. was killed in action at Stono Ferry; Lt. Col. Samuel Watson promoted to full colonel at this time)

June 20, 1779, circa June 6, 1780—No known battles during this period of time

Colonel, Bratton's Regiment, Sumter's Brigade

June 8, 1780	Mobley's Meeting House, Fairfield County, SC
June 17, 1780	Hill's Iron Works, York County, SC
June 20, 1780	Ramsour's Mill, Lincoln County, NC
July 12, 1780	Williamson's Plantation, York County, SC
July 30, 1780	Rocky Mount, Fairfield County, SC
August 6, 1780	Hanging Rock, Lancaster County, SC
August 18, 1780	Fishing Creek, Chester County, SC
September 26, 1780	Bigger's Ferry, York County, SC
November 9–10, 1780	Fishdam Ford, Chester County, SC
November 20, 1780	Blackstock's Plantation, Union County, SC
February 19–21, 1781	Fort Granby (Friday's Fort), Lexington County, SC
February 24, 1781	Fort Motte (Buckhead), Calhoun County, SC
February 27–28, 1781	Fort Watson (Wright's Bluff), Clarendon County, SC
March 6, 1781	Scape Hoar-Radcliffe's Bridge, Lee County, SC
April 7, 1781	Four Hole Swap, Dorchester County, SC
July 16, 1781	Biggin's Bridge/Biggin's Church, Berkeley, SC
July 17, 1781	Quinby's Bridge/Shubrick's Plantation, Berkeley County, SC
September 8, 1781	Eutaw Springs, Orangeburg County, SC

Sources for William Bratton's military service:

William Bratton left no written account of his campaigns and military services during the American Revolution. The information above was taken primarily from statements made by soldiers who served under him during the war, and is contained in the hundreds of South Carolina audited accounts and federal pension applications filed by these veterans in the years between 1783 and 1845.

1. Revolutionary War Federal Pension Applications, Microfilm Series M804. National Archives and Records Administration, Washington, D.C. Microfilm Reels RW I—RW 2848, South Carolina Department of Archives and History, Columbia, SC. Microfilm copies on file at Southern Revolutionary War Institute, York, SC.

2. South Carolina Accounts Audited for Claims Growing out of the American Revolution. Microfilm Reels RW 2685—2848, South Carolina Department of Archives and History, Columbia, SC. Microfilm copies on file at Southern Revolutionary War Institute, York, SC.

II. Civil Service, 1769-1797

1769–1772	Road Overseer, Tryon County, NC
1776–1784	Justice of the Peace, New Acquisition District, SC
1777–1784	Tax Inquirer and Collector, New Acquisition District, SC
1785–1795	Justice of the Peace and County Court Judge York County, SC
1785–1790	York County Representative, SC Assembly
	Sixth General Assembly, 1785–1786
	Seventh General Assembly, 1785–1786
	Eighth General Assembly, 1789–1790

1786	Commissioner, Aera Iron Works, York County, SC
1790	York County Delegate, SC Constitutional Convention
1791	Commissioner for Jail and Courthouse Construction, Pinckney District, SC
1791–1795	York County Senator, SC General Assembly
	Ninth General Assembly, 1791
	Tenth General Assembly, 1792–1794
	Eleventh General Assembly, 1794–1795[1]
1795–1798	Sheriff, Pinckney District
	Three terms: 1795, 1797, 1798
1797	Trustee, Alexandria College, Pinckney District, SC

Sources for William Bratton's civil service:

1. Bailey, N. Louise, and Elizabeth Ivey Cooper. *Biographical Directory of the South Carolina House of Representatives, Volume III: 1775–1790.* Columbia, SC: University of South Carolina Press, 1981.
2. Holcomb, Brent H. South Carolina and Deed Abstracts, 1773–1778, books F-4 through X-4. Columbia, SC: South Carolina Magazine of Ancestral Research, 1993. Holcomb, Brent A. *Tryon County, North Carolina Minutes of the Court of Pleas and Quarter Sessions, 1769–1779.* Columbia, SC: South Carolina Magazine of Ancestral Research, 1994.

---

1   Bratton resigned as state senator upon his election as sheriff of Pinckney District, SC, December 19, 1794.

3. Reynolds, Emily Ellinger, and Joan Reynolds Faunt. *Biographical Directory of the Senate of the State of South Carolina, 1776–1965.* Columbia, SC: South Carolina Archives Department, 1964.
4. Wells, Laurence K. *York County, South Carolina Minutes of the County Court, 1786–1797.* Columbia, SC: South Carolina Magazine of Ancestral Research, 1981.

Reprinted with minor changes to titles and subtitles with permission from Michael Scoggins.

Appendix B: The Bratton Family at the Homestead, A Personal Look

Joseph H. Rainey, Curator, October 3, 1978

SOME SEVENTEEN YEARS AFTER the completion of the Homestead, Dr. John Simpson Bratton died unexpectedly in April 1843. Fourteen of his fifteen children and his wife survived him. At his death, Dr. Bratton had the largest plantation in the county, some 9,000 acres, and was also the largest slaveholder, owning around 143 slaves. Other than his medical profession and his plantation, Dr. Bratton owned at least two mercantile establishments, one in Brattonsville and one in Yorkville. Known as a financier of sort, he had on loan at the time of his death some $50,000. Although many people wrote him for advice and put great confidence in him, Bratton would not accept any powerful political office, although asked to run for Senate.

Always interested in education, sometime before 1838 he established a fine classical school at Brattonsville for the education not only of his children, but neighboring plantation children as well. He hired French and Italian tutors as teachers, and by 1840 his school was well known throughout the upcountry (records show thirty pupils in 1840). Looking towards expansion of his school, Dr. Bratton contracted just before his death, the building of a large brick house to be used dually as a school and as a store. Records show that O. S. Crawford complied with his contract and was paid by J. Rufus Bratton and John S. Bratton II, administrators of their father's estate. According to the diary of J. Rufus Bratton, his brother John discontinued his study of medicine because of the numerous duties concerning the settlement of the estate.

Since Dr. Bratton died intestate, his entire estate was divided amongst his wife and children.

Harriet Rainey Bratton continued to live in the Homestead until her death in 1874. Unlike many widows, Harriet did not go into seclusion. She did quite the reverse. She managed the plantation, using an overseer, renovated the Homestead, and remained active for the next thirty-one years of her life.

At the outbreak of the War Between the States, Harriet Bratton pledged her support to the Confederacy. Her brother, Samuel Lawrence Rainey, had signed the Ordinance of Secession of South Carolina from the Union as a delegate from York County. He was the oldest member of the secession delegation. Before the war would end some four years later, Harriet Bratton would have been one of the largest contributors of wheat, barley, and corn to the Confederate Army in York County.

Three of her sons went to the wars, while the fourth became a member of the South Carolina Legislature. Of her sons, Dr. J. Rufus Bratton was the most famous. [At] the end of the war, Rufus was head surgeon of the Confederate Hospitals in Georgia. He was captured by Sherman's Army and held prisoner until the entire Union Army had passed from the state of Georgia. He then walked from Georgia back to his home in Yorkville, only to hear of Lee's surrender and the end of the war.

The last ten years of Harriet Bratton's life were anything but pleasant. Reconstruction in York County was worse than four years of war. Federal troops were brought in to curb all "rebellious activities." Particularly notorious was the captain of the black militia who was backed in all he did by the Federal authorities. Formerly known as Jim Rainey, he called himself Jim Williams. According to testimony of witnesses at *The Yorkville Clan Trials*, Williams held a special grudge against the Bratton family and "intended to burn Brattonsville to the ground." He was also quoted as saying, "In case we don't succeed in carrying the next election, we will kill from the cradle to the grave, and we will apply the torch in every direction; we will lay waste to this country generally." He supposedly made these statements on March 4 of 1871. The same night, he and his militia burned the summer house at Brattonsville. On March 6, Jim Williams was taken from his house about ten o'clock at night and hanged. The Ku Klux Klan was held responsible for this act, and both John S. Bratton and Dr. J. Rufus Bratton were forced to flee York County for their alleged leadership in "this brutal act." Federal warrants for their arrest were issued, and Federal guards were stationed at Brattonsville in hopes of capturing the two brothers upon their return home. However, realizing their precarious situation, the Brattons fled to Canada, where they had friends.

Harriet Rainey Bratton did not live to see her eldest son, Rufus, return home. Although she constantly sought his pardon from officials in Washington, her requests were mostly ignored until some four years after her death. John S. Bratton II was pardoned and returned home. Dr. J. Rufus returned to his home in 1878, some seven years after the Jim Williams incident.

From the time of Harriet's death in 1874 until 1898, the Homestead had no regular occupant. Although its ownership passed to Dr. J. Rufus Bratton, he had purchased a home in Yorkville in 1845, and the Homestead was closed until Dr. Bratton's son, Moultrie, was married in 1898. Moultrie married his first cousin, Virginia Bratton, daughter of Napolean Bonaparte and Minnie Mason Bratton, and they lived in the Homestead until 1914, when they moved to Yorkville. This move was made so that Virginia's parents, who were quite old by this time and who had also resided at Brattonsville in the house known as "The Bricks," could be close to physicians care in Yorkville.

Both the Homestead and The Bricks were rented to tenants soon after the Brattons left Brattonsville. Both fell into disrepair quite rapidly and were finally vacated in the early 1950s. From that time until the late 1960s, vandalism ran rampant, especially at the Homestead. The Bricks was sold in the early 1960s by the heirs of Virginia Bratton to Samuel B. Mendenhall, while the Homestead remained in the possession of Dr. J. Rufus Bratton II. Through the efforts of Judge Mendenhall, the Homestead was orally leased to the York County Historical Commission for restoration in 1969, while actual restoration began in May of 1976. A written lease with a perpetual clause of historical usage was signed in March 1977.

Courtesy of the Fairfield County Museum, Winnsboro, SC

Appendix C: John Bratton's Military and Civil Service

I. Military Service and Battles, 1775-1782

John Bratton enlisted April 1, 1861, as a private in Company C of the Sixth Carolina Infantry, promoted a month later to captain. On April 22, 1862, he became a colonel of the Sixth Regiment.

September 20, 1861	Battle of Dranesville, VA
May 4–5, 1862	Battle of Williamsburg/Fort MacGruder, VA
May 31–June 1, 1862	Battle of Seven Pines, VA
Dec 11–15, 1862	Battle of Fredricksburg, VA
April 11–May 4, 1863	Siege of Suffolk, VA
October 28–29, 1863	Battles of Wauhatchie, TN
November 16, 1863	Battle of Campbell's Station, TN

Promoted to brigadier general as of May 6, 1864

May 5–7, 1864	Battle of the Wilderness, VA
May 8–21	Battle of Spotsylvania Court House, VA
May 31–June 12, 1864	Battle of Cold Harbor, VA
June 9, 1864–April 2, 1865	Siege of Petersburg, VA
Oct 13, 1864	Battle of Darbytown Road, VA

II. Political Service

September 1865	State Constitutional Convention, delegate
1865–1866	South Carolina State Senator
November 1867	Conservative (Democratic) Convention, delegate & vice president
1871, 1874	Taxpayers' Conventions of South Carolina, delegate, executive committee in 1874
1876	Democratic National Convention, delegate
1876–1880	Fairfield County Democratic Party, Chairman in 1880
1879	Commissioner of Phosphates
1880–1882	Comptroller General of South Carolina
1882, 1890	Candidate for the Governor of South Carolina
December 1884– March 3, 1885	U.S. House of Representatives, 48th Congress
1894	Conservative Democratic Convention, executive committeeman

III. Civic Service

1876—?	Grange & State Agricultural Society, member
1868—?	Fairfield Soldiers' Relief Association
1869	Survivors' Association of the Sixth Regiment, president, delegate to the state Survivors Association Convention in 1869

1880	South Carolina Historical Society, member
1881–1882, 1889	South Carolina College Alumni Association, vice president
1886–1888	South Carolina College, elective trustee
1888–1890	University of South Carolina, elective trustee
1894	Piedmont Colonization Society of South Carolina Convention, delegate
1896	South Carolina Society of the Sons of the American revolution, member of the board of managers

Appendix D: Some Historical Notes on South Carolina's Brattons
Elliot Bratton, October 2015

IN THE MID-1970S, I asked my father, Noble C. Bratton Jr., to interview his uncle, my great-uncle James M. "Uncle Jim" Bratton (1887–1979), about our family history. Before this time, all my father and I knew about our South Carolina ancestors prior to Uncle Jim's generation was that a Civil War general and enslaved people were involved. From my dad's interview with Uncle Jim, we learned that this general was Brigadier General John Bratton, C.S.A. (1831–1898), a slave owner who fathered Uncle Jim's dad, Ruffus Bratton (1855–circa 1913). According to the 1860 Slave Schedule (U.S. Census), John Bratton owned two males about age six and six females ages twenty-two to thirty-five; I believe Ruffus was one of the boys and his mother (unknown by name) was likely one of the six women.

Uncle Jim informed my dad of the close relationship between his father, Ruffus, and his father's half-brother, Bishop Theodore DuBose Bratton (1862–1944), and half-sister, Isabel Bratton Crisler (1873–1933). He also related that another half-brother, William Bratton, had died in an accident on a ship. Uncle Jim said Ruffus and his younger half-brother Theodore were "best friends." He also observed that Isabel was fond of Ruffus. The 1880 U.S. Census reveals that Isabel, age seven and having lost her mother at age two, was then living with her aunt and uncle, Col. Edward and Mrs. Mary Bratton Noble.

I believe all these connections were what led my great-grandfather Ruffus to name a daughter Isabel, a son William, and two more of his sons John Edward and Isaac Noble (the latter being my grandfather who, at some point, changed his name to Noble C. Bratton, Sr.).

While the 1880 Census confirms that Ruffus was able to read and write, any letters that may have passed between Theodore or Isabel and him have likely been lost. No writings by Ruffus have survived in my part of the family, and Theodore's grandson, John Bratton of Sewanee, Tennessee, told me that most of his grandfather's early papers were lost in a fire around 1918. It is likely that the close connection between Ruffus and Theodore was interrupted when both men left South Carolina for good. Ruffus moved his family nearer to his wife's sisters in Mecklenburg County, North Carolina, in 1902 after his wife, Kate Beaty Bratton, died in childbirth with their tenth child, my great-aunt Katherine. Meanwhile, Theodore, then living in Raleigh, North Carolina, moved his family (including Isabel) to Mississippi in 1903 after being elected Bishop of Mississippi.

Uncle Jim said that his father, Ruffus, had "died farming." Ruffus's date of death may only be estimated by the fact that most of his children, who had helped with his farm, started moving north sometime between 1910 and 1917.

Reprinted with permission from Elliot Bratton

Noble C. Bratton Sr. (1899–1982), youngest son of Ruffus Bratton. Courtesy of Cornelius Jenkins and Elliot Bratton.

Appendix E: A Tale of Two Families
John Gass Bratton, September 2000

B OTH THE BRATTONS AND the Gasses emigrated from County Antrim in Ireland and settled in the Piedmont of South Carolina.

The Gasses

The Gasses came to Sewanee first. Benjamin Gass, the emigrant, died in Greenville, South Carolina, and his widow married Henry Markley; a carriage maker who sent his newly adopted sons, John and Charles, to Sewanee in 1872. They were not yet of college age and were admitted to the Sewanee Grammar School just four years after the school's first students were enrolled. John Gass was graduated from the Sewanee Grammar School, the college, and the seminary. He had a successful career, dying at a young age while rector of St. Luke's Church in Atlanta.

My mother, Ivy, and two of her siblings, Henry and John Gass, were left at a young age without a father. My grandfather, Bishop Bratton, whose wife, Lucy, had died, married Ivy Gass. [Ivy was the first name of both the Rev. John Gass's wife and his daughter. Bishop Bratton married Mr. Gass's widow.] Their home was Battle Hill in Jackson, Mississippi. My mother and father, William DuBose Bratton [son of Bishop Bratton and his first wife, Lucy], though stepbrother and sister, were married and began a complication of these family ties.

Henry Gass, my uncle, was a classics professor at Sewanee when we moved to the Mountain following the tragic and unexpected death of my father, William DuBose Bratton. The home in which I still reside was built as a residence for us by Uncle Henry and his brother, the Rev.

John Gass, who was rector of the Church of the Incarnation in New York City, the parish of the President Franklin Roosevelt his mother, Sarah Delano Roosevelt. Uncle Henry was Sewanee's first Rhodes scholar in 1907 and maintained for decades the highest grade point average of any Sewanee graduate. He served Sewanee as Dean of Men and Acting Vice-Chancellor on the death of Alexander Guerry in the fall of 1947. Dr. Guerry died just after addressing the Rotary Club of Knoxville on the professional direction taken by collegiate football, of which he strongly disapproved.

Uncle Henry was known to the students as "Major Gass," a title he brought to the college from the Sewanee Military Academy where he taught and was headmaster. He was a popular figure on campus, and his humorous observations were often quoted by students who liked to imitate his high-pitched and peculiar inflections. My mother, Ivy, was gracious and had many friends. The KA fraternity had members living in the house, and members visited her daily for a number of years. She served at the Robert E. Lee teas, and once, when I was home on vacation, there was a supper for her at the Sewanee Inn.

When Uncle Henry and Aunt Marguerite's son, Currin, married Elizabeth Connor of Houston, Bishop Bratton's granddaughter, the second intermarriage occurred, thus further complicating the relationships of its members. Currin and Elizabeth's children are my double first cousins. Both Currin and his brother, John, graduated from Sewanee after serving in World War II, Currin in the Navy and John in the Marines.

The Brattons

When the Brattons emigrated from County Antrim to Pennsylvania, they settled there with proximity to Chester, Lancaster, and York. From there, the descendants of British emigrants and later the Brattons went to South Carolina, giving the towns they established these same names in the Piedmont. My direct ancestors settled near York and established an estate known to this day as Brattonsville.

If you were to travel to Brattonsville, you would find this place in the country very much as it was in the eighteenth century. Crops and animals are genetically similar to the original species, farmed with the same type of implements, and the original Bratton furnishings may be found along with other pieces of the period. Brattonsville is open year -round. There are performed re-enactments of the Battle of Houck's Defeat, the first victory over the British in South Carolina, and soon there will be a Colonial Christmas observed with descendants and others in period costumes in the John Bratton manor house. Because of these original houses, still standing, and the colonial integrity of the farm and surrounding area, Brattonsville was chosen for the site of the filming of *The Patriot* with Mel Gibson in the title role.

While Colonel William Bratton was out seeking to engage Colonel Houck, British soldiers occupied the house and insisted that Martha make a meal for them. Afterwards a British soldier took a scythe from the wall and held it to her throat, threatening to kill her if she would not disclose the whereabouts of her husband. She refused, but fortunately an officer came to her rescue. After the skirmish was over, Martha in turn saved the officer's life, as he was to have been executed along with several other officers.

Colonel Bratton's eldest son, William, moved from Brattonsville to Fairfield County near Columbia and married Isabella Means, a descendant of Francis Marion's sister. Here the Sewanee connections begin. Their son, John Bratton, a graduate of the Medical College of South Carolina with no military training, joined the state militia and rose through the Confederate ranks from private to general, remaining with the South Carolina Sixth Regiment all the way from Fort Sumter to Appomattox. All during the war, he wrote letters to his wife Elizabeth Porcher DuBose, the sister of William Porcher DuBose, then a Confederate officer and later chaplain. Dr. DuBose founded the School of Theology at Sewanee and the student governing body of the University known as the Order of Gownsmen. Right around the corner from where we are meeting, in nearby Monteagle, was Fairmount School for girls. Dr. DuBose' first wife was a Peronneau, also of Huguenot descent. His second wife, a Yerger, was a member of a distinguished Mississippi family and she was head of Fairmount School. Dr. DuBose joined her in the administration of the school. My mother attended Fairmount, and it is well known that Mme Chang Kai-shek and her sister were present there for at least one summer.

Theodore DuBose Bratton, son of John and also my grandfather, was Dr. DuBose' nephew. Entering Sewanee in 1874, he joined John Gass in the Sewanee Grammar School and was in attendance with him through college and seminary. They were close friends and ATO fraternity brothers.

In 1903 Grandfather was elected Bishop of Mississippi and served in this office until 1938. During World War I, my grandfather and father served as chaplains in the Army in France.

The year we moved to Sewanee was 1938, and Bishop Bratton was Chancellor. He had persuaded Alexander Guerry, then president of the University of Chattanooga, to accept the Vice-Chancellorship after he had previously declined. Dr. Guerry told me as a child that Grandfather had taken his election by the Board of Trustees to Chattanooga with these words: "Alex, I want you to save Sewanee." John, this was a challenge I could not refuse."

Bishop Bratton was far ahead of his time in his quest for education and advancement for African Americans. In 1922 he authored *Wanted-Leaders! A Study of Negro Development* published by the Episcopal Church in New York City. Tracing the tribes from their origins in Africa, he deals with misconceptions about the "backwardness" of blacks and ends with a call for black leadership and a plea for racial justice and tolerance. He established a trade school for blacks in Mississippi and was heavily involved with the support of Okolona College.

Bishop Bratton was also the founder of All Saints' College in Vicksburg, and he became the leading scholar on the theology of William Porcher DuBose (*An Apostle of Reality*).

Although I have no current means of authenticating my recollections, I remember reading at one time or another that Grandfather had once intervened with a lynch mob in Mississippi, negotiated a labor dispute in Jackson, and I clearly recall that at the time, he was the only clergyman whose portrait was in the Mississippi Hall of Fame. His portrait hanging there was painted by Vice-Chancellor Edward McCrady.

In Sewanee there are three memorials to Bishop Bratton: a bridge behind my house in Abbo's Alley, Lake Bratton near Proctor's Hall, and a new academic building at St. Andrews-Sewanee School, Bishop

Bratton Hall, dedicated September 30, 2000, and donated by the John Brattons of Raleigh, N.C.

To bring this family report current since my talk to Rotary, John Gass and his wife, Tibbie, of Chattanooga, and Currin and Elizabeth Gass of Salisbury, Maryland, have made provision for the most recent stained glass window to be placed in All Saints' Chapel. This window will be a memorial to Henry and Marguerite Gass. It will be the second clerestory window over the north isle, and the glass will display the art-ist's view of vision of Saint John accounted in the Book of Revelations. Other panels depict the fate of Christian martyrs in the first century. The windows will be installed in the summer and dedicated in the fall of 2001.

Lightly edited by author, and reprinted with permission from John Gass Bratton

Notes

CHAPTER ONE
Colonel William Bratton

1.   There are no known records at this time that indicate exactly when William emigrated or when he was born. His date of birth, as stated in family recordings, cemetery internment records, and other records, was between 1740–1742; for this book's purposes we will list it as 1742. Since family statements indicate that he emigrated with his father as a boy, William would have arrived sometime between 1742 and 1760.

2.   R. F. Foster, *Modern Ireland, 1600–1972* (New York: Penguin, 1988), 153.

3.   Gottlieb Mittelberger, *Gottlieb Mittelberger's Journey to Pennsylvania in the Year 1750 and Return to Germany in the Year 1754 : Containing Not Only a Description of the Country According to Its Present Condition, but Also a Detailed Account of the Sad and Unfortunate Circumstances of Most of the Germans That Have Emigrated, or Are Emigrating to That Country*, translated by Carl T. Eben, (Philadelphia: J. J. McVey, 1898), 23, from *Library of Congress* website, accessed September 17, 2015, https://archive.org/details/gottliebmittelbe00gott. Hereafter cited as *Mittelberger*.

4.   Ibid., 20.

5.   Alan Taylor, *American Colonies: The Settling of North America*, (New York, Penguin, 2001), 317.

6.   Michael C. Scoggins, "The Life and Times of William Bratton, Part 1," paragraph 2, email to author July 23, 2015. This is part 1 of a four-part series that appeared in *YC Magazine* (York County, SC) in February, March, April and May of 2011.

7.   Ibid., paragraph 7.

8.   *Mittelberger*, 118–119. First quote located on p. 118, second quote on p. 119.

9.   Michael C. Scoggins, "The Life and Times of William Bratton, Part 1," paragraph 8.

10.   Lyman Chalkey, *Chronicles of the Scotch-Irish Settlement in Virginia*, extracted from the original court records of Augusta County 1745–1800, vol. 1, Adam Bratton: 172, 178, 185, 201, 388; Ann Bratton: 54, 67, 298, 388; George Bratton: 215, 216, 225; James Bratton: 188, 198, 201, 215, 221, 223, 272, 276, 278; John Bratton: 188; Peter Bratton: 284; Robert Bratton: 30, 33, 49, 51, 54, 67, 72, 120, 123, 134, 148, 178, 298, 335, 368, 388, 498, 529; Thomas Bratton: 221; and William Bratton: 281, 416, from US GenWeb Project e-book, accessed July 24, 2015, http://www.rootsweb.ancestry.com/~chalkley/. Hereafter cited as *Chalkey's Chronicles*.

11.   Oren F. Morton, *A History of Rockbridge County, Virginia* (Staunton, VA: McClure Co., 1920,), 89, California Digital Library e-book, accessed August 5, 2015, https://archive.org/details/historyofrockbri00mortrich.

12.   *Chalkey's Chronicles*, 281 (1795), 416 (1800). The first entry (1795): "Called Court on William Bratton for larceny--discharged." The second entry (1800): "William Bratton vs. Frederick Shaver.--Petition, 28th November, 1799. Defendant no inhabitant."

13.   Joseph A. Waddell, "Indian Wars from 1756 to 1758," in *Waddell's Annals of Augusta County, Virginia from 1726 to 1871*, 2nd ed. (Rockwood, TN: EagleRidge Technologies, 1902), 155, electronic resource with various versions available for viewing or downloading, accessed September 17, 2017, https://archive.org/details/annalsofaugustac00wadd.

14.   John H. Logan, "William Bratton Biography and Obituary," Lyman C. Draper Manuscript Collection, State Historical Society, Wis., vol. 16, series 55, 174 (16VV154), paragraph 1, compiled by Michael C. Scoggins, 2002, email to author July 23, 2015. Dr. John H. Logan interviewed Harriet Bratton in the 1850s.

15.   John H. Logan, "William Bratton Biography and Obituary," Lyman C. Draper Manuscript Collection, State Historical Society, WI, 11VV33–336, paragraph 1, compiled by Michael C. Scoggins, 2002, email to author July 23, 2015. Notes regarding reminiscences of Dr. James Rufus Bratton regarding his father.

16.   Michael C. Scoggins, "The Life and Times of William Bratton, Part 2," paragraph 6.

17.   Ibid, paragraph 2.

18.   Pettus, Louise, "What is the 'Waxhaws'?" Rootsweb, accessed July 21, 2015, http://freepages.genealogy.rootsweb.ancestry.com/~waxhaw/.

19.   Michael C. Scoggins, "The Life and Times of William Bratton, Part 2," paragraph 1. Last sentence in paragraph.

20.   Ibid., paragraphs 2–3, 5–6.

21.   Richard J. Hooker, *The Carolina Backcountry on the Eve of the Revolution* (Chapel Hill: University of North Carolina Press, 1953), 13–14. I have included the original wording for the sake of authenticity, in this and in other quotes cited. Hereafter cited as Hooker, *The Carolina Backcountry*.

22.   Ibid., 25.

23.   Ibid., 45, 30.

24.   Walter B. Edgar, *South Carolina: A History*. (Columbia, SC: University of South Carolina Press, 1998), 186.

25.   Hooker, *The Carolina Backcountry*, 118.

26.   Michael C. Scoggins, "The Life and Times of William Bratton, Part 2," paragraphs 4–5, 7, 10.

27.   Ibid., paragraph 9.

28.   PBS, "The Slave Experience: Living Conditions," pbs.org, accessed August 13, 2015, http://www.pbs.org/wnet/slavery/experience/living /history2.html.

29.   Rachel N. Klein. *Unification of a Slave State: the Rise of the Planter Class in the South Carolina Backcountry, 1760–1801* (Chapel Hill: University of North Carolina Press, 1990), 9.

30.   Ibid., 41. The parish of St. Mark was the only backcountry parish in 1765, and contained the only two slots represented by the backcountry.

31.   Scoggins, Michael, "The Life and Times of William Bratton, Part 3," paragraph 2.

32.   Rachel N. Klein. *Unification of a Slave State …* , 45.

33.   Ibid., 41.

34.   Michael C. Scoggins, "A Brief History of the New Acquisition Militia," York County Historical Center, May 2002, paragraph 1, from New Acquisition Militia website, accessed April 24, 2015,http://newacquisitionmilitia.com/brief-history -new-acquisition-militia/. Hereafter cited as Scoggins, *New Acquisition Militia*.

35.   Michael C. Scoggins, "The Life and Times of William Bratton, Part 3," paragraph 3.

36.   See list of battles in appendix A, William Bratton's Military and Civil Service, compiled by Michael C. Scoggins, December 2008.

37.   Michael C. Scoggins, "The Life and Times of William Bratton, Part 3," paragraph 3.

38.   John W. Gordon, *South Carolina and the American Revolution: A Battlefield History* (Columbia, SC: University of South Carolina Press, 2003), 45–47. Hereafter cited as Gordon, *South Carolina and the American Revolution*.

39.   A. S. Salley, Jr., *The History of Orangeburg County, South Carolina* (Orangeburg, SC: H. Lewis Berry, 1898), 21. Copy found at Fairfield County Museum June 25, 2015, in Bratton Family files. Reference refers to preceding sentence only.

40.   Michael C. Scoggins, "The Life and Times of William Bratton, Part 3," paragraph 4.

41.   Gordon, *South Carolina and the American Revolution*, 67–69.

42.   Michael C. Scoggins, "The Life and Times of William Bratton, Part 3," paragraphs 7–9.

43.   Michael C. Scoggins, *The Day it Rained Militia: Huck's Defeat and the Revolution in the South Carolina Backcountry, May-July 1780* (Charleston, SC: History Press, 2005), kindle edition, locations 1269, 1277, 1285. Hereafter cited as Scoggins, *The Day it Rained Militia*.

44.   Ibid., location 1837.

45.   Gordon, *South Carolina and the American Revolution*, 89.

46.   Scoggins, *The Day it Rained Militia*, location 2231.

47.   Scoggins, *The Day it Rained Militia*, 1-6, kindle locations 2455, 2459, 2467, 2468, 2475, 2486. Mr. Scoggins's source for the interview was "Huck's Defeat: Dr. William Bratton's Story," (unpublished manuscript, n.d., Winnsboro, SC).

48.   Culture & Heritage Museums, "African American History," paragraph 2, from Culture & Heritage Museums website, accessed April 24, 2015, http://www .chmuseums.org/african-american-history-hb/.

49.   *Proceedings of a Celebration of Huck's Defeat, at Brattonsville, York District, South Carolina, July 12, 1839,* (Tucker Printing House, 1839), 5–6, Published by request of the Committee of Arrangements.

50.   Elizabeth F. Ellet, *The Women of the American Revolution*. (New York: Baker and Scribner, 1848), 244. Hereafter cited as Ellet, *The Women of the American Revolution*.

51.   Scoggins, *The Day it Rained Militia*, location 2617.

52.   Ellet, *The Women of the American Revolution*, 242.

53.   Scoggins, *New Acquisition Militia*, paragraph 6.

54.   Robert M. Dunkerly, *Women of the Revolution: Bravery and Sacrifice on the Southern Battlefields*. (Charleston, SC, The History Press, 2007), 63–65.

55.   Michael Scoggins, "The Life and Times of William Bratton, Part 4," paragraph 1.

56. J. D. Lewis, "The American Revolution in South Carolina: Fishdam Ford," from Carolana website, accessed August 14, 2015, http://www.carolana.com/SC /Revolution/revolution_battle_of_fishdam_ford.html.

57. Gordon, *South Carolina and the American Revolution,* 120–123.

58. Michael Scoggins, "The Life and Times of William Bratton, Part 4," paragraph 6.

59. Gordon, *South Carolina and the American Revolution,* 166.

60. Ibid., 1.

61. Michael Scoggins, "The Life and Times of William Bratton, Part 3," paragraph 3.

62. Jerome Nadelhaft, "The'Havoc of War' and its Aftermath in Revolutionary South Carolina," from *Histoire Sociale* website, 107, accessed August 18, 2015, http://hssh.journals.yorku.ca/index.php/hssh/article/viewFile/38975/35363.

63. Ibid., 115. Mr. Nadelhaft referenced his source as "Bratton to Gov. Gerard," February 13, 1784, Penal System (SCA).

64. Culture & Heritage Museums, "Early Physicians: Healing in the Backcountry," from Culture & Heritage Museums website, accessed August 18, 2015, http://docs.chmuseums.org/Early_physicians.pdf.

65. Findagrave.com, "Infant Daughter Bratton," from Find a Grave website, accessed July 2, 2015, http://www.findagrave.com/cgi-bin/fg.cgi?page=gr &GSln=Bratton&GSfn=+&GSiman =1&GScid=2179680&GRid=132998741&. Website shows tombstone of Martha Bratton and indicates this infant is one of three unknown infants buried in the same plot.

66. Culture & Heritage Museums, "Colonel William Bratton House, 1760s," from Culture & Heritage Museums website, accessed June 19, 2015, http://chmuseums.org/historic-structures-hb/#s2. Hereafter cited as Colonel Bratton House.

67. See list of civil service position held in appendix A, William Bratton's Military and Civil Service, compiled by Michael C. Scoggins, December 2008.

68. Michael C. Scoggins, "The Life and Times of William Bratton, Part 4," paragraph 9.

69. Jerome Nadelhaft, "The'Havoc of War' and its Aftermath in Revolutionary South Carolina," vol. 12, no. 23 (1979): 108, from *Histoire Sociale* website, accessed August 24, 2015, http://hssh.journals.yorku.ca/index.php/hssh/article /view/38975/35363.

70. Ibid., 118.

71. Michael C. Scoggins, "The Life and Times of William Bratton, Part 4," paragraph 11.

72. Pettus, Louise, "William Hills Iron Plantation," from Rootsweb website, accessed August 20, 2015, http://www.rootsweb.ancestry.com/~scyork/LouisePettus/whill.htm.

73. "William Bratton," *Biographical Directory of the United States Congress, 1774–984, Bicentennial Edition*, (United States Government Printing Office, 1989), South Carolina Department of Archives and History, Columbia, SC, 182–183.

74. Ibid.

75. Colonel Bratton House.

76. "Will of William Bratton," South Carolina Department of Archives and History, Columbia, SC, South Carolina Will Transcripts, microcopy, estate packet, case no. 9, file 378 (3 frames).

77. Ibid.

78. "William Bratton Estate Inventory," transcribed by Michael C. Scoggins, *York County Inventories, Appraisement and Sales Book 1, 1813–1828*, 67.

79. The Bratton Family, "The Bratton Family: David Sadler," from www1.tribalpages.com website, accessed September 17, 2015, http://www1.tribalpages.com/tribe/rowse?view=0&rand=349780939&pid=1239&userid=jbratton; Michael C. Scoggins, *The Day it Rained Militia: Huck's Defeat and the Revolution in the South Carolina Backcountry, May–July 1780*, Charleston, SC: History Press, 2005, kindle edition, location 3575.

80. Culture & Heritage Museums, "The Brattons: A Family of Physicians," from Culture & Heritage Museums website, accessed May 24, 2015, http://docs.chmuseums.org/Brattons_Family_of_Physicans.pdf.

81. Joseph H. Rainey. "The Bratton Family at the Homestead: A Personal Look," 1. Unpublished four-page document located in Bratton Family Collection, Fairfield County Museum, Winnsboro, SC.

82. Ibid., paragraph 1.

83. Culture & Heritage Museums, "African American History," from Culture & Heritage Museums website, accessed June 19, 2015, http://chmuseums.org/african-american-history-hb/.

84. "Rooted in Brattonsville," *The Herald*, December 24, 2008, from the Herald Online website, accessed April 24, 2015, http://www.heraldonline.com/news/local/article12245525.html.

85. "William Bratton Biography and Obituary," transcribed by Michael C. Scoggins, 1–2.

CHAPTER TWO
General John Bratton

1.   Fairfield County, SC, "History of Fairfield County," paragraphs 5–6, from Fairfield County, SC, website, accessed September 3, 2015, http://fairfieldchamber .sc/viewPage.php?ID=History#winnsboro.

2.   Fitz Hugh McMaster, *History of Fairfield County South Carolina: From "Before the White Man Came" to 1942* (Spartanburg, SC: Reprint Company Publishers, 1980), 6. Cited hereafter as McMaster, *History of Fairfield County*.

3.   *Cyclopedia of Eminent and Representative Men of the Carolinas of the Nineteenth Century,*vol. 1 (Madison, WI: Brant and Fuller, 1892), 433–34. Hereafter cited as *Cyclopedia of Eminent and Representative Men*.

4.   The Bratton Family, "The Bratton Family: Bratton, William (Jr)," from The Bratton Family website, accessed May 24, 2015, http://www1.tribalpages. com/tribe/browse?userid=jbratton&view=0&pid=1166&ver=456#moreinfo_. Sources listed on website: Acts & Resolutions, 1831, 25. Book X, 123; Census, 1800, York Dist., 962; Census, 1810, Fairfield Dist., 181; Census, 1820, Fairfield Dist., 158; Census, 1830, Fairfield Dist., 355; Census, 1850, Fairfield Dist., 238; Fairfield County (WPA) Epitaps, Sion Presbyterian Church, E48:24; Brent Holcomb, York, South Carolina, Newspaper Marriage & Death Notices, 1823-1865 (Spartanburg, SC, 1981),12; House Committee Book, 1820, 1822; SCHM, 44: 151; 72: 179.

5.   "Index of Implied Families of Fairfield County, SC," from Deed Books 1785–1884," compiled by Linda M. Malone, August 2002, from the Fairfield County Museum, Genealogical Resource Library, Winnsboro, SC.

6.   *Cyclopedia of Eminent and Representative Men*, 434. A statement is made that Dr. Bratton and Christine Winn had four children, but I have only been able to locate information on the three that are buried in Winnsboro; Email from Michael Scoggins to Fairfield Museum (Winnsboro, SC) dated May 26, 2013, and found in the Bratton Family Files there states, "According to my information, there were four children born to [William Bratton] and three by his second wife ... " but no source is cited.

7.   Ibid., 434. Means was Isabella's maiden name. Her father was John Means, who moved with his parents from Boston, Massachusetts to South Carolina; Rootsweb, "Facts for Hilliard Judge (1787–1820)," from Rootsweb website, accessed September 16, 2015, http://freepages.genealogy.rootsweb.ancestry. com/~klfowler/Refs_Judge_Hilliard_1787.html.

8.   South Carolina Probate Court (Fairfield County), *Miscellaneous Probate Records, 1780-1868; General Index, 1780–1865*, 71–74, Fairfield, SC. This four-page Last Will and Testament by Isabella J. Bratton dated August 20, 1847, appears to have been written in her handwriting and mentions the names of her children, including deceased son Hillard M. Judge. It also refers to her son, John, as John M. Bratton. Hereafter cited as Isabella Bratton's Will.

9.   Ancestry.com, 1830 United States Federal Census; Census Place: Fairfield, South Carolina; Series: M19; Roll: 169; Page: 356; Family History Library Film: 0022503, from Ancestry.com website (Provo, UT: Ancestry.com Operations, Inc., 2009); 1840 United States Federal Census; Census Place: Fairfield, South Carolina; Roll: 511; Page: 151; Image: 312; Family History Library Film: 0022509, from Ancestry.com website (Provo, UT: Ancestry.com Operations, Inc., 2010), accessed September 17, 2015, http://person.ancestry.com/tree/78639377/person/44389357851/facts.

10.   McMaster, *History of Fairfield County*, 31.

11.   United States Congress, "John Bratton." *Biographical Directory of the United States Congress, 1774–1984, Bicentennial Edition* (United States Government Printing Office, 1989), 180, South Carolina Department of Archives and History, Columbia, SC. Hereafter cited as Bratton, *Biographical Directory of the United States Congress*.

12.   Culture & Heritage Museums, "The Brattons: A Family of Physicians," from Culture & Heritage Museums website, accessed May 24, 2015, http://docs.chmuseums.org/Brattons_Family_of_Physicans.pdf; "Gen. Bratton Dead," *The News and Herald* (Winnsboro, SC), January 19, 1868, from the Library of Congress website Chronicling America: Historic American Newspapers, accessed May 25, 2015, http://chroniclingamerica.loc.gov/lccn/2012218613/1898-01-19/ed-1/seq-2.pdf.

13.   Encyclopedia.com, "1850–1877: Science and Medicine: Overview," *American Eras, 1997*, accessed September 6, 2015, http://www.encyclopedia.com/doc/1G2-2536601487.html.

14.   Elaine G. Breslaw, "What Was Healthcare Like in the 1800s?" from History News Network website, accessed September 6, 2015, http://historynewsnetwork.org/article/149661.

15.   Isabella Bratton's Will, 71.

16.   Luke J. Austin, *General John Bratton: Sumter to Appomattox, in Letters to His Wife*, (Sewanee, TN: Proctor's Hall Press, 2003), 3. Hereafter cited as *General John Bratton*; "Fairfield County, South Carolina: Largest Slaveholders from 1860 Slave Census," transcribed by Tom Blake, 2001, from Rootsweb website, accessed September 17, 2015, http://freepages.genealogy.rootsweb.ancestry.com/~ajac/scfairfield.htm.

17.   US Genweb Archives, "Statewide Marriage Records: Marriage Records, 1844-1860," compiled by Paul R. Sarrett Jr. and submitted on December 1997, extracted from the *South Carolina Magazine of Ancestral Research*, Vol 11, no. 2, 4, from US Genweb Archives website, accessed September 15, 2015, http://www.usgwarchives.net/sc/statewide/marriages.htm.

18.   Theodore DuBose Bratton, *An Apostle of Reality; the Life and Thought of the Reverend William Porcher DuBose*, (London, New York: Longmans, Green and Company, 1936), 3–4, a series of lectures on the DuBose Foundation, delivered at The University of the South by the Rt. Rev. Theodore DuBose Bratton. Hereafter cited as Bratton, *Apostle of Reality*.

19.   Library of Congress, "Jim Henry, Ex-Slave, 77 Years Old," *Slave Narratives: A Folk History of Slavery in the United States From Interviews with Former Slaves, 1936-1938*, vol. 14, part 2: 266–270, South Carolina Narratives, Prepared by the Federal Writers' Project of the Works Progress Administration, from the *Library of Congress* website, accessed July 7, 2015, http://memory.loc.gov/mss/mesn/142/142.pdf.

20.   Library of Congress, "Phillip Evans, Ex-Slave, 85 Years Old," *Slave Narratives: A Folk History of Slavery in the United States From Interviews with Former Slaves, 1936–1938*, vol. 14, part 2: 34–37, South Carolina Narratives, Prepared by the Federal Writers' Project of the Works Progress Administration, Library of Congress, accessed July 7, 2015, http://memory.loc.gov/mss/mesn/142/142.pdf.

21.   Ibid. Refers to this quote and all information and quotes in the four preceding paragraphs.

22.   Library of Congress, "Louisa Davis. Ex-Slave 106 Years Old." *Born in Slavery: Slave Narratives from the Federal Writers' Project, 1936-1938*, vol. 14, part 1: 299–303, South Carolina Narratives, Prepared by the Federal Writers' Project of the Works Progress Administration, Library of Congress, accessed July 20, 2015, http://memory.loc.gov/cgi-bin/ampage?collId=mesn&fileName=141/mesn141.db&recNum=301&itemLink=D?mesnbib:1:./temp/~ammem_Vqjs:: Cited hereafter as Davis, *Slave Narratives*.

23.   Ibid.

24.   Library of Congress, "Ned Walker, Ex-Slave 83 Years Old." *Born in Slavery: Slave Narratives from the Federal Writers' Project, 1936–1938*, vol. 14, part 4: 174-180, South Carolina Narratives, Prepared by the Federal Writers' Project of the Works Progress Administration, Library of Congress, accessed July 20, 2015. http://memory.loc.gov/cgi-bin/ampage?collId=mesn&fileName=144/mesn144.db&recNum=177&itemLink=D?mesnbib:1:./temp/~ammem_u4Dn::

25.   Personal email received from Elliot Bratton on October 4, 2015. Reference refers to entire paragraph, including quotes. See Appendix D for complete narrative by Elliot Bratton.

26.   David M. Potter, *The Impending Crisis, 1848–1861: America Before the Civil War* (New York: Harper Collins, 2011), 44-45.

27.   *General John Bratton*, 5–6.

28.   Ibid, 5–23.

29.   Ibid. Quote is on p. 10; "Hon. John Bratton," *Cyclopedia of Eminent and Representative Men of the Carolinas of the Nineteenth Century*, vol. I (Madison, WI: Brant and Fuller, 1892), 434.

30.   *General John Bratton*, 29–30.

31.   John Bratton to Bettie Bratton, July 23, 1861, "Confederate War Letters of General John Bratton," 1861–1865 (unpublished collection of letters), Southern Historical Collection, University of North Carolina. Letters written from John to Bettie Bratton, his wife, during the Civil War. Hereafter cited as Bratton, "Confederate War Letters," with the date of the letter.

32.   Bratton, "Confederate War Letters," September 5, 1861.

33.   *Cyclopedia of Eminent and Representative Men of the Carolinas of the Nineteenth Century*, "Hon. John Bratton," vol. I (Madison, WI: Brant and Fuller, 1892), 434. Refers to quote only; *General John Bratton*, 47–51.

34.   *General John Bratton*, 67.

35.   Ibid., 71–73.

36.   Ibid., 81–93. This and preceding paragraph.

37.   Shelby Foote, *The Civil War, : A Narrative*, (New York: Random House, 1963), 3 vols., 2: 234–35, 38. Hereafter cited as Foote, *The Civil War*.

38.   *General John Bratton*, 93–94.

39.   "The Late Capt William M. Bratton," *The Yorkville Inquirer* (Yorkville, SC), July 17, 1862, from the Library of Congress, Chronicling America: Historic American Newspapers, accessed September 10, 2015, http://chroniclingamerica.loc.gov/lccn/sn84026925/1862-07-17/ed-1/seq-2/.

40.   *General John Bratton*, 101–102.

41.   Ibid., 108–110.

42.   Bratton, "Confederate War Letters," December 26 and 27, 1862. Last two sentences.

43.   *General John Bratton*, 113–115.

44.   Ibid., 166–123.

45. Mark St. John Erickson, "Siege of Suffolk, Envelops Hampton Roads," *Daily Press*, April 14, 2013, accessed September 11, 2015, http://articles.dailypress.com/2013-04-14/features /dp-nws-civil-war-siege-of-suffolk-20130414_1_suffolk-malvern-hill-confederate.

46. Foote, *The Civil War*, 2: 569–584.

47. Bratton, "Confederate War Letters," October 16, 1863.

48. *General John Bratton*, 151–158.

49. Ibid., 163–177.

50. Bratton, "Confederate War Letters," January 4–9, 1864.

51. *Cyclopedia of Eminent and Representative Men of the Carolinas*, 1: 45 (Madison, Wis: Brant and Fuller), 1892.

52. Foote, *The Civil War*, 3: 188–189.

53. Ibid., 241–242.

54. "Cold Harbor National Cemetery, Mechanicsville, Virginia," from the National Park Service website, accessed September 14, 2015, http://www.nps.gov /nr/travel/national_cemeteries/virginia/Cold_Harbor_National_Cemetery.html.

55. *General John Bratton*, 214.

56. Bratton, "Confederate War Letters," June 5 and June 8, 1864.

57. *General John Bratton*, 216–241.

58. Bratton, "Confederate War Letters," January 27, 1865.

59. William Ederington and B. H. Rosson, "Sherman in Winnsboro," *History of Fairfield County, South Carolina* (Charleston, SC: Nabu Press, 2010), 19.

60. "Ravages of the Enemy in South Carolina," *The Daily Dispatch* (Richmond, VA), March 30, 1865, Library of Congress, Chronicling America, accessed September 15, 2015, http://chroniclingamerica.loc.gov/lccn /sn84024738/1865-03-30/ed-1/seq-2/; "Fairfield Remembers Sherman," Fairfield County Genealogy Society Special Edition Newsletter 2015, vol. 26, no. 1, January 2015, 8-14.

61. Julian Stevenson Bolick, *A Fairfield Sketchbook* (Clinton, SC: Jacobs Brothers, circa 1963), 144.

62. Foote: *The Civil War*, 2: 893–894.

63. Ibid., 912–930.

64.   Southern Historical Society, *Paroles Of The Army Of Northern Virginia: R. E. Lee, Gen., C.S.A., Commanding, Surrendered At Appomattox C. H., Va., April 9, 1865, to Lieutenant General U. S. Grant, Commanding Armies Of The U. S.,* vol. 15, 144 (CreateSpace Independent Publishing Platform, June 21, 2012); *Cyclopedia of Eminent and Representative Men of the Carolinas,* 1: 45 (Madison, WI: Brant and Fuller, 1892).

65.   "Hon. John Bratton," *Cyclopedia of Eminent and Representative Men of the Carolinas of the Nineteenth Century,* vol. I (Madison, WI: Brant and Fuller, 1892), 435.

66.   Ancestry.com, "Confederate Applications for Presidential pardons, 1865–1867," Original data: Case Files of Applications From Former Confederates for Presidential Pardons ("Amnesty Papers"); 1865–1867; (National Archives Microfilm Publication M1003, 73 rolls); Records of the Adjutant General's Office, 1780's–1917, Record Group 94; National Archives, Washington, D.C., from Ancestry.com (Provo, UT: Ancestry.com Operations Inc., 2008), accessed September 17, 2015, http://person.ancestry.com/tree/78639377 /person/44389357850/facts.

67.   *New York Times,* "Reconstruction in South Carolina," *New York Times,* September 13, 1865, from *New York Times* website, accessed May 21, 2015, http://www.nytimes.com/1865/09/13/news/reconstruction-in-south-carolina .html.

68.   Bratton, *Apostle of Reality,* 72.

69.   Ibid., 74-75.

70.   Julian Stevenson Bolick, *A Fairfield Sketchbook,* (Clinton, SC: Jacobs Brothers, circa 1963), 11.

71.   Fitz Hugh McMaster, "Low Country Families Influence Fairfield," *State,* July 31, 1938, from YCL Digital Collections, accessed September 16, 2015, https://dspace.ychistory.org/bitstream/handle/11030/71212/00001054.pdf?sequence=1 . Refers to sentence preceding quote; "Ella E. Gooding, 80 Years Old (White) and Robert C. Gooding, 82 Years Old (White)," *Slave Narratives: A Folk History of Slavery in the United States, 1936–1938,* 4, *Library of Congress,* accessed April 30, 2015, http://www.loc.gov/resource/wpalh3.30082108. Refers to quote.

72.   United States Congress, "Bratton," *Biographical Directory of the United States Congress,* 180.

73.   Danielle DuBose, (unnamed article), Fairfield Genealogical Society Newsletter, vol. 20, no. 4 (December 2007), 2.

74. Wynne Dee Plantation was inherited by John Bratton from his mother. It is unclear when or if he owned Canaan Plantation, but his ownership was mentioned in a June 22, 2015 interview with one of his descendants, Johnny Bratton, of Raleigh, N.C., and during an interview with Phillip Evans, ex-slave in "Jim Henry, Ex-Slave, 77 Years Old," *Slave Narratives: A Folk History of Slavery in the United States From Interviews with Former Slaves, 1936-1938*, vol. 14, South Carolina Narratives, part 2, 266-270, Library of Congress, accessed July 7, 2015, http://memory.loc.gov/mss/mesn/142/142.pdf; and the name "Bratton" is listed as owner of Canaan Plantation on the South Carolina Plantations website: http://south-carolina-plantations.com/fairfield/canaan.html.

75. "DuBose Genealogy," compiled by Dorothy Kelly MacDowell, (unpublished manuscript, n.d.), 232, Bratton Family Collection, Fairfield County Museum, Winnsboro, SC.

76. Sharon Goff Avery, *History of Saint John's Episcopal Church, Winnsboro, South Carolina, 1839–1989* (Spartanburg, SC: The Reprint Company, 1995), 324.

77. Bratton, *Biographical Directory of the United States Congress*, 180.

78. Michael Trinkley, "South Carolina African Americans: Major Events in Reconstruction Politics," from SCIWAY website, accessed September 22, 2015, http://www.sciway.net/afam/reconstruction/majorevents.html.

79. Richard Zuckzek, *State of Rebellion: Reconstruction in South Carolina*, (Columbia, SC: University of South Carolina Press, 1966), 11.

80. "Articles of Agreement" [Freedman's Agreement] between John S. Bratton and the Freedman or Freedmen residing on his plantation. Copy found at Fairfield County Museum, Winnsboro, SC, June 25, 2015, Bratton Family Collection.

81. Lisa M. Bratton, "Green and Matilda Bratton: From Enslavement to Land Ownership in Historic Brattonsville," (unpublished booklet sold at Historic Brattonsville, McConnells, SC), 31.

82. "Constitutional Convention, 1868," *Constitution of 1868*, S 131081, State Department of Archives and History, Columbia, South Carolina.

83. "The Conservative Convention," *The Yorkville Inquirer* (Yorkville, SC), November 14, 1867, from the Library of Congress, Chronicling America: Historic American Newspapers website, accessed September 23, 2015, http://chroniclingamerica.loc.gov/lccn/sn84026925/1867-11-14/ed-1/seq-2/.

84. "The Conservative Convention: Address to the People of South Carolina," *The Charleston Daily News*, vol. 5, no. 694, From the Library of Congress, Chronicling America: Historic American Newspapers website, accessed September 23, 2015, http://chroniclingamerica.loc.gov/lccn/sn84026994/1867-11-09/ed-1/seq-1.pdf.

85. Ibid. This paragraph, including quotations.

86. Ibid., Chestnut quotation.

87. Ibid., Hamilton quotation.

88. Bratton, *Biographical Directory*, 181; "Standing Committees of the [SC] Senate, 1866," (South Carolina: General Assembly, 1866), from the South Carolina Library, Digital Collections website, accessed September 22, 2015, http://digital.tcl.sc.edu/cdm/ref/collection/bro/id/1099.

89. John Bratton, "Letter to the Soldiers' Meeting at Walhalla," *The Tri-Weekly News* (Winnsboro, SC), from the Library of Congress, Chronicling America: Historic American Newspapers website, accessed October 1, 2015, http://chroniclingamerica.loc.gov/lccn/sn84026922/1866-10-18/ed-1/seq-2/.

90. "Meeting of the Fairfield Soldiers' Relief Association" *The Daily Phoenix* (Columbia, SC), from the Library of Congress, Chronicling America: Historic American Newspapers website, accessed April 24, 2014, http://chroniclingamerica.loc.gov/lccn/sn84027008/1868-09-16/ed-1/seq-1/.

91. Bratton, *Biographical Directory*, 181.

92. Lou Falkner Williams, *The Great South Carolina Ku Klux Klan Trials, 1871–1872* (Athens, GA: University of Georgia Press, 2004), 19. Hereafter cited as Williams, *The Klan.*

93. Library of Congress, "Ella E. Gooding, 80 Years Old (White) and Robert C. Gooding, 82 Years Old (White)," *Slave Narratives: A Folk History of Slavery in the United States, 1936-1938*, 3-4, from the *Library of Congress* website, accessed April 30, 2015, http://www.loc.gov/resource/wpalh3.30082108.

94. Williams, *The Klan*, 20–29.

95. "Life History of Gen. Bratton," *The News and Herald* (Winnsboro, SC), September 19, 1935. This and quote in previous paragraph. Copy of article courtesy of John Bratton, Sewanee, TN. Refers to quotes and information in paragraph.

96. Bratton, *Biographical Directory*, 181.

97. *Tax-payers' Convention of South Carolina: Columbia* (Charleston, SC: E. Perry, printer, 1871), HathiTrust Digital Library, pdf, accessed October 2, 2015, http://hdl.handle.net/2027/loc.ark:/13960/t5m90h585; Tax-payers' Convention of South Carolina: Columbia (Charleston, SC: The News and Courier Job Presses, 1874), accessed October 2, 2015, http://hdl.handle.net/2027/loc.ark:/13960/t5m90h585.

98. R. Means Davis, ed., "Wednesday Morning: December 16, 1874," (*Fairfield Herald* (Winnsboro, SC), December 16, 1874, from the Library of Congress, Chronicling America: Historic American Newspapers website, accessed May 25, 2015, http://chroniclingamerica.loc.gov/lccn/sn84026923/1874-12-16/ed-1/seq-2/pdf. Indented quote and quote in preceding paragraph.

99. "Death of Mrs. John Bratton," *The Fairfield Herald*, June 30, 1875, from the Library of Congress, Find a Grave website, accessed April 24, 2015, http://chroniclingamerica.loc.gov/lccn/sn84026923/1875-06-30/ed-1/seq-3/.

100. "Democratic Convention," *The Fairfield Herald* (Winnsboro, SC), April 25, 1876, from the Library of Congress website Chronicling America: Historic American Newspapers website, accessed April 25, 2015, http://chroniclingamerica .loc.gov/lccn/sn84026923/1876-04-26/ed-1/seq-3.pdf.

101. "Wednesday, August 16," *Yorkville Enquirer* (Yorkville, SC), August 24, 1876, from the Library of Congress, Chronicling America: Historic American Newspapers website, accessed April 25, 2015, http://chroniclingamerica.loc.gov /lccn/sn84026925/1876-08-24/ed-1/seq-3/.

102. Richard Zuckzek, *State of Rebellion: Reconstruction in South Carolina*. Columbia, SC: University of South Carolina Press, 1966, 159–188. Hereafter cited as Zucknez, *State of Rebellion*; William Arthur Sheppard, *Red Shirts Remembered: Southern Brigadiers of the Reconstruction Period* (Atlanta, GA: Printed by Ruralsit Press, Inc., 1940), 122.

103. Davis, *Slave Narratives*, 300.

104. Zucknez, *State of Rebellion*, 188–210.

105. William R. Cooper, *The Conservative Regime: South Carolina, 1877–1890* (Baton Rouge: Louisiana State University Press, 1991). Quote is found on p. 34, the remainder of the reference on p. 33. Hereafter cited as Cooper, *The Conservative Regime*.

106. Bratton, *Biographical Directory*, 181.

107. "Former Comptroller," SC Comptroller General, from the South Carolina Comptroller General website, accessed April 2, 2015, http://www.cg.sc.gov /meetcgeckstrom/Pages/formercomptrollers.aspx. Former sentence.; "For Governor: General John Bratton," *The Newberry Herald and News* (Newberry, SC), June 9, 1886, from the Library of Congress, Chronicling America: Historic American Newspapers website, accessed May 25, 2015, http://chroniclingamerica .loc.gov/lccn/sn93067777/1886-06-09/ed-1/seq-2/. Latter sentence and quote.

108. "The State Convention," *The Anderson Intelligencer* (Anderson Court house, SC), August 10, 1882, from the Library of Congress, Chronicling America: Historic American Newspapers website, accessed October 6, 2015, http://chroniclingamerica.loc.gov/lccn/sn84026965/1882-08-10/ed-1/seq-1.pdf.

109. Cooper, *The Conservative Regime*, 66–67.

110. Bratton, *Biographical Directory*, 181.

111. "The Hon. John G. Bratton," *Yorkville Inquirer* (Yorkville, SC), August 10, 1882, from the Library of Congress, Chronicling America: Historic American Newspapers website, accessed May 25, 2015, http://chroniclingamerica.loc.gov /lccn/sn84026925/1882-08-10/ed-1/seq-1.pdf ; "For Governor: General John Bratton," *The Newberry Herald and News* (Newberry, SC), June 9, 1886, from the Library of Congress, Chronicling America: Historic American Newspapers website, accessed May 25, 2015, http://chroniclingamerica.loc.gov/lccn /sn93067777/1886-06-09/ed-1/seq-2/.

112. "Local Items," *The Fairfield Herald* (Winnsboro, SC), January 5, 1876, from the Library of Congress, Chronicling America: Historic American Newspapers website, accessed July 24, 2015, http://chroniclingamerica.loc.gov/lccn/sn84026923 /1876-01-05/ed-1/seq-3.pdf

113. "Flocks and Herds," *The News and Herald* (Winnsboro, SC), August 23, 1877, from the Library of Congress, Chronicling America: Historic American Newspapers website, accessed July 7, 2015, http://chroniclingamerica.loc.gov/lccn /sn93067705/1877-08-23/ed-1/seq-1.pdf.

114. Kristina A. Shuler and Ralph Bailey Jr., "A History of the Phosphate Mining Industry in the South Carolina Lowcountry," (Mount Pleasant, SC), from the nationalregister.sc.gov website, accessed October 6, 2015, http://nationalregister .sc.gov/SurveyReports/hyphosphatesindustryLowcountry2SM.pdf.

115. Ibid; E. B. Murray, ed., "Thursday Morning, January 23, 1879," *The Anderson Intelligencer (Anderson County Courthouse, SC)*, from the Library of Congress, Chronicling America: Historic American Newspapers website, accessed May 25, 2015, http://chroniclingamerica.loc.gov/lccn/sn84026965/1879-01-23/ed-2 /seq-2.pdf. Refers to first quote. "Phosphates Commissioner and Agent," *The Yorkville Enquirer, (Yorkville, SC)*, December 4, 1879, from the Library of Congress, Chronicling America: Historic American Newspapers website, Accessed May 25, 2015, http://chroniclingamerica.loc.gov./lccn/sn84026925/1879-12-04/ed-1 /seq-1.pdf. Refers to second quote.

116. Cooper, *The Conservative Regime*, 119–125.

117. Bratton, *Biographical Directory*, 181.

118. Cooper, *The Conservative Regime*, 43 (quote), 159.

119. Encylopedia.com, "Farmers' Protest Movements: 1870–1900," *Gale Enclyclopedia of U.S. Economic History, 1999*, from the Encyclopedia.com website, 2000, accessed October 13, 2015, http://www.encyclopedia.com/doc/1G2-3406400307.html.

120. Faust, Patricia L., ed., *Historical Times Illustrated Encyclopedia of the Civil War* (New York, 1986), 125.

121. Cooper, *The Conservative Regime*, 206. Quote from the *News and Courier*, June 13, 1890.

122. *Encyclopaedia Britannica*, "Benjamin R. Tillman," from the Encyclopaedia Britannica website, accessed October 13, 2015, http://www.britannica.com /EBchecked/topic/595880/Benjamin-R-Tillman.

123. Cooper, *The Conservative Regime*, 168–172.

124. Ibid., 172.

125. Bratton, *Biographical Directory*, 181. First part of sentence ending in 1894; "South Carolina Democrats," California Digital Newspaper Collection, *Los Angeles Herald*, vol. 42, no. 162, September 1894, accessed October 13, 2014, http://cdnc.ucr.edu/cgi-bin/cdnc?a=d&d=LAH18940920.2.8.

126. "Piedmont Colonization Society," *Yorkville Enquirer* (Yorkville, SC), September 26, 1894, from the Library of Congress website Chronicling America: Historic American Newspapers website, accessed October 14, 2015, http://chroniclingamerica.loc.gov/lccn/sn84026925/1894-09-26/ed-1/seq-3.pdf. Refers to latter sentence.

127. Bratton, *Biographical Directory*, 181. Last sentence of paragraph.

128. "Life History of Gen. Bratton," *The News and Herald* (Winnsboro, SC), September 19, 1935. Copy of article courtesy of John Bratton, Sewanee, TN.

129. "Fine Plantations for Sale," *Fairfield County Genealogy Society Newsletter*, vol. 11, no. 3, September 1998, 12. Reprinted from *The Fairfield Herald* (Winnsboro, SC), September 22, 1889.

130. "Dr. William D. Bratton," *The Fairfield News and Herald* (Winnsboro, SC), October 6, 1896, accessed June 9, 2015, http://chroniclingamerica.loc.gov /lccn/2012218613/1897-10-06/ed-1/seq-3/. Hereafter cited as Dr. William D. Bratton, *The Fairfield News and Herald*.

131. "South Carolina's Sponsor," *Fairfield News and Herald* (Winnsboro, SC), June 30, 1897, from the Library of Congress website Chronicling America: Historic American Newspapers *website*, accessed October 14, 2015, http://chroniclingamerica.loc.gov/lccn/2012218613/1897-06-30/ed-1/seq-2.pdf.

132. "A Tribute," *The Fairfield News and Herald* (Winnsboro, SC), October 13, 1897, from the Library of Congress website Chronicling America: Historic American Newspapers *website*, accessed June 9, 2015, http://chroniclingamerica. loc.gov/lccn/2012218613/1897-10-13/ed-1/seq-3.pdf.

133. "Gen. Bratton Dead: Fairfield's Most Distinguished Citizen Passes Away Suddenly," *Fairfield News and Herald*, June 19, 1898, from the Library of Congress website Chronicling America: Historic American Newspapers *website*, accessed June 9, 2015, http://chroniclingamerica.loc.gov/lccn/2012218613 /1898-01-19/ed-1/seq-2.pdf. Reference refers to indented quote and quotes in preceding paragraph.

134. "Life History of Gen. Bratton," *The News and Herald* (Winnsboro, SC), September 19, 1935. Refers to indented quote, as well as quotes in preceding paragraph. Copy of article courtesy of John Bratton, Sewanee, TN.

135. Ibid; Ancestry.com, *South Carolina Wills and Probate Records, 1670–1980*, Fairfield County, South Carolina Estate Papers, Ca. 1865–1915; Probate Court, Fairfield, South Carolina, from Ancestry.com (Provo, UT: Ancestry.com Operations, 2015), accessed September 17, 2015, http://person.ancestry.com/tree/78639377/person/44389357850/facts.

Chapter Three
The Rt. Rev. Theodore DuBose Bratton

1. Holly Wilberforce Wells, *Recollections of Theodore DuBose Bratton* (Vicksburg, MS: All Saints' Episcopal College, 1951), 5. Hereafter cited as Wells, *Recollections*.

2. "Fairfield County, South Carolina: Largest Slaveholders from 1860 Slave Census," transcribed by Tom Blake, 2001, from the Rootsweb website, accessed September 17, 2015, http://freepages.genealogy.rootsweb.ancestry.com/~ajac/scfairfield.htm.

3. Theodore DuBose Bratton, *An Apostle of Reality; the Life and Thought of the Reverend William Porcher DuBose*, S.T.D., D.C.L., A series of lectures on the DuBose Foundation, delivered at The University of the South by the Rt. Rev. Theodore DuBose Bratton (London, New York: Longmans, Green and Company, 1936.), 5. Hereafter cited as Bratton, *An Apostle of Reality*.

4. Frederick Sullens, *Jackson Daily News*, June 27, 1944, 7.

5. Bratton, *An Apostle of Reality*, 22.

6. Ibid., 17.

7. Ibid., 79.

8. Ancestry.com and The Church of Jesus Christ of Latter-day Saints, "1880 United States Federal Census" from Ancestry.com (Provo, UT: Ancestry.com Operations, 2010), accessed September 17, 2015, http://person.ancestry.com/tree/78639377/person/44392222322/facts.

9. Mark A. Noll, *A History of Christianity in the United States and Canada* (Grand Rapids, MI: W. B. Edermans, circa 1992), 286–310.

10. David L. Holmes, *A Brief History of the Episcopal Church* (Valley Forge, PA: Trinity Press International, circa 1993), 80. Hereafter cited as Holmes, *Episcopal Church*.

11. Rowland, *Heart of the South*, vol. 2, 596.

12. Bratton, *An Apostle of Reality*, 93.

13. Sydney E. Ahlstrom, *A Religious History of the American People* (New Haven: Yale University Press, circa 2004), 726–727.

14. Ibid., 85.

15. Ibid., 116.

16. Bratton, *An Apostle of Reality*, v.

17. Ibid., 137.

18. Martha Stoops, *The Heritage: The Education of Women at St. Mary's College, Raleigh, North Carolina, 1842–1982* (Raleigh, NC: Saint Mary's College, 1984), 136. Hereafter cited as Martha Stoops, *The Heritage*.

19. Alex McKeigney, "Bratton Observes 36th Anniversary Here," name of newspaper unknown, n.d.(circa 1939), copy of newspaper article courtesy of John Gass Bratton, Sewanee, TN.

20. Dunbar Rowland, *History of Mississippi, Heart of the South*, vol. 4 (Spartanburg, SC: The Reprint Co., 1978), 678. Includes quote and information in preceding paragraph. Hereafter cited as Rowland, *Heart of the South*.

21. Theodore D. Bratton, Vertical file, Mississippi Department of Archives and History, Jacksonville, MS, February 6, 1924. Hereafter cited as Bratton file, Mississippi Archives.

22. Personal communication (email), December 8, 2015. John Gass Bratton, a member of the Sewanee Trust for Historic Preservation, indicated that The University of the South Archives Department provided the information for the Trust.

23. "Theodore DuBose Bratton," Episcopal Church.org, from The Episcopal Church website, accessed November 6, 2015, http://www.episcopalchurch.org /library/glossary/bratton-theodore-dubose.

24. Rowland, *Heart of the South*, 679.

25. Sharon Goff Avery, *History of Saint John's Episcopal Church, Winnsboro, South Carolina, 1839-1989* (Spartanburg, SC: The Reprint Company, 1995), 212; Rowland, *Heart of the South*, 679.

26. Wells, *Recollections*, 5-6.

27. John B. Edmunds, *The Episcopal Church of the Advent: History and Records, 1848–1998*, (Spartanburg, SC: The Reprint Company, 1998), 31. Hereafter cited as Edmunds, *The Episcopal Church of the Advent*.

28. South Carolina Department of Archives and History, "Church of the Advent, Spartanburg County," from the South Carolina Department of Archives and History website, accessed November 6, 2015, http://www.nationalregister .sc.gov/spartanburg/S10817742044/. Preceding paragraph except for first line.

29. Edmunds, *The Episcopal Church of the Advent*, 30.

30. "Brief History of the Church of the Advent," *Herald-Journal* (Spartanburg, SC), October 10, 1948.

31. Edmunds, *The Episcopal Church of the Advent*, 35.

32. Rowland, *Heart of the South*, 679.

33. South Carolina Department of Archives and History, "Converse College Historic District, Spartanburg County," from the South Carolina Department of Archives and History website, accessed November 8, 2015, http://www .nationalregister.sc.gov/spartanburg/S10817742013/.

34. Randolph Family Papers, 1820-1978, State Archives of Florida Online Catalogue, accessed November 6, 2015, http://archivescatalog.info.florida.gov/default.asp?IDCFile=/fsa/detailss .idc,SPECIFIC=2539,DATABASE=SERIES.

35. Holmes, *Episcopal Church*, 76–78. Refers to preceding sentence.

36. "Circular Announcing Death of Passed Assistant Surgeon W. D. Bratton, U.S. Marine Hospital Service," St. Louis Medical and Surgical Journal, Volumes 74–75, 119-120.

37. "Rev. T. D. Bratton Accepts," *The News and Herald* (Winnsboro, SC), June 3, 1899, from the Library of Congress, Chronicling America: Historic American Newspapers website, accessed July 5, 2015, http://chroniclingamerica.loc.gov/lccn /sn93067705/1899-06-03/ed-1/seq-4.pdf.

38. Martha Stoops, *The Heritage*, 136-137.

39. Mary Virginia Swain, "Founders' Day Honors 173 Years of Saint Mary's History," Saint Mary's School blog posted October 29, 2014, accessed November 9, 2015, http://www.sms.edu/news/item/index.aspx?LinkId=4235&ModuleId=34. Includes preceding quote.

40. Martha Stoops, *The Heritage*, 139.

41. Ibid.

42. Ibid., 141–149.

43. "St. Mary's High School and College," 1901, 1903, and 1904, from NCGenWebDigital Bookshelf website, accessed November 9, 2015, http://ncgenweb.us/nc/bookshelf/yearbooks/.

44. Sororityhistories.wordpress.com, "Alpha Kappa Psi-History through Alpha Chapter," accessed November 11, 2015, https://sororityhistories.wordpress.com/2015/05/13/alpha-kappa-psi-history-through-alpha-chapter/.

45. "St. Mary's High School and College," 1901, 1903, and 1904, from NCGenWebDigital Bookshelf website, accessed November 9, 2015, http://ncgenweb.us/nc/bookshelf/yearbooks/.

46. Episcopal Church, Diocese of Mississippi, *The Episcopal Church in Mississippi: 1763–1992* (Jackson: Episcopal Diocese of Mississippi, circa1992), 47. Hereafter cited as *The Episcopal Church in Mississippi.*

47. Ibid., 62.

48. Ibid., 73; Rowland, *Heart of the South*, vol. 2, 597.

49. Ibid., 79.

50. David Stetson Langdon, "The Episcopate of Theodore DuBose Bratton, Third Bishop of Mississippi." Thesis, University of the South, 1999, 81–82. Hereafter cited as Langdon, *The Episcopate of Theodore DuBose Bratton.*

51. Episcopal Church, Diocese of Mississippi. "Bishop's Address," *Journals of the Diocese of Mississippi: 1902–1945,* Jackson Archives, Jessie Ball DuPont Library, University of the South, Sewanee, TN, (1904), 43–50.

52. *The Episcopal Church in Mississippi,* 74.

53. 'Death of Mrs. Bratton," *Palestine Daily Herald (Palestine, TX),* January 7, 1905, from the Library of Congress, Chronicling America: Historic American Newspapers website, accessed January 19, 2016, http://chroniclingamerica.loc.gov/lccn/sn86090383/1905-01-07/ed-1/seq-3.pdf

54. Martha Stoops, *The Heritage,* 149.

55. Find a Grave, "Lucy Randolph Bratton," from Find a Grave website, accessed November 10, 2015, http://www.findagrave.com/cgi-bin/fg.cgi?page=gr&GRid=12908009.

56. "Bishop Bratton Weds," *Clarion Ledger* (Jackson, MS), July 22, 1906, Bratton file, Mississippi Archives.

57. "The Late Battle, *Abbeville Press and Banner (Abbeville, SC),*May 15, 1863, from the Library of Congress, Chronicling America: Historic American Newspapers website, accessed November 10, 2015, http://chroniclingamerica.loc.gov/lccn/sn85042527/1863-05-15/ed-1/seq-1.pdf.

58. Sharon Goff Avery, *History of Saint John's Episcopal Church, Winnsboro, South Carolina, 1839–1989* (Spartanburg, SC: The Reprint Company, 1995), 105. Refers to preceding sentence.

59. Ibid., 101. Cause of death provided by John Gass Bratton, Sewanee, TN, personal communication.

60.   Ivy Gass Bratton, biographical file, Department of Archives and Special Collections, Jessie Ball DuPont Library, University of the South, Sewanee, TN.

61.   *The Episcopal Church in Mississippi*, 76; Langdon, *The Episcopate of Theodore DuBose Bratton*, 46–47.

62.   Ibid.

63.   Martha Stoops, *The Heritage*, 149, cited from Walter B. Capers, "A Personal Tribute to Bishop Bratton," *Bulletin*, St. Andrews Episcopal Church, Jackson, MS, July 1944, 4.

64.   *The Episcopal Church in Mississippi*, 76.

65.   Ibid.

66.   I. A. Newby, ed., *The Development of Segregationist Thought, 1931–*. (Homewood, Ill: Dorsey Press, 1968), 106–107.

67.   Ibid.

68.   Theodore DuBose Bratton, "The Christian South and Negro Education," *Sewanee Review*, vol. xvi, July, 1908), 291–292. Hereafter cited as Bratton, *The Christian South and Negro Education*.

69.   Ibid., 294.

70.   Ibid.

71.   Shattuck, *Episcopalians and Race*, 23.

72.   Bishop Theodore DuBose Bratton, "Race Cooperation in Church Work," in *Battling for Social Betterment: Southern Sociological Congress, Memphis, Tennessee, May 6-10, 1914*, ed. James Edward McCullock, ed., 145–153. (Whitefish, MT: Kessinger Publishing, LLC, 2008), quotes on 147, 149, 152–153.

73.   Bishop Theodore D. Bratton, "An Open Door to Industry on the Basis of Efficiency," in *Democracy in Earnest, Southern Sociological Congress: 1916–1918*, James E. McCulloch, ed., 235–242 (Washington: Southern Sociological Congress, 1918), quotes on 237, 240–241.

74.   "Bishop Bratton Speaks," *Chicago Defender*, May 6, 1916, col. 3, microfilm copy, Davis Library, University of North Carolina.

75.   "Bill Introduced to Bar White Teachers: Bishop Bratton Addresses Letters to Author of Bill," *Chicago Defender*, February 26, 1916, 7, microfilm copy, Davis Library, University of North Carolina.

76.   Proquest.com, "Commission on Interracial Cooperation, 1919–1944," from the Proquest.com website, accessed March 20, 2016, http://www.proquest.com /products-services/Interracial-Cooperation-20.html.

77. "Life's Other Side," *Clayton's Weekly* (Seattle, WA), September 27, 1919, vol. 4, no. 15, from the Library of Congress, Chronicling America: Historic American Newspapers website, accessed July 20, 2015, http://chroniclingamerica .loc.gov/lccn/sn87093353/1919-09-27/ed-1/seq-1.pdf.

78. Dennis J. Mitchell, *A New History of Mississippi* (University Press of Mississippi, 2014) e-book preview, accessed October 27, 2015, https://books .google.com/books?id=zgAbBwAAQBAJ&pg=PT421&lpg=PT421&dq= Theodore+DuBose+Bratton+children&source=bl&ots=Ou5vjT6eJE&sig=Fzw HalyVe2UXcVnezJwsBHEwP0c&hl=en&sa=X&ved=0CDoQ6AEwBWoVC hMItcPh9oPkyAIVBjo-Ch29vgm0#v=onepage&q=Theodore%20DuBose%20 Bratton%20children&f=false.

79. Barbara Beadle Barber, *By Faith: A Century of Progress* (Bloomington, IN: iUniverse, Inc., 2009), 23.

80. Theodore DuBose Bratton, *Wanted-Leaders! A Study of Negro Development* (New York: Presiding Bishop and Council, Department of Missions and Church Extension, 1922), 218–219. Refers to indented quote and quote in previous paragraph.

81. Gardiner H. Shattuck, *Episcopalians and Race: Civil War to Civil Rights* (Lexington, KY: The University Press of Kentucky, 2000), 18. Hereafter cited as Shattuck, *Episcopalians and Race.*

82. Theodore DuBose Bratton, *Wanted-Leaders! A Study of Negro Development* (New York: Presiding Bishop and Council, Department of Missions and Church Extension, 1922), 228–229.

83. Rowland, *Heart of the South*, vol. 2, 506.

84. Shattuck, *Episcopalians and Race,* 20.

85. The Episcopal Church, "American Church Institute," from The Episcopal Church website, accessed November 18, 2015, http://www.episcopalarchives.org /Afro-Anglican_history/exhibit/divergence/acin.php.

86. *The Episcopal Church in Mississippi,* 77.

87. Lena Mitchel, "History of Okolona College Added to Mississippi Historical Trail," *Daily Journal Corinth Bureau*, posted July 27, 2014, accessed November 18, 2015, http://djournal.com/news /history-okolona-college-added-mississippi-historical-trail/.

88. *Journal of the Diocese of Mississippi: 1944,* epitaph in the Frontispiece containing Bishop Bratton's photograph and tribute.

89. "Bishop Bratton Visits Industrial School," *Okolona Messenger* (Okolona, MS), December 23, 1920, Chronicling America, from the Library of Congress, Chronicling America: Historic American Newspapers website, accessed November 16, 2015, http://chroniclingamerica.loc.gov/lccn/sn87065462/1920-12-23/ed-1 /seq-8.pdf.

90. *The Episcopal Church in Mississippi*, 80.

91. Dolly Dalrymple, "Bishop Bratton Says Womanhood Is Foundation of Civilization," circa 1919-1920, col. 4, unknown newspaper clipping courtesy of John Gass Bratton, Sewanee, TN. Hereafter cited as Dalrymple, "Womanhood."

92. *Southern Women and Race Cooperation. A Story of the Memphis Conference, October Sixth and Seventh, Nineteen Hundred and Twenty,*(Atlanta: Commission on Interracial Cooperation, 1921), first ed., electronic edition, accessed October 21, 2015, https://archive.org/details/southernwomenrac00comm.

93. *The Episcopal Church in Mississippi*, 80.

94. Dalrymple, "Womanhood," col. 3–4.

95. Rowland, *Heart of the South*, vol. 4, 679.

96. Sydney E. Ahlstrom, *A Religious History of the American People* (New Haven: Yale University Press, circa 2004), 889.

97. *The Episcopal Church in Mississippi*, 80.

98. Frederick Sullens, "Rites Planned Thursday for Bishop T. D. Bratton," *Jackson Daily*, June 27, 1944, Bratton file, Mississippi Archives.

99. Langdon, *The Episcopate of Theodore DuBose Bratton*, 32–38.

100. Ancestry.com, "William DuBose Bratton," U.S., World War I Draft Registration Cards, 1917-1918, from Ancestry.com (Provo, UT: Ancestry.com Operations, Inc., 2005), accessed September 17, 2015, http://person.ancestry.com /tree/78639377/person/44392228058/facts

101. Langdon, *The Episcopate of Theodore DuBose Bratton*, 95.

102. Ibid., 33.

103. *The Episcopal Church in Mississippi*, 82.

104. Langdon, *The Episcopate of Theodore DuBose Bratton*, 35.

105. *The Episcopal Church in Mississippi*, 83.

106. "Says Church Faces Plain Responsibility," *Lexington Dispatch-News*, September 17, 1919, from the Library of Congress, Chronicling America: Historic American Newspapers website, accessed July 17, 2015, http:// chroniclingamerica.loc.gov/lccn/sn92065503/1919-09-17/ed-1/seq-15.pdf. Refers to all quotes in paragraph.

107. *The Episcopal Church in Mississippi*, 84–86. Refers to all quotes in paragraph.

108. Ibid., 88.

109. Barbara Beadle Barber, *By Faith: A Century of Progress* (Bloomington, IN: iUniverse, Inc., 2009), 23.

110. *The Episcopal Church in Mississippi*, 88.

111. *Journals of the Diocese of Mississippi: 1912*, 72–73.

112. John Gass Bratton, personal communication (email), November 18, 2015.

113. Elizabeth N. Chitty, "Chancellors Nine and Ten: Bishop Theodore DuBose Bratton," *The Sewanee Mountain Messenger*, March 30, 2000.

114. John Gass Bratton, "Dr. Alexander Guerry," March 24, 2004, Theodore DuBose Bratton, Biographical file, Department of Archives and Special Collections, Jessie Ball DuPont Library, University of the South, Sewanee, TN.

115. Elizabeth N. Chitty, "Chancellors Nine and Ten: Bishop Theodore DuBose Bratton," *The Sewanee Mountain Messenger*, March 30, 2000.

116. Sewanee, The University of the South, "Previous Vice-Chancellors," Sewanee, from Sewanee, The University of the South website, accessed November 26, 2015, http://www.sewanee.edu/about/vc/previous-vice-chancellors/.

117. John Gass Bratton, personal communication (email) November 18, 2015.

118. Samuel R. Williamson, *Sewanee Sesquicentennial History: The Making of the University of the South* (Sewanee, TN: The University of the South, 2008), 177.

119. Reference to Rotary Club is contained in: Bratton file, Mississippi Archives, February 26, 1924; quote and remaining information taken from Rowland, *Heart of the South*, 679.

120. Interview by the author with James Lyles, Winnsboro, SC, June 25, 2015.

121. "War Veteran Dies By His Own Hand: Bratton Funeral Arrangements Pending Word From Bishop," Winnsboro, August 7, 1937, (name of newspaper unknown), copy of article courtesy of John Gass Bratton, Sewanee, TN. Refers to three preceding quotes in paragraph.

122. Bratton Family Collection, Fairfield County Museum, Winnsboro, SC. The file contains several letters to Eula, at least one to his son, Randolph, when Randolph was overseas during the war, and two or three to his sister, Isabel, all filled with much love and affection.

123. "The Rev. W. D. Bratton Takes Life in Plunge From Harrahan Bridge," name of newspaper unknown, n.d., copy of newspaper article from William DuBose Bratton Biographical file, Department of Archives and Special Collections, Jessie Ball DuPont Library, University of the South, Sewanee, TN.

124. Ivy Gass Bratton, Biographical file, Department of Archives and Special Collections, Jessie Ball duPont Library, University of the South, Sewanee, TN.

125. Theodore DuBose Bratton, "The Bishop's Message to the Council," January 18, 1938, Episcopal Church, Diocese of Mississippi, Council. *Journals of the Diocese of Mississippi 1938*, Jackson Archives, Jessie Ball DuPont Library, University of the South, Sewanee, TN.

126. "Bishop's Anniversary Celebration Monday: Rt. Rev. Theodore DuBose Bratton Has Served Diocese 27 Years; Recalls Happy Events," name of newspaper unknown, September 28, 1939, Bratton file, Mississippi Archives. Refers to all quotes in paragraph.

127. "Wife of Retired Mississippi Bishop Succumbs at Home of Daughter," *Delta Democrat Times (Greenville, MS)*, December 11, 1938, Bratton file, Mississippi Archives. Refers to all quotes in paragraph.

128. Frederick Sullens, "Rites Planned Thursday For Bishop T. D. Bratton," *Jackson Times*, n.d., Bratton file, Mississippi Archives.

129. "Services for Bishop Bratton Thursday From St. Andrews," *Clarion Ledger* (Jackson, MS), June 28, 1944.

130. "Bishop Bratton Dies at Jackson After Heart Attack," *Clarion Ledger*, (Jackson, MS), June 27, 1944, Bratton file, Mississippi Archives. This and preceding paragraph.

131. "Dr. Capers Pays High Tribute to Late Bishop Theodore D. Bratton," *Jackson Daily News* (Jackson, MS), July 4, 1944, Bratton file, Mississippi Archives.

132. Rev. James W. Emerson, "Bishop Theodore DuBose Bratton," *All Saints' Bulletin* (Tupelo, MS), July 13, 1944, Bratton file, Mississippi Archives.

133. P. I. Lipsey, "A Memorial to Bishop Bratton," *Baptist Record*, July 27, 1944, 1, 5, Bratton file, Mississippi Archives.

134. "The Proposed All Saints' Chapel Theodore DuBose Bratton Memorial," circa November 1946, pamphlet Bratton file, Mississippi Archives.

135. Information about the portrait in the Hall of Fame, memorial bridge and bench, Bratton Hall, and the portrait presented to Sewanee are from the John Gass Bratton personal files containing newspaper articles, programs, and pamphlets; information on the tablet from newspaper article, "Bratton Memorial," name of newspaper unknown, circa 1948, Bratton file, Mississippi Archives.

136. John Gass Bratton, "Dedication of Bishop Bratton Portrait," May 4, 2010, pamphlet, John Gass Bratton personal files.

Chapter Four
John Bratton Jr.

1.   History, "The Roaring Twenties," from the History website, accessed January 29, 2016, http://www.history.com/topics/roaring-twenties.

2.   "Anne Bratton Obituary," published in theAdvocate.com from January 23 to January 24, 2005, personal communication (email), January 26, 2016, from Glyn Oliver, Assistant Archivist, Clarendon County Archives and History Center, Manning, SC. Canaan Plantation was owned by General John Bratton, Anne's great-grandfather.

3.   Ancestry.com, "U.S., World War I Draft Registration Cards, 1917–1918," original source: Registration State: South Carolina; Registration County: Fairfield; Roll: 1877592, accessed January 26, 2016, http://person.ancestry.com /tree/78639377/person/44392228056/facts. Hereafter cited as John Bratton Sr. WWI Draft Card.

4.   Ancestry.com, "U.S. School Yearbooks, 1880–2012" from Ancestry.com (Provo, UT: Ancestry.com Operations, 2010), accessed January 26, 2016, http:// person.ancestry.com/tree/78639377/person/44392228056/facts.

5.   John Bratton Sr. WWI Draft Card.

6.   Ancestry.com, "1920 United States Federal Census," from Ancestry.com (Provo, UT: Ancestry.com Operations, 2004). Census data for John Bratton, age 27; "1910 United States Federal Census." Census data for Ann Lewis Drake, age 15; "U.S. City Directories, 1822–1995." Raleigh, North Carolina, City Directory, 1928. Refers to John Bratton (Sr.) address and occupation. All items from Ancestry. com website, accessed January 27, 2016, http://person.ancestry.com /tree/78639377/person/44392228056/facts.

7.   Ancestry.com, "1920 United States Census," from Ancestry.com (Provo, UT: Ancestry.com Operations, 2010), accessed January 27, 2016, http://person.ancestry.com/tree/78639377/person/44392228056/facts.

8.   David C. Wheelock, "The Great Depression: An Overview," from the North Carolina Museum of History, the 1930s in NC, Session I, [web archive], accessed January 29, 2016, http://ncmuseumofhistory.org.

9.   Interview with Johnny Bratton, Sam Bratton, and Tom Oxholm at Wake Stone Corporation, Knightdale, North Carolina, June 29, 2015. Hereafter cited as Bratton: Interviews at Wake Stone.

10.   Find a Grave"Ann Lewis Drake Bratton," Find a Grave website, accessed January 22, 2016, http://www.findagrave.com/cgi-bin /fg.cgi?page=gr&GRid=24131736.

11.   Ancestry.com, "1930 United States Federal Census," Ancestry.com (Provo, UT: Ancestry.com Operations, 2002). Census data for John Bratton, age 37. From Ancestry.com website, accessed January 27, 2016, http://person.ancestry.com /tree/78639377/person/44392228056/facts.

12.   Raleigh Historic Development Commission, "Hayes Barton Historic District," from the Raleigh Historic Development Commission website, accessed February 3, 2016, http://rhdc.org/hayes-barton-historic-district.

13.   Telephone interview with Lucy Bratton Doak, January 14, 2016. Hereafter cited as Lucy Doak interview.

14.   Ibid.

15.   "John Bratton Jr.," [obituary], *The Wilson Times*, accessed January 21, 2016, http://obituaries.wilsontimes.com/john-bratton-jr. Hereafter cited as John Bratton Jr. obituary.

16.   North Carolina State University, "Agromeck Yearbook (Raleigh, NC), Class of 1943," from e-yearbook.com, accessed June 19, 2015, http://www.e-yearbook.com/sp/eybb?school=4&year=1943&flavor=ncsu.

17.   Ancestry.com, "U.S. WWII Draft Cards Young Men, 1940-1947, Contains John Bratton Jr's draft card in 1941, including his address, and is taken from The National Archives Southeast Region; Atlanta, GA; Records of the Selective Service System, 1926-1975; Record Group: RG 147; Class: RG147, North Carolina World War II Draft Registration Cards; Box Number: 40; "Anne Lewis Bratton in the U.S., School Yearbooks, 1880-2012." Refers to Anne; "Lewis Palmer Bratton in the U.S., School Yearbooks, 1880-2012." Refers to Lewis. From Ancestry.com (Provo, UT: Ancestry.com Operations, Inc., 2010), accessed January 27, 2016, http://person.ancestry.com/tree/78639377/person/44392228056/facts.

18.   Ancestry.com, "U.S. WWII Draft Cards Young Men, 1940-1947. John Bratton Jr.'s WWI Draft Card. From Ancestry.com (Provo, UT: Ancestry.com Operations, Inc. 2011), http://person.ancestry.com/tree/78639377 /person/44392228056/facts.

19.   "Anne Bratton Obituary," published in theAdvocate.com from January 23 to January 24, 2005, personal communication (email), January 26, 2016, from Glyn Oliver, Assistant Archivist, Clarendon County Archives and History Center, Manning, SC.

20.   Ancestry.com, "U.S. Marine Corps Muster Rolls, 1798–1958" Ancestry.com (Provo, UT: Ancestry.com Operations, Inc. 2007), John Bratton Jr enrolled as Private First Class, Station Platoon Leaders' Unit, Sixth Reserve District, Mbnyd, Charleston, SC. Refers to first sentence; John Bratton Jr. obituary. Refers to first sentence; Edward Martin, "Solid as a Rock," *Business North Carolina*, June 1999, from Wake Stone Corporation website, accessed February 19, 2016, http://www .wakestonecorp.com/wakestonecorp/News2.html. Refers to second sentence indicating he built roads and airports in China.

21.   Bratton: Interviews at Wake Stone.

22.   Ancestry.com, "North Carolina Marriage Records, 1741–2011, from Ancestry.com (Provo, UT: Ancestry.com Operations, Inc., 2011), accessed January 27, 2016, http://person.ancestry.com/tree/78639377/person/44392545319/facts. Image of marriage license issued October 12, 1944, from the Office of Register of Deeds, Wake County.

23.   Ancestry.com, "Historical Newspapers, Birth, Marriage & Death Announcements, 1851–2003," from Ancestry.com (Provo, UT: Ancestry.com Operations, Inc., 2006), taken from the *New York Times* (1851-2001) article, "Mary Telfair Fiancée: Scarsdale Girl Is Engaged to Lt. John Bratton Jr., Marines."

24.   Ancestry.com, "Historical Newspapers, Birth, Marriage, & Death Announcements, 1851–2003," from Ancestry.com (Provo, UT: Ancestry.com Operations, Inc., 2011), taken from the *New York Times*, (1857-Current file), article "Samuel Telfair, 62, Fordham Professor" [obituary].

25.   "Last Rites for Thomas E. Warren Largely Attended," obituary dated March 12, 1931, (name of newspaper unknown) posted on Ancestry.com December 9, 2010, accessed February 4, 2016, http://mv.ancestry.com/viewer/915af283-6385-4029-bd30-19eaf7199 4a3/78639377/44566730650?_phsrc=kKI14&usePUBJs=true.

26.   Digital History, "Overview of the Post-War Era," accessed February 15, 2016, http://www.digitalhistory.uh.edu/era.cfm?eraid=16&smtid=1.

27.   Raleighnc.gov, "History of Raleigh," from raleighnc.gov website, accessed June 29, 2016, https://www.raleighnc.gov/home/content/PubAffairs/Articles /Historic.html.

28.   History.com, "Cold War History," from history.com website, accessed February 18, 2016, http://www.history.com/topics/cold-war/cold-war-history.

29.   History.com, "The 1960s," , from history.com website, accessed February 23, 2016, http://www.history.com/topics/1960s.

30.   Bratton: Interviews at Wake Stone.

31.   Lucy Doak interview.

32.   Michelle Telfair Bratton, "Presentation of the Smedes Memorial tablet," Saint Mary's School, *Saint Mary's School Bulletin*, 1944–1949, from Mocavo website, accessed January 21, 2016, http://www.mocavo.com/St-Marys-School-Bulletin -Raleigh-1944–1949-Volume-December–1944-June-1949/953997/486.

33.   Martin Marietta, "Martin Marietta Materials: Company History, from Martin Marietta website, "accessed February 16, 2016, http://www.martinmarietta .com/about-us/company-history/.

34.   Frank Atlee, "Wake Stone: Exemplifying the Good Neighbor Policy," *Stone Review*, April 1987, 10.

35.   Bratton: Interviews at Wake Stone.

36.   Ibid.

37.   Tom Oxholm, personal communication (email), March 28, 2016. Mr. Oxholm said that Wake Stone had grown from being in the top sixty to the top forty quarries in the United States.

38.   Bratton: Interviews at Wake Stone.

39.   Tom Brokaw, *The Greatest Generation* (New York: Random House, 1998), xxx.

40.   John Bratton Jr. obituary; "North Carolina Aggregates Association 2014– 2016 Membership Directory," North Carolina Aggregates Association, accessed June 18, 2015, http://www.ncaggregates.org/assets/pdf/Directory-2014-FINAL -REVISED-3.pdf?

41.   Felicia Lewis, "Carving a Career in Stone," *Triangle Business Journal*, December 8–15, 1986.

42.   "Wake Stone Corporation 40th Anniversary," 2, 2010 Corporate history publication provided by Wake Stone (also found at www.wakestonecorp.com). Hereafter cited as Wake Stone Corporation 40th Anniversary.

43.   Frank Atlee, "Wake Stone: Exemplifying the Good Neighbor Policy," *Stone Review*, April 1987, 10: Refers to Jane, Connie, and Michelle; Personal communication (email) with Lucy Doak Bratton, February 26, 2016. Refers to Lucy.

44.   Edward Martin, "Solid as a Rock," *Business North Carolina*, June 1999, from Wake Stone Corporation website, accessed February 19, 2016, http://www.wakestonecorp.com/wakestonecorp/News2.html.

45.   Personal communication (email) with Johnny Bratton, February 25, 2016.

46.   Frank Atlee, "Wake Stone: Exemplifying the Good Neighbor Policy and Reaping the Rewards," *Stone Review*, 1987, 11. Copy provided by Johnny Bratton.

47.   Wake Stone Corporation 40th Anniversary, 27.

48.　Felicia Lewis, "Carving a Career in Stone," *Triangle Business Journal*, December 8-15, 1986.

49.　Lee Weisbecker, "Rock Solid Operation," *Triangle Business Journal*, April 16, 2007; "Being a Good Steward of the Land Has Many Rewards," *Stone Review*, April 1996. Refers to the quarry pit in Knightdale, NC.

50.　Wake Stone Corporation, "Wake Stone Company Awards," from Wake Stone Corporation website, accessed February 19, 2016, http://www.wakestonecorp.com/wakestonecorp/News.html.

51.　Felicia Lewis, "Carving a Career in Stone," *Triangle Business Journal*, December 8–15, 1986.

52.　Bratton: Interviews at Wake Stone.

53.　Ibid.

54.　Ibid; More information can be found at "Oakwood Cemetery: Board of Directors," from Oakwood Cemetery website, accessed January 21, 2016, http://historicoakwoodcemetery.org/contact-us.asp.

55.　Bratton: Interviews at Wake Stone.

56.　"Bratton Descendant Founds Historic Brattonsville Fund," *Keepers*, (York County Culture & Heritage Museums, Winter Issue, 1999). Copy of publication courtesy of John Bratton, Sewanee, TN.

57.　Classic American Homes Preservation Trust, "Annual Report, 2009: 2009 Donors," from the Classic American Homes Preservation Trust website, accessed May 15, 2015, 10, http://3rr5m4277iau4460932day88.wpengine.netdna-cdn.com/wp-content/uploads/CAHPT_AR_2009.pdf. Donation was $1,000; Joellane.org, "Joel Lane Museum House/Joel Lane Historical Society Donors Jan. 1 to Dec. 31, 2009," 5, accessed May 15, 2015, http://www.joellane.org/images/uploads/Annual_Report.Final_.for_2009_.2010_.02_.09_.pdf. Donation was between $5,000-$9,999; UNC TV, "North Carolina's WWII Experience: Funders," from UNC TN website, accessed February 25, 2016, http://wwii.unctv.org. Note on website indicates that "major funding" was provided by John Bratton Jr. and Michelle T. Bratton.

58.　The Society of the Cincinnatti, "About the Society," from The Society of the Cincinnatti website, accessed February 25, 2016, http://www.societyofthecincinnati.org.

59.　Ibid.

60.　Lucy Doak interview.

61.　Saint Mary's School, "Saint Mary's History," from Saint Mary's School website, accessed July 15, 2015, http://www.sms.edu/about-us/saint-marys-history.

62. "Bratton Hall Dedicated: Family Honors Its Long-Standing Tradition at Saint Mary's with $1 million Gift," *Saint Mary's*, 3. Copy of article courtesy of John Gass Bratton, Sewanee, TN.

63. "The Dedication of Harvey House & Bishop Bratton Hall," St. Andrew's School, September 30, 2000. Pamphlet about the dedication, apparently published by SAS, courtesy of John Gass Bratton, Sewanee, TN. The pamphlet indicates that John R. Bratton (Johnny Bratton) would be providing remarks during the ceremony.

64. Bratton: Interviews at Wake Stone.

65. John Bratton Jr. obituary.

66. Hospice of Wake County, "Hospice of Wake County: Annual Report 2007," accessed January 21, 2016, http://hospice.poweredbyeden.com/files/750/35223.pdf; Wake Med Foundation, "2005 Love Light Tree Donors," *Developments*, Spring 2006, from Wake Med Foundation website, accessed January 21, 2016, http://www.wakemedfoundation.org/document.doc?id=6; Wakebcg.org, "40 Years of Inspiring Our Youth: 2007 Annual Report," 26, Boys & Girls Clubs of Wake County, pdf downloaded from Internet, accessed January 21, 2016, www.wakebgc.org; Duke Pratt School of Engineering, "Honor Roll-Half Century Club," March 16, 2006, from Duke Pratt School of Engineering website, accessed June 19, 2015, http://www.pratt.duke.edu/news/honor-roll-half-century-club.

67. Lucy Doak interview.

68. John Bratton Jr. obituary.

69. Bratton: Interviews at Wake Stone

70. Lucy Doak Interview.

Bibliography

I. Primary Sources

Bratton Family Papers, 1764–1983. South Caroliniana Library, University of South Carolina, Columbia, SC.

Bratton, Ivy Gass. Biographical file. Department of Archives and Special Collections, Jessie Ball duPont Library, University of the South, Sewanee, TN.

Bratton, John Gass. Biographical file. Department of Archives and Special Collections, Jessie Ball duPont Library, University of the South, Sewanee, TN.

Bratton, Theodore DuBose. Biographical file. Department of Archives and Special Collections, Jessie Ball duPont Library, University of the South, Sewanee, TN.

Bratton, Theodore D. Vertical file, Mississippi Department of Archives and History, Jacksonville, MS, February 6, 1922.

Bratton, Theodore DuBose. *An Apostle of Reality; the Life and Thought of the Reverend William Porcher DuBose*, S.T.D., D.C.L. A series of lectures on the DuBose Foundation, delivered at the University of the South by the Rt. Rev. Theodore DuBose Bratton. London, New York: Longmans, Green and Company, 1936.

———. *Best Method of Work for Colored People: 1–9*. Address delivered at the Missionary Council of Sewanee, Montgomery, AL, November 10, 1909. Davis Library, Rare Book Collection, University of North Carolina, Chapel Hill, circa 1909, text-fiche, 778105.

———. "Life History of Gen. Bratton: Interesting Story of Incidents in Life of South Carolina Pioneer and Soldier." In *The News and Herald* (Winnsboro, SC), September 19, 1935.

———. "Race Co-operation in Church Work." In *Battling for Social Betterment: Southern Sociological Congress, Memphis, Tennessee, May 6–10, 1914*. Edited by James Edward McCullock: 145–153. Whitefish, MT: Kessinger Publishing, LLC, 2008.

———. *Wanted-Leaders! A Study of Negro Development*. New York: Presiding Bishop and Council, Department of Missions and Church Extension, 1922.

———. "The Christian South and Negro Education," *Sewanee Review*. Vol. 14. July 1908: 290–297.

Bratton, William DuBose. Biographical file. Department of Archives and Special Collections, Jessie Ball duPont Library, University of the South, Sewanee, TN.

Bratton Family Collection. Fairfield County Museum, Winnsboro, SC.

Brown, James C. "Printed Hearings of the House of Representatives Found Among its Committee Records in the National Archives of the United States, 1824–1958." Special list no. 35. *National Archives and Records Service, General Services Administration.* Washington: 1974.

Chalkely, Lyman. *Chronicles of the Scotch-Irish Settlement in Virginia.* The Crucible of Civil War and Reconstruction in the Experience of William Porcher DuBose. Vol. 1. Extracted from the Original Court Records of Augusta County 1745–1800. US GenWeb Project. Accessed August 4, 2015. http://www.world-net.net/home/sakirk/documents/State%20of%20Virginia/Chronicles%20of%20the%20Scotch.pdf.

Chicago Daily Tribune. "Charges Against a Bishop." September 17, 1904: 5.

Chicago Defender. "Bill Introduced to Bar White Teachers: Bishop Theodore Bratton Addresses Letters to Author of Bill." February 26, 1916.

"Constitutional Convention, 1868." *Constitution of 1868*, S 131081. State Department of Archives and History, Columbia, South Carolina.

Episcopal Church, Diocese of Mississippi, Council. *Journals of the Diocese of Mississippi 1903–1944.* Jackson Archives. Jessie Ball duPont Library, University of the South, Sewanee, TN.

Episcopal Church, Diocese of Mississippi. *Journals of the Diocese of Mississippi: 1902–1945.* Jackson Archives, Jessie Ball duPont Library, University of the South, Sewanee, TN.

Library of Congress. "Ella E. Gooding, 80 Years Old, and Robert E. Gooding, 82 Years Old (White)." In *Slave Narratives: A Folk History of Slavery in the United States, 1936–1938.* Accessed April 30, 2015. http://www.loc.gov/resource/wpalh3.30082108.

Library of Congress. "Jim Henry, Ex-Slave, 77 Years Old," 266–270. In *Slave Narratives: A Folk History of Slavery in the United States From Interviews with Former Slaves, 1936–1938.* Vol. 14, part 2. South Carolina Narratives. Prepared by the Federal Writers' Project of the Works Progress Administration, 1941. Accessed July 7, 2015. http://memory.loc.gov/mss/mesn/142/142.pdf.

Library of Congress. "Louisa Davis. Ex-Slave 106 Years Old." In *Born in Slavery: Slave Narratives from the Federal Writers' Project, 1936–1938.* Prepared by the Federal Writers' Project of the Works Progress Administration, 1941. Accessed July 20, 2015. http://memory.loc.gov/cgi-bin/ampage?collId=mesn&fileName=141/mesn141.db&recNum=301&itemLink=D?mesnbib:1:./temp/~ammem_Vqjs::.

Library of Congress. "Ned Walker, Ex-Slave 83 Years Old." In *Born in Slavery: Slave Narratives from the Federal Writers' Project, 1936–1938.* Prepared by the Federal Writers' Project of the Works Progress Administration, 1941. Accessed July 20, 2015. http://memory.loc.gov/cgi-bin/ampage?collId=mesn&fileName=144/mesn144.db&recNum=177&itemLink=D?mesnbib:1:./temp/~ammem_u4Dn::

Library of Congress. "Phillip Evans, Ex-Slave, 85 Years Old." In *Slave Narratives: A Folk History of Slavery in the United States From Interviews with Former Slaves, 1936–1938*. Vol. 14, part 2. South Carolina Narratives. Prepared by the Federal Writers' Project of the Works Progress Administration, 1941. Accessed July 7, 2015. http://memory.loc.gov/mss/mesn/142/142.pdf.

Logan, John H. "William Bratton Biography and Obituary." Compiled by Michael C. Scoggins, 2002. From the Lyman C. Draper Manuscript Collection. Vol. 16, series 55, 174 (16VV154). State Historical Society, WI.

Mittelberger, Gottlieb. *Gottlieb Mittelberger's Journey to Pennsylvania in the Year 1750 and Return to Germany in the Year 1754 : Containing Not Only a Description of the Country According to Its Present Condition, but Also a Detailed Account of the Sad and Unfortunate Circumstances of Most of the Germans That Have Emigrated, or Are Emigrating to That Country*, translated by Carl T. Eben. Philadelphia: J. J. McVey, 1898. *Library of Congress*. https://archive.org/details/gottliebmittelbe00gott.

Salley, A. S. *The History of Orangeburg Count, South Carolina*. Orangeburg, SC: H. Lewis Berry, 1898. Copy found at Fairfield County Museum in Bratton Family Collection.

Wells, Holly Wilberforce. *Recollections of Theodore DuBose Bratton*. Vicksburg, Miss: All Saints' Episcopal College, 1951.

"Will of William Bratton." South Carolina Department of Archives and History, Columbia, SC. South Carlina will transcripts, estate packet, case no. 9, file 378 (3 frames).

II. Secondary Sources

Ahlstrom, Sydney E. *A Religious History of the American People*. New Haven: Yale University Press, circa 2004.

Anderson, Agnes. "Logging Time." In *A Place Called Mississippi: Collected Narratives*. Edited by Marion Barnwell, 245. Jackson: University Press of Mississippi, 1997.

Andrew, Rod. *Wade Hampton: Confederate Warrior to Southern Redeemer*. Chapel Hill: University of North Carolina Press, 2008.

Armentrout, Donald S. *A DuBose Reader: Selections from the Writings of William Porcher DuBose*. Sewanee, TN: University of the South, 1984.

Atlee, Frank. "Wake Stone: Exemplifying the Good Neighbor Policy and Reaping the Rewards." *Stone Review*. April 1987: 1–13.

Austin, J. Luke. *General John Bratton: Sumter to Appomattox. In Letters to His Wife*. Sewanee, TN: Proctor's Hall Press, 2003.

Avery, Sharon Goff. *History of Saint John's Episcopal Church, Winnsboro, South Carolina, 1839–1989*. Spartanburg, SC: The Reprint Company, 1995.

Bailey, N. Louise, Mary L. Morgan, and Carolyn R. Taylor. *Biographical Directory of the South Carolina Senate, 1776–1985.* Vol. 1. Columbia, SC: University of South Carolina Press, 1986.

Barber, Barbara Beadle. *By Faith: A Century of Progress.* Bloomington, IN: iUniverse, Inc., 2009.

Biographical Directory of the South Carolina House of Representatives, Volume III, House of Representatives, 1775–1790. Edited by N. Louise Bailey. Columbia: University of South Carolina Press, 1981.

Biographical Directory of the United States Congress, 1774–1984, Bicentennial Edition, s.v. "John Bratton." United States Government Printing Office, 1989. South Carolina Department of Archives and History, Columbia, SC.

Bolick, Julian Stevenson. *A Fairfield Sketchbook.* Clinton, SC: Jacobs Brothers, circa 1963.

Bratton, Lisa M. "Green and Matilda Bratton: From Enslavement to Land Ownership in Historic Brattonsville," n.d., circa 2014. Unpublished booklet sold at Historic Brattonsville, McConnells, SC.

Cauthen, Charles Edward. *South Carolina Goes to War, 1860–1865.* Columbia: University of South Carolina Press, 2005.

Cooper, William R. *The Conservative Regime: South Carolina, 1877–1890.* Baton Rouge: Louisiana State University Press, 1991.

Cothen, Charles Edward. *South Carolina Goes to War, 1860–1865.* Columbia, SC: Columbia Press, 2005.

Cyclopedia of Eminent and Representative Men of the Carolinas of the Nineteenth Century. Vol. I, s.v. "Hon. John Bratton." Madison, WI: Brant and Fuller, 1892.

DuBose, Daniel. "Mrs. Mary Dolly DuBose Macklin." *Fairfield Genealogical Society Newsletter.* Vol. 2: 2–3, no. 4 (December 2007).

"DuBose Genealogy." Compiled by Dorothy Kelly MacDowell, (unpublished manuscript, n.d.), 232. Bratton Family Collection, Fairfield County Museum, Winnsboro, SC.

DuBose, William Porcher. *A DuBose Reader: Selections from the Writings of William Porcher DuBose.* Introduced and compiled by Donald S. Armentrout. Sewanee, TN: University of the South, 1984.

Dunkerly, Robert. *Women of the Revolution: Bravery and Sacrifice on the Southern Battlefields.* Charleston, SC: The History Press, 2007.

Ederington, William, and B. H. Rosson, *History of Fairfield County, South Carolina.* Charleston, SC: Nabu Press, 2010.

Edgar, Walter B. *South Carolina: A History.* Columbia: University of South Carolina Press, 1998.

Edmunds, John B. *The Episcopal Church of the Advent: History and Records, 1848–1998.* Spartanburg, SC: The Reprint Company, 1998.

Ellet, Elizabeth F. *The Women of the American Revolution.* New York: Baker and Scribner, 1848.

Episcopal Church, Diocese of Mississippi. *The Episcopal Church in Mississippi: 1763–1992.* Jackson: Episcopal Diocese of Mississippi, 1992.

Fairfield County Cemeteries, Vol 2: Eastern Section of County. Winnsboro, SC: Fairfield Genealogical Society, circa 1991.

Foote, Shelby. *Civil War: A Narrative.* Vol. 2. New York: Random House, 1963.

Foster, R. F. *Modern Ireland, 1600–1972.* New York, NY: Penguin Books, 1988. Columbia, SC.: University of South Carolina Press, 2003.

Hendricks, J. Edwin and Christopher E. Hendricks. "Expanding to the West: Settlement of the Piedmont Region, 1730 to 1775." *Tar Heel Junior Historian.* no. 2 (Spring 1995).

Hollis, John Porter. *Early Period of Reconstruction in South Carolina.* Baltimore: The John Hopkins Press, 1905.

Holmes, David L. *A Brief History of the Episcopal Church.* Valley Forge, PA: Trinity Press International, circa 1993.

Hooker, Richard J. *The Carolina Backcountry on the Eve of the Revolution.* Chapel Hill: University of North Carolina Press, 1953.

Kantrowitz, Stephen David. *Ben Tillman & the Reconstruction of White Supremacy.* Chapel Hill: University of North Carolina Press, 2000.

Keepers. "Bratton Descendant Founds Historic Brattonsville Fund." Winter 1999: 6.

Klein, Rachel N. *Unification of a Slave State: the Rise of the Planter Class in the South Carolina Backcountry, 1760–1801.* Vol. 1. Chapel Hill: University of North Carolina Press, 1990.

Langdon, David Stetson. "The Episcopate of Theodore DuBose Bratton, Third Bishop of Mississippi." Thesis, University of the South, 1999.

Lewis, Felicia. "Carving a Career in Stone: John Bratton Aims to be 'A Good Steward of the Land.'" *Triangle Business Journal,* December 8–15, 1986.

Luker, Ralph. "Liberal Theology and Social Conservatism: A Southern Tradition, 1840–1920. *Church History.* Vol. 50, no. 2 (June 1981): 193–2014. Accessed May 12, 2015. http://jstor.org/stable/3166883.

———. "The Crucible of Civil War and Reconstruction in the Experience of William Porcher DuBose." *The South Carolina Historical Magazine.* Vol. 83, no. 1. January 1982: 50–71.

Martin, Edward. "Solid as a Rock: How Does a Small, Family Owned Quarry Company Compete with Giant Corporations? It's the Pits." *Business North Carolina,* June 1999.

Mathews, Donald G. *Religion in the Old South.* Chicago: University of Chicago Press, 1977.

McCrady, Edward, and Samuel A. Ashe. *Cyclopedia of Eminent and Representative Men of the Carolinas of the Nineteenth Century.* Vol. 1. Madison, WI: Brant & Fuller, 1892.

McMaster, Fitz Hugh. *History of Fairfield County South Carolina: From "Before the White Man Came" to 1942.* Spartanburg, SC: Reprint Company Publishers, 1980.

Merriweather, Robert L. *The Expansion of South Carolina: 1729–1765.* Kingsport, TN: Southern Publishers, Inc, 1940.

Morton, Oren Frederic. *A History of Rockbridge County, Virginia, 1857–1926.* Staunton, VA: McClure Co., 1920. https://archive.org/details/historyofrockbri00mortrich.

Newby, I. A., ed. *The Development of Segregationist Thought, 1931–.* Homewood, Ill: Dorsey Press, 1968.

Noll, Mark A. *A History of Christianity in the United States and Canada .* Grand Rapids: MI: W. B. Edermans, circa 1992.

Phillips, Mrs. Herman. "Early History of U. D. C. Chapter: Historian of Society Furnishes Data of Value and Interest To Our Readers." *The News and Herald* (Winnsboro, SC), September 19, 1985.

Potter, David M. *The Impending Crisis, 1848–1861: America Before the Civil War.* New York: Harper Collins, 2011.

Proceedings of a Celebration of Huck's Defeat, at Brattonsville, York District, South Carolina, July 12, 1839. Tucker Printing House, 1839. Published by request of the Committee of Arrangements.

Rowland, Dunbar. *History of Mississippi, Heart of the South.* Spartanburg, SC: The Reprint Co., 1978.

Saint Mary's. "Bratton Hall Dedicated." Vol. 85, no. 2 (Fall 1997), 2–3.

Scoggins, Michael C. *The Day it Rained Militia: Huck's Defeat and the Revolution in the South Carolina Backcountry, May–July 1780.* Charleston, SC: History Press, 2005.

Shattuck, Gardiner H. Episcopalians and Race: Civil War to Civil Rights. Lexington, KY: The University Press of Kentucky, 2000.

Sheppard, William Arthur. *Red Shirts Remembered: Southern Brigadiers of the Reconstruction Period.* Atlanta, Ga.: Printed by Ruralsit Press, Inc., 1940.

Simkins, Francis Butler. *Pitchfork Ben Tillman: South Carolinian.* Baton Rouge: Louisiana State University Press, 1944.

Simms, William Gilmore. *The Revolutionary War in South Carolina:* An anthology: compiled from the writings of William Gilmore Simms. Compiled by Stephen Eats. Columbia: University of South Carolina, 1975.

Stone Review. "Being a 'Good Steward of the Land' Has Many Rewards." April 1996.

Stoops, Martha. *The Heritage: The Education of Women at St. Mary's College, Raleigh, North Carolina, 1842–1982.* Raleigh, NC: Saint Mary's College, 1984.

Sullens, Frederick. "Rites Planned Thursday for Bishop T. D. Bratton." *Jackson Daily* (Jackson, MS), June 27, 1944.

The Parchment Press. "The Honor Plaque." Vol. 2, no. 2 (Summer 2008).

The Sewanee Mountain Messenger. "Chancellor Bratton's Portrait Dedicated." May 13, 2010.

United States Congress. "William Bratton." *Biographical Directory of the United States Congress, 1774–1984, Bicentennial Edition.* United States Government Printing Office, 1989. South Carolina Department of Archives and History, Columbia, SC.

West, Jerry Lee. *The Reconstruction Ku Klux Klan in York County, South Carolina, 1865–1877.* Jefferson, NC: McFarland & Co., 2002.

"Wife of Bishop Bratton Dies." *Courier-Journal* (Louisville, KY: 1869), January 6, 1905: 6.

Williams, Lou Falkner. *The Great South Carolina Ku Klux Klan Trials, 1871–1872.* Athens: University of Georgia Press, 2004.

Williamson, Samuel R., Jr. *Sewanee Sesquicentennial History: The Making of the University of the South.* Sewanee, TN: The University of the South, 2008.

Yerkes, Royden Keith, and Arthur Ben Chitty. "The Beginnings of the Graduate School of Theology of the University of the South." *Historical Magazine of the Protestant Episcopal Church.* Vol. 29, no. 4 (December 1960). Accessed May 12, 2015. http://www.jstor.org/stable/42974535.

Zuckzek, Richard. *State of Rebellion: Reconstruction in South Carolina.* Columbia, SC: University of South Carolina Press, 1966.

Index